Resilience at Work

C000078865

The world of work is in a constant state of flux. *Resilience at Work: Practical Tools for Career Success* is an essential guide to maintaining resilience in this ever-changing environment, whether you are working in a turbulent field, navigating the job market or simply trying to realise your career ambitions.

Based on the author's own experience of working under extreme circumstances in post-earthquake Christchurch, New Zealand and enhanced by collaboration with leading resilience experts from around the world, this book is packed with stories, resources and personal coaching to support you to:

- learn about the importance of **emotional honesty** as a foundation for true resilience
- explore how your levels of **self-care** influence your ability to re-energise and stay strong
- consider how having the right sort of **connections** play a part in your ability to flourish
- reflect on how you have been **learning** (and changing) along your journey to resilience

This is an invaluable resource for organisations looking to support employees by giving them the tools for self-managed resilience at work. It is also ideal for career coaches, counsellors and other professionals who are working with clients facing their own crisis of resilience, whether they are starting out or well-advanced on their career journey.

Kathryn Jackson's unique coaching style enables readers to truly personalise the approach they choose to take, using the stories, the frameworks and the research to create a unique voyage towards building *Resilience at Work*.

Kathryn Jackson is an experienced learning and development coach, specialising in supporting professionals who want to build confidence, achieve career success and grow resilience.

Resilience at Work

Practical Tools for Career Success

Kathryn Jackson

LONDON AND NEW YORK

First published 2019
by Routledge
2 Park Square, Milton Park, Abingdon, Oxon OX14 4RN

and by Routledge
52 Vanderbilt Avenue, New York, NY 10017

Routledge is an imprint of the Taylor & Francis Group, an informa business

2019 Kathryn Jackson

The right of Kathryn Jackson to be identified as author of this work
has been asserted by her in accordance with sections 77 and 78 of the
Copyright, Designs and Patents Act 1988.

All rights reserved. No part of this book may be reprinted or reproduced or
utilised in any form or by any electronic, mechanical, or other means, now
known or hereafter invented, including photocopying and recording, or in
any information storage or retrieval system, without permission in writing
from the publishers.

Trademark notice: Product or corporate names may be trademarks or
registered trademarks, and are used only for identification and explanation
without intent to infringe.

British Library Cataloguing in Publication Data
A catalogue record for this book is available from the British Library

Library of Congress Cataloging in Publication Data
Names: Jackson, Kathryn, 1972- author.
Title: Resilience at work : practical tools for career success / Kathryn
 Jackson.
Description: Abingdon, Oxon ; New York, NY : Routledge, 2018.
Identifiers: LCCN 2018014848| ISBN 9781138305403 (hardback) | ISBN
 9781138305120 (pbk.) | ISBN 9780203729038 (ebook)
 Subjects: LCSH: Resilience (Personality trait) | Work—Psychological
 aspects. | Career development.
Classification: LCC BF698.35.R47 J33 2018 | DDC 155.2/4—dc23
LC record available at https://lccn.loc.gov/2018014848

ISBN: 978-1-138-30540-3 (hbk)
ISBN: 978-1-138-30512-0 (pbk)
ISBN: 978-0-203-72903-8 (ebk)

Typeset in Bembo
by Swales & Willis Ltd, Exeter, Devon, UK

Contents

PART IV
Concluding thoughts 275

Illustrations

Figures

Tables

Acknowledgements

Thank you

This book is for everyone who is committed to exploring how to grow strength and resilience in a world where uncertainty at work flourishes.

Especially . . .

- **The teams at Stronger Christchurch.** You inspired me to look constantly for ways to disrupt normal standards and set the bar higher, even though the world in which we worked together was filled with unpredictability.

- **The researchers and consultants at Resilient Organisations.** Your diligent work to understand what creates resilience at work and in life inspired me to look for ways to share your story and contributed to the framework for this book.

I also want to thank the HR professionals, Business leaders, researchers and Career coaches from around the world who contributed to my surveys and questions; inspiring Coaching tales and informing my research.

To my clients for agreeing to share their personal stories of resilience. Your insights, advice and ideas will make an incredible difference to the resilience of others everywhere; thank you.

Thanks to my team of reviewers for giving your time and your radical honesty. You have made the content even stronger.

And to my wonderful husband for creating the quiet place I needed for my thinking and writing by caring for our little family, for helping me stay true to my ideas and finding the resilience that I needed myself to write this book. Oh, and for bringing me gin. You are awesome.

Finally, I would like to add a thank you to my parents.

Mum and Dad, you taught me so much about the foundations for resilience while I was growing up in a world of extreme change, without me even realising. Thank you for laying the groundwork and encouraging me to continue to explore the importance of resilience throughout my life.

Thank you all, from the bottom of my heart.

Extra-special thank you

Thank you for reading my book. I know that you have other resources to choose from when learning about resilience at work, so it means an awful lot to me that you've picked mine.

I also know that to read a book takes a great deal of time and thinking space, and finding time for both these things represents an enormous commitment.

Knowing that there will be more people at work, who have these Resilience Frameworks to help them overcome the obstacles and hurdles along the way is enormous; the research and learning from the Christchurch experience will continue to leave its legacy.

Writing a book like this takes its own special resilience; it's important to have the right mix of people who will support you, challenge you and help you to build on your thinking.

The following people have been absolute Rockstars throughout the six months it has taken to pull together the research and writing for this book.

These wonderful people have taken my ideas, shaped them with me and made them stronger.

To the team at University of Canterbury, Resilient Organisations, the SCIRT Peak Performance team, my amazing academic reviewers, the members of my LinkedIn groups who completed surveys and inspired the Coaching tales, my publishing team and my wonderful global gang of peer reviewers; thank you.

The Resilient Organisations team

- Dr Venkataraman Nilakant, NZ
- Dr John Vargo, NZ
- Dr Bernard Walker, NZ
- Dr Joanne Kuntz, NZ
- Dr Sanna Malinen, NZ
- Dr Katharina Naswall, NZ
- Dr Kate van Heugten
- Dr Rosemary Baird
- Dr Herb de Vries

The SCIRT Peak Performance team

- Belinda de Zwart, NZ
- Ruth Donde, NZ
- Leah Kininmonth, NZ
- Moira Mallon, NZ
- Mason Tollerton, NZ
- Tia Chakravarty, NZ
- David "Sav" Savage, NZ

Academic reviewers

- Dr Lucy Hone, NZ
- Dr Lehan Stemmet, NZ

Peer reviewers

- Sara Bagheri-Tanner, NZ
- Ella Farrell, NZ
- Jenny Harris, NZ
- Allison O'Neill, NZ
- Andrew Jackson, NZ
- Janna Kealy, Australia
- Tracy Keith, NZ
- Liz Morgan, UAE
- Kevin Nolan, UK
- Jessie Snowdon, NZ
- Angela Winkler, USA

Massive thanks to my awesome publishing team: to Susannah Frearson for recognising the opportunity to share the stories of this book, Lucinda Knight for supporting and mentoring my writing, Matt Bickerton for diligently helping me meet the professional standards required and the incredible team of marketing experts for taking time to understand the story behind Resilience at Work. And of course, my wonderful graphic designer M. J. Steffens for taking my ideas and turning them into amazing illustrations.

Part I

An introduction to resilience at work

1   My resilience story

There have been so many plot twists in my life that I have lost count . . . I'm pretty sure that you have had similar experiences, particularly if you're choosing to read this book.

My own story of resilience so far includes; life in Cold War Europe, unplanned career choices and most recently the demise of our home and my business thanks to the Christchurch earthquakes. Has some of it been terrifying? Devastating? Infuriating? Absolutely . . . but do you know what? I'm grateful for everything that has not quite gone to plan – because I'm rather fond of the person I've become and the people that I've met along the way as a result of life's curveballs.

Understanding and strengthening our Resilience Quotient (RQ) is starting to become viewed as a holy grail of life. A utopian place where we can supposedly handle anything that the world throws at us with a smile on our face and a spring in our step.

As a result, an enormous amount of resource is emerging to support us as we navigate the highs and lows of life and work, and RQ measures will surely soon become as desirable as Intelligence Quotient (IQ) and Emotional Quotient (EQ) measures in both recruitment processes and organisational development as businesses seek to grow the resilience of their workforce.

- Plans at work haven't worked out? No problem, I've got resilience.
- Life not going to in the right direction? Never fear, I'm resilient.
- World falling apart? Don't worry about me, I'm resilient.
- Volatile? Uncertain? Complex? Ambiguous? Bring on the world of change . . . I'm ready!!

From a personal perspective, I've learned more about resilience during the last five years than I ever imagined. And trust me, I thought I had resilience nailed already:

I spent the first eighteen years of my life growing up in a variety of cultures across Europe and Asia, starting a new school every three or four years, experiencing the beauty of exotic cultures and learning the value of miles-apart-friendships.

I also travelled to school on a train protected by armed guards, experienced multiple terrorist threats first-hand and supported school friends who lost family members during the conflicts of the 1980s.

After enjoying a corporate career in the UK, where I experienced the usual ups and downs of working in the finance industry, I decided to turn a personal experience of redundancy into something amazing and emigrated to Christchurch, New Zealand with my husband.

I launched my coaching practice in early 2007, and began enjoying the unique resilience challenges that go along with the decision to step into self-employment.

I had the confidence of a person who has a place to go, a plan to get there and the tools and resources to achieve it.

Then, in 2010, my confidence was rocked (literally) to the core.

The first earthquake in September damaged our home beyond repair. We lived without a working toilet for almost six months, albeit we were eventually allocated a shared portable toilet at our front gate, so we were amongst the lucky ones. Our front door became an office nook because it could no longer be opened . . . and we grew accustomed to the constant rolling of enormous aftershocks.

Then, the February 2011 earthquake changed everything.

On a geotechnical scale, the earthquake itself shattered previous New Zealand records of ground-shaking, with the Peak Ground Acceleration creating almost simultaneous vertical and horizontal ground movement at 1.8 times the acceleration of gravity. Quite simply, this means buildings were getting pushed up with enormous pressure and were literally in freefall as the ground was pushed down faster than the natural fall of gravity.

The city faced estimates of over NZ$50 billion of reconstruction, including roads, buildings and infrastructure. Approximately 250,000 homes faced rebuild or repair with around 8,000 of these zoned as "red" meaning that the land was no longer stable enough for sustaining a house.

Ours was one of these homes.

Anybody who has ever been through a significant natural disaster like an earthquake will no doubt confirm that you are never the same again.

This is one of the first things that I learned about resilience.

Despite many popular opinions; you do not "bounce back". There is no "recovery".

Physiologically you can return to a normal state of heart rate, blood pressure and adrenalin levels, but you are a different person.

You find ways of making the different person part of who you are now; look for the lessons and gifts the experience has given you, celebrate the new connections that are formed and find a way to move forward from this new and unexpected place.

The immediate impact, was that my coaching practice imploded. The client base I had worked so hard to create was too busy focussing on ensuring the longevity of their own businesses and lives to be concerned about mine, so I was quickly forced to rethink how I used my skills.

Because my office was in the Central Business District (CBD) of the city (and off limits for years to come, eventually scheduled to be demolished) I discovered that I was eligible for some financial support from my insurer, and from the government. As a result, I offered my professional coaching skills free to support locals who were faced with immediate decisions about whether to stay in the city or relocate to a new life elsewhere.

I also accessed the psychosocial support that was offered to Christchurch residents, to ensure my own mental house was "in order" before providing support to others. This decision resulted in meeting some amazing psychologists who were not only instrumental in growing my personal interest in understanding resilience but who also still play a critical role in supporting my work and who contributed to this book.

As the rebuild began, so too the opportunities for coaching skills came back to the fore – in a new environment of uncertainty.

The Stronger Christchurch Infrastructure Rebuild Team (SCIRT) was a virtual organisation launched in 2011 to rebuild civil infrastructure. The plan to deliver more than $2 billion of rebuild was unprecedented in New Zealand, and required five construction companies to work together within a non-financially incentivised model to deliver the work.

To support this, a team of five Peak Performance coaches was employed – with the specific aim of exploring, understanding and growing resilience to support the capability of leaders operating in an environment of extreme uncertainty. High performance was deliberately designed into the model for how SCIRT operated.

I was one of those Peak Performance coaches.

During this time, all our work was consciously aligned to the work of Resilient Organisations; a research and consulting group including a virtual organisation of researchers and students, and a team who translate the science into meaningful action within organisations, industries and economies.

Learning from their findings was (and continues to be) a privilege and all references in this book to their research and frameworks are with my absolute gratitude.

I noticed that although their company specific "Adaptive Resilience" framework was supporting our work at SCIRT and designed explicitly for developing organisational resilience, it inspired me to learn more about how the lessons learned could be adapted and applied to develop personal and emotional resilience at work, for those whose career goals were not bearing fruit.

I noticed that the foundations of the Adaptive Resilience framework could be easily applied to exploring career resilience, to create the foundations of strength for those navigating a career path within an organisation, or to support those who are searching for something new, and for whom the journey is not going to plan.

So, I decided to explore this in more detail and look for ways to share what I learned. The book you are now holding is the result of that explorative journey.

I have shared my personal story of resilience at the start of this book for three simple reasons:

1   To reassure you that I am not simply writing an academic book about how to cultivate resilience. I have personally had to use the tools, resources and ideas shared in this book to support my own journey. I have tried them, adapted them and learned from them.

2   To reinforce that resilience isn't a thing that just happens, nor is it something that can be relied on to be ready when you need it. You need to constantly nurture your resilience muscles; dialling them up and down as you need them and fine tuning them, because they must already be strong and well-oiled when you call them in to play for more significant challenges.

3   To encourage you to consider that everybody can grow their resilience for a variety of circumstances. Do not wait until there has been a disaster and then whip out your resilience. Use the things that happen to you every day of your life, at work, to sharpen your resilient approach.

A desire to develop resilience can come from several sources; a need to overcome specific adversity, a desire to handle better the everyday pressures we all face, a requirement to make it through bigger pressures that we sometimes face and a desire proactively to learn and do things a bit better and with a bit more strength.

Whatever your reason for starting this journey, using the coaching tools, resources and stories of this book will teach you how to create a story of resilience that's about you.

The Christchurch context

How can we make sure that when people return to their employer at the end of this collaborative project, they are even stronger than when they first arrive?

With this question, the HR Manager at SCIRT inspired something quite unique.

For five years, the SCIRT alliance project challenged existing boundaries and standards; contributing to changing legislation and raising benchmarks across the construction industry in New Zealand.

The team decided not just to rebuild and recover from the earthquakes, but to grow from the experience and leave a legacy of improved systems, safer legislation and stronger leaders.

SCIRT was a collaboration of employees from different organisations who came together to rebuild the city after the earthquakes destroyed Christchurch's infrastructure. They came from their employing organisation into a virtual team, committed to rebuilding the city's infrastructure.

In my role in the SCIRT team as one of five Peak Performance coaches, I was invited to work beside these virtual construction teams, challenging, supporting and sometimes guiding them along the way.

At every possible moment, we examined "the way we do things around here" and there was no such thing as a Business as Usual response to this question.

Every activity we undertook was designed with resilience in mind, because we were not only working on a project which had been activated in response to a critical event (the Christchurch earthquakes) but we also faced five years of working in Volatility, Uncertainty, Complexity and Ambiguity (VUCA).

It was exceptionally hard work, it took a very long time and it required a lot of resilience.

As the project entered the final phase in 2016 we wanted to understand how we could apply the very same principals of peak performance which had driven the project as employees returned to their "normal" place of work at the end of their collaborative work.

We wanted to transition employees into their next role back with their employer, in a way that also raised the standards of what was normal at the end of a construction project. Instead of just transitioning them back to their employer we wanted to do something better.

So, we asked the organisations that had supplied our virtual team what they wanted.

They told us:

- We'd like employees who are more certain about what they would like to achieve in their career, and who are self-motivated to achieve these goals at our workplace regardless of obstacles.
- We'd like employees who are skilled to make better connections, both inside and outside our organisation to continue to broaden their thinking about how we get the job done.
- We'd like employees who understand what it takes to be resilient in our workplace so that they can more confidently navigate the change and uncertainty that exists in our business world every day.

We designed several solutions to meet these needs, which became part of the Strength to Strength programme and which were met with outstanding feedback.

These solutions form part of the original inspiration for this book.

In retrospect, it would have been amazing to have been able to share the information covered in this book at the start of our SCIRT project.

Imagine the additional potential and engagement we could have created if all our employees had been empowered with knowledge about how to recognise, and then dial up or down the Resilience Foundations as they stepped into the unknown? Sharing the same language? Supporting each other and recognising when a colleague might not be operating from a place of resilience?

Instead, we worked with what we had, sharing knowledge where it became available and offering training and development for all team members (not just leaders) when we recognised the need.

We learned that developing resilience at work does not just mean mindfulness training, nor does it mean simply talking to somebody about how you feel.

Both approaches can play a part in growing your coping strategies, but will not by themselves help you to move forward, stronger than before. Resilience at work then, is a very personal blend of the four Resilience Foundations, which are continually reviewed and adjusted as the journey evolves.

This book is an opportunity to share what we learned about supporting resilience at SCIRT, what we did and why we did it; adding extra ideas, stories and research from around the world to make sure that the content is both academically sound and practically applicable.

You can learn from the journey that we took, and can use our stories to support the people in your organisation, benefiting from our lessons learned.

This story is intended for every employee in the workplace to learn from; it is not limited to the leadership or management team where so much resilience training is currently targeted.

We want to contribute to the ever-growing conversation about the power of resilience to support career ambitions; by sharing amongst our global findings, the research-based case study of the impact it has had in Christchurch.

What a great contribution to the experience of employees at work around the world, and what a marvellous legacy from the SCIRT project that would be.

The elephants in the book

There are several metaphorical elephants in the room (and the book), when it comes to writing about resilience.

From the outset, this book was going to be a controversial topic; from the impending overuse of the word "resilience" in our workplaces and our world, through to questions about "whose fault is it anyway?" otherwise known as; what has caused a need to be more resilient at work in the first place?

In researching this book and gathering thought and theory from professionals and academics all around the world, this controversy was further underlined for me personally.

- I was advised to steer clear of using the word "resilience".
- I was warned that the topic was too hard and too large to define.
- I was cautioned that by focussing on a resource for everybody at work, I ran the risk of suggesting that it was no longer the responsibility of employers to find ways of supporting their employees in their career ambitions.
- It was suggested that I might alienate academics if the content of the book was too mainstream and alienate everyday readers if the content was too research focussed.

While these points are very valid concerns, have been explored throughout the book in the "elephant" section of every chapter and have contributed to making sure the discussions in this book are robust, they shouldn't stop us from learning about how we might "do" resilience better in our workplaces and our job searches.

I decided to keep writing anyway, because it is more important to me that something in this book might help somebody at some level.

So, my search went on for more thought and theory . . . and I didn't find a single recommendation that we should be giving up on resilience and just letting it go.

Instead, I began also to hear from professionals and academics who are dedicated to understanding and growing resilience at work and who share my belief that there is a bit of a gap in this area of resilience research right now; that of linking resilience to understanding pressure at (and because of) work.

These professionals and academics are proud of the work they are contributing which supports companies that want consciously to create cultures that support resilience, and they are excited to play a part in widening the understanding of what contributes to our career resilience beyond leadership training.

While we are talking about elephants in the room, there is also a need to acknowledge a growing "Global Resilience Fatigue" from the start. Everywhere we look there seems to be a resilience programme about something; resilient farming, resilient cities, resilience alliances. They are all doing amazing work, and they all rely on the tireless efforts of investors, researchers and supporters to achieve their admirable goals.

It is worth considering whether every single one of these programmes really is about building resilience (as a means of learning and growing from circumstances) or more about sustainability (as a way of ensuring continued success).

Perhaps we are becoming tired of resilience, not because it is so widely publicised, but because we know we can never be 100% resilient in all areas of our life, for every moment of every day the thought of even beginning to focus on it is too overwhelming. This is a key message from the global surveys that contributed to this book.

The New York Times published an article in December 2016 called, "The profound emptiness of resilience", encouraging us to consider that the overuse of the term is draining it of its very strength and meaning. Resilience is becoming a word squeezed into mission statements, political broadcasts and employer brand descriptions.

However, the article also defines the opportunities that come with resilience should we choose to embrace its true meaning; proclaiming, "It's not just strength to stay the course – but to question it (the course) and propose other courses, not just to survive but to thrive". Herein lies the strength of resilience.

So, the purpose of this book is to simplify resilience specifically to help you achieve your career ambitions. Not just to achieve your career goals, but to regularly check they are the right ones, consider alternative journeys and thrive in whatever you choose to do.

What you learn will be personalised and planned so you can break down the building process for your resilience into bite sized chunks. After all, that's the best way to eat an elephant, isn't it?

Let's emphasise from the start:

- Sometimes, it is our workplace that causes pressure from a variety of sources, which results in our need to be resilient. Without which, we might already be as resilient as we need to be.
- Sometimes, it is our life that causes pressure from a variety of sources, which results in our need to be resilient. Without which, we might already be as resilient as we need to be.
- Resilience is an incredibly personal subject; a level of resilience that is good enough for one person will not be enough for another person in the same circumstances. The path towards greater resilience will be totally different for every single person who reads this book, and this is reflected in how it has been designed.

This is a book which is aimed at helping us to learn and thrive from failure to achieve our career ambitions and is therefore targeted at building resilience at work.

It has not been written to support the very few who want to learn and thrive as a result of significant trauma.

Figure 1.1 Word cloud: resilience

In choosing to personalise resilience, you may decide to call it by another name that's more meaningful to you, one that will support you in your journey to grow stronger as a result of what you face.

You may decide to focus on strengthening just one Resilience Foundation, or you may realise that you have been placing too much emphasis on another Resilience Foundation.

Let's journey together, learning from the science, the stories and the SCIRT experience and explore the impact that resilience might have on our own career success.

Tell me more!

- Earthquake: Christchurch 22 February 2011. The Press, Christchurch. www.stuff.co.nz/the-press/news/christchurch-earthquake-2011/
- Christchurch Ruptures. Katie Pickles, 2016
- The Earthquake Hazard in Christchurch: A detailed evaluation. D. Elder, I. McCahon and M. Yetton, March 2011. www.eqc.govt.nz/research/research-papers/the-earthquake-hazard-in-christchurch-a-detailed-evaluation
- Post-earthquake Christchurch: The facts, the figures, the forecast. Peter Townsend. Business Day, August 2016. www.stuff.co.nz/business/opinion-analysis/83063469/peter-townsend-postearthquake-the-facts-the-figures-the-forecast
- Stronger Christchurch Infrastructure Rebuild Team (SCIRT): The lessons learned from rebuilding the city. www.scirtlearninglegacy.org.nz
- Resilient Organisations. www.resorgs.org.nz

2 How to use this book

A book that's just a little bit different

This book combines academic research with a coaching approach to create a mix of theoretical learning and practical application.

The book presents evidence, introduces frameworks, shares case studies, asks questions and invites you to consider what you are learning and what you're going to do with what you've learned.

You can reflect upon the book alone or consider it with the support of a colleague, friend or coach. Choose somebody who is going to listen to your thoughts and ask questions to encourage you – not somebody who will just tell you what they think you should do.

Throughout the book, we hear the stories and anecdotes of others who have stood where we are standing, and who have stayed strong, or grown their resilience.

It's been designed so that you can "choose your own resilience adventure", completing the exercises and tools most relevant to you so that you can design your own personal coaching programme. You will get the most value from reading the entire book, and designing a holistic approach to developing your resilience, but I wanted to respect that some of you may want a quicker result – so use the resilience quiz section to decide which chapters will be best suited to achieving your personal resilience plan.

Ideally you will need to be in a helpful emotional state to create the optimum conditions for learning and growth, which is why Emotional Honesty is the first of our Resilience Foundations. We can then check into the remaining Resilience Foundations, dialling them up or down as required to help us achieve optimal conditions for achieving success at work.

The book has been created for two main types of reader:

- **Ambitious employees** – Whether you are getting frustrated with achieving your career objectives in the job you are doing right now, or are finding it tricky to stay strong while looking for your next role in another company. Look upon this book as your best friend. It will ask you the questions you need to consider, introduce you to tools and resources to support you and share stories of fellow job hunters who have been where you are right now.

- **HR professionals, Career coaches and Career counsellors** – HR, Business and Career professionals from around the world have directly contributed to developing this resource; sharing their wisdom, advice and lessons learned. Consider this book your ultimate handbook for supporting the ambitious employees who work with you as their guide.

Ultimately, here's what I hope we will achieve together – regardless of whether you're an ambitious employee, an HR professional, a Career coach, a Career counsellor or any other type of reader:

- Celebrate how resilient you already are, and consciously build on this.
- Explore tools for becoming more resilient at work; develop more expertise and find more energy for achieving your career ambitions.
- Hear stories of resilience from other ambitious employees, HR and Business professionals, Career coaches and Career counsellors.

Our employer can to some extent provide the environment which assists us to grow our resilience at work; training leaders, presenting opportunities for career progression, supporting our development plans. Except, if we aren't lucky enough to work somewhere that offers this (or if our employer is the reason we need to be more resilient) then learning from the science of resilience seems to me to be a very empowering place to start.

Throughout this book there are several features to help you to explore what you're learning and create practical steps to support your resilience.

These include:

- The **My story** accounts have been written by the people whom they introduce. All were given the opportunity to change their name and/or gender if they desired anonymity.
- The **Coaching tales** are designed around people that global career coaches have worked with or talked to, but are entirely fictional. They have been inspired by circumstances outlined on professional social media website, my own experience and conversations with colleagues.
- The **HR and Business reflect** comments have been provided with the permission of the real HR and Business professionals who responded to online surveys.
- The **Coaching moments** have been designed to help you reflect on what you are learning, and how you will adapt what you learn to your own circumstances. They include exercises, tools and resources that have been suggested by global Career coaches.
- The **Management corner** suggestions have been designed to help you consider how you might talk with your team about the chapter content if you manage a team.

- The **Tell me more!** resources have been shared in the hope of inspiring you to learn more about what you have read in my book.
- The chapters include an action focussed **Personal Plan** to help you decide what you're going to do to support your learning, to make sure you don't just read ideas and then go back to normal.

The use of a coaching approach throughout the book is intended to encourage you to reflect on how the ideas and resources could be used or adapted to help YOUR personal circumstances.

Nobody can tell you what you must do to grow your own resilience, because it's so personal to you. There will be factors in your life and work that only you will be aware of, which will influence the success of your journey. However, there is amazing information available to support us from the world of academia and business, should we wish to make it our own.

This is what coaching helps us to achieve.

Please know that all information presented in this book is grounded in academic research or the practical experience of professionals; and I hope that the content inspires you to deepen your own understanding, challenge the ideas I've presented or just find out a little bit more.

My own specific credentials which are relevant to the information presented in this book include:

- Individual Accreditation with the European Mentoring and Coaching Council (Senior Practitioner)
- Fellow of the Chartered Institute of Personnel and Development (CIPD)
- Career Coach Training with Career Engagement Group, New Zealand
- Neuro Linguistics Training for Business Applications
- Coach Training with the Oxford School of Coaching and Mentoring, UK
- MA specialising in Motivation at Work, London
- First Class (Honours) degree in Human Resource Management and Sociology, Stirling and Texas A&M University.

The GRID coaching difference

A framework to personalise your learning

In working with this book, we are exploring some of the newest and most robust studies of resilience and examining how their learnings might be applied in a blended approach to our personal circumstances at work.

The phrase "personal circumstances" is the most critical thing to consider as we start our journey together. Your life is personal to you, and it's unlikely that anybody (not even your closest friends and family) can ever have absolute information about your circumstances.

You have a totally unique set of values, cultural background, aspirations, beliefs, skills and experiences. I want to respect that.

As a result, I believe it is well meaning and kind for me to suggest actions to help you research to inspire your thinking and stories for you to reflect upon, but only you can make choices about what is helpful, and what is not – and therefore what you are going to do with what you learn here.

I hope that the information presented in this book ignites a desire in you to find out more, to play with and enhance the tools and resources and share what you learn with others.

Introducing GRID

GRID is a conversation framework that I designed while working at SCIRT.

It is an adaptation (with permission) of the exceptional, widely used and easily understood Goal, Reality, Options and Will/Way Forward (GROW) coaching model, which was modified to meet the requirements of my SCIRT audience.

- The **Goal** part of the conversation represents what we are trying to achieve – we define where we would like to go, and how we'll know that we've arrived.
- The **Reality** part of the conversation refers to what we've already done and the place where we are right now. It helps us to consider action we've already taken, lessons we've learned along the way and appreciate where we might have achieved a similar goal in the past.
- The **Ideas** part of the conversation allows us to create possibilities. We think as widely as we can about what we might do to achieve our Goal, including consideration of what other people, organisations etc. have done to achieve something similar.
- The **Do** part of the conversation commits us to action. We consider all of the Ideas and decide which ones we are going to progress, how and by when so that we can achieve our Goal.

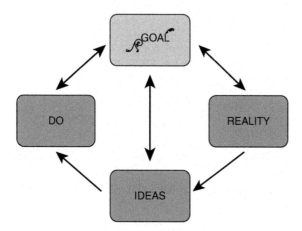

Figure 2.1 GRID coaching framework

Throughout the conversation, we constantly check back into the Goal to make sure it hasn't changed because of our discussion.

In most of our normal, non-coaching discussions we tend to focus on action and support, this equates to the Ideas and Do part of our GRID framework.

For example, you might share a career **Goal** with a friend; "I'd love to be my own boss – and get the heck away from organisation politics". A non-coaching conversation is going to likely result shortly after this comment with a whole heap of wonderful Ideas and advice for what you should Do. Or it might lead to a long discussion about how the person you shared this goal with also would like to be their own boss, and hates office politics too – their shared Reality.

Another example might be sharing your **Reality** with a colleague; "I'm really stressed at work right now and it's making me sick". A non-coaching conversation will likely result in a great deal of sympathy with you, and kind suggestions about what you should do to resolve your stress.

Yet another example might be where you share your job-related **Ideas**; "I think I might apply for an MBA or a post grad diploma to give me the credentials for a promotion". A non-coaching conversation might recommend where you should study, or other academic options to consider.

Finally, you might share what you plan to **Do** for your career; "I'm going to apply for a job in another business, I've had it with this place". A non-coaching conversation might agree that this place really is tough to work in, and you're making a great decision to leave.

GRID coaching conversations are very different.

You start anywhere on the GRID framework (Goal, Reality, Ideas, Do), and then the first place you check into is your Goal.

For the four examples we just considered, your conversation might change a little to something like this:

- "I'd love to be my own boss – and get the heck away from organisation politics"
- (Goal) "How would being your own boss help you avoid organisation politics?"

    o   "I'm really stressed at work right now and it's making me sick"
    o   **(Goal) "What would you like to change about your work so it makes you less stressed?"**

- "I think I might apply for an MBA or a post grad diploma to give me the credentials for a promotion"
- (Goal) "What sort of role are you hoping to be promoted into?"

    o   "I'm going to apply for a job in another business, I've had it with this place"
    o   **(Goal) "What do you hope will be different about the new job in another business?"**

Once you're a little clearer about the Goal that you're hoping to achieve, you can then check into each of the sections of the GRID framework to make sure that your conversation considers how things already are (your Reality), the things you could consider doing to achieve your Goal (your Ideas) and then from these Ideas you can choose the action you are going to take (what you will Do).

Sounds a bit obvious, doesn't it? Surely this is common sense . . . perhaps you're wondering whether you really need to follow the steps of the GRID coaching framework? It's worth considering:

- Failing to consider your Goal might result in amazing things, but they may not necessarily take you in the direction you'd like to go. A goal is like your personal compass, guiding you towards what you're looking to achieve. Without it you might get lost or you might miss your destination. Goals aren't set in stone, and can be amended, adapted or written off at any time.
- Failing to contemplate your Reality might lead to great actions but may miss what you've already achieved, or how you've previously handled something similar successfully. Your Reality represents the wisdom that you've already got – the strength that already exists within you.
- Failing to generate Ideas might overlook potentially better-but-less-obvious solutions for achieving your Goal. Increasing the possibility of paths that you might be able to take could be done alone or with other people.
- Neglecting to commit to what you will Do is likely to lead to total inaction, and result in continued frustration with not achieving your Goal.

We all have our happy place in the GRID framework, which we can start to notice if we become more conscious of our conversations. For example, you might notice that you spend much of your time sharing your Reality; what's happening in your life right now. You might be super energised by creating Ideas; spend hours perfecting your Goal or endless lists of what you will Do.

Similarly, we all have a weak spot in the GRID. For example, we might find it hard to work out what we're aiming for, or prefer avoiding talking about what's happening in our world. We might struggle to think of ideas or avoid committing to action.

This is where working with an independent person can help. At work, this might be your manager, your HR contact or a good friend you can trust. Outside work it might be friends or family, or a Career professional like a coach or counsellor.

Coaching moments

Today, listen carefully to conversations around you, and to conversations that you are part of. See whether you can identify the flow of conversations and consider:

1   Where on the GRID coaching framework do the conversations begin?
2   How do the conversations flow?
3   If any section of the GRID framework is missed, what impact does this have on the conversation?

Coaching tales: Barbara

Barbara wanted to start her conversation with a coach by sharing her **Reality** about work.

She felt that she was being overlooked in her role on the projects that she led. Her manager was not giving her any feedback about the work she delivered and was choosing other project leaders to deliver new work instead of Barbara. This was very frustrating for Barbara and in response she withdrew from her manager even further.

For the first two coaching conversations with Barbara she chose to focus on how she felt stuck in her **Reality**. The impact on her was very negative and she was even more despondent by her second meeting. It was important for Barbara to consider this effect fully before she moved forward, and to be emotionally honest about the impact her situation was having on her. She felt that she had not been able to do this until she began her coaching journey.

Throughout all her coaching discussions, Barbara wanted to talk about **Ideas** for leaving her employer and in between coaching, she frequently chatted to friends about possible opportunities in new companies. Her friends agreed that she should look for a new job, because she was losing her confidence at work and frequently sent her adverts from local job boards for her to consider. They were being kind, and they were behaving like good friends do.

By using a GRID coaching approach, Barbara's coach discussed the importance of clarifying her **Goals** before further exploring any of the **Ideas** that had been suggested. Her coach persuaded Barbara that by doing so, she could be more certain that anything she decided to **Do** was going to take her closer to what she wanted, and not just what her friends thought she should do.

After working through the GRID framework, Barbara realised that she wanted to be taken more seriously at work and be considered for senior roles and new projects; she didn't want to leave her employer after all.

This totally changed the **Ideas** that Barbara considered and in turn what she decided to **Do**; she was no longer looking for a new employer, she was redefining who she was at work.

Reflection: sometimes the path to resilience that we choose changes as the goal we hope to achieve is more clearly defined.

It is now just over three years since Barbara had that first conversation about her work.

Barbara is now one of the best regarded project leaders in her organisation, and is heading up a multi-million dollar team. She is frequently sought after for her input when other leaders are having challenges within their team, because she's now seen as one of the best performing leaders in the company.

Of course, Barbara could have taken the advice of her well meaning friends, left her employer and enjoyed an equally wonderful career in another organisation, but what if her dented confidence had left her underperforming during interviews, or prevented her from believing she had the skills to apply for the more senior role that she dreamed of?

During her GRID coaching conversations, Barbara realised that this had happened before in other organisations. She had perceived her manager to be overlooking her, and had decided to leave. She realised that this was one of the patterns she had created for herself at work, and she concluded it was neither helpful nor resilient. To create a more resilient approach she needed to look for the learning and growth, so she handled the situation differently the next time it happened.

Strengthening Barbara's resilience was not an overnight feat, and she understands that maintaining her resilience will be an ongoing project forever as life and work brings its usual ups and downs. But Barbara now has a personal resilience toolkit of resources to help her.

Coaching tales: Patrick

Patrick was unemployed and desperately searching for a new job. He had been turned down over and over again and approached a coach out of sheer desperation to help him rewrite his CV. He was exhausted over it and very specific that a revised CV was what he wanted to **Do**.

Instead of simply starting work on his CV, the coach asked Patrick what sort of job he was hoping to get (his **Goal**), and discovered it was in a totally different industry to the one he had just left.

(continued)

(continued)

Working together, they explored how Patrick was identifying possible new roles, and discovered that he was simply sending his CV to jobs that were advertised on search engines. The **Reality** was that he was stuck in doing the same thing over and over again, without any success.

Instead, they considered the impact that different approaches might have, new **Ideas** like; attending conferences or talks that were being organised by employers in the new industry, arranging to meet friends or acquaintances who worked in the new industry and talking to recruiters who specialised in hiring employees into the new industry Patrick wanted to join.

After a couple of weeks, Patrick realised that he didn't need a CV he needed a new job searching approach.

Armed with feedback and advice from his new connections he simply included a short paragraph about why he was making the transition from his old industry onto his CV, and submitted it directly to a couple of employers he had talked to.

With this small change, Patrick scored his first interview.

Reflection: resilience isn't about having the persistence to do the same thing over and over without losing energy. It's about stopping to learn from what is (or isn't) happening, and finding new ways to try instead.

For the remainder of the book we're going to build your own personal resilience toolkit, and each chapter has been designed using the GRID coaching framework to help you achieve this.

Whether you recognise your own story in Barbara's or Patrick's story or whether you are exploring resilience for very different reasons, I'm sure that you will enjoy playing with the GRID coaching framework as you consider how you will apply what you learn about resilience to achieve your own career ambitions.

Tell me more!

If you're curious about coaching and want to learn about the different tools and frameworks to grow your coaching skills further, please consider visiting these excellent resources:

Read

- Coaching for Performance. Sir John Whitmore, 2009
- Quiet Leadership. David Rock, 2009

- The Manager's Pocket Guide to Workplace Coaching. Daniel A. Feldman, 2001
- Change Your Questions, Change Your Life. Marilee Adams, 2016
- Coaching People: Expert solutions for everyday challenges. Patty McManus, 2006
- Essential Questions to GROW Your Team. Kathryn Jackson, 2017

Watch

- www.coachingatwork.com (A complete online resource for leaders and managers who coach including articles, research and videos.)

Part II

Resilience mindsets and frameworks

3   How to become more resilient

Resilience is built over time, by
continuously reflecting and then
more consciously acting

One of the fundamental assumptions that I am making in this book is that you believe that you can become more resilient. Research shows us that you will much better deal with pressure and stress at work (and out of work) as a result.

I have presumed that you think in one of these ways:

- You truly believe that you already have the resources (physically, emotionally and spiritually) to deal with pressure and want to learn how to be more conscious about using them.
- You want to learn about building the resources (physically, emotionally and spiritually) to deal with pressure, and more consciously use what you learn to build your resilience.

So, let's check my assumptions before we go any further.

To help us, we'll consider the decades of research by Stanford University psychologist, Carol Dweck, who invites us to consider whether we have a predominantly fixed mindset or growth mindset.

"I am not resilient"

Is this A FACT set in stone or your starting point?

In the former, **Fixed mindset**, we have a belief that intelligence or talent is static. With this mindset, our desire is to look smart, and we tend to avoid challenges, give up easily, see effort as fruitless, ignore criticism and feel threatened by the development of others. We will believe that the levels of resilience we have right now are all that we are capable of.

In the latter, **Growth mindset**; we have a belief that intelligence or talent can be developed. With this mindset, our desire is to learn and therefore we embrace challenge, persist in the face of setbacks, view effort as part of the journey to proficiency, learn from criticism and find inspiration in the success of others. You know that effort is going to result in personal growth and your thinking is likely to be more along the lines of *"I am not resilient yet"*.

As you might suspect, a growth mindset is preferable for creating the conditions where you believe that you can influence and develop your resilience capabilities. This mindset has also been found to be the more resilient of the two, so not only will you believe in your capability to develop resilience; you will also already be more resilient because you'll be constantly looking for learning moments. Double High Five!

Dweck's research found that we can all dive deeply into both mindsets under the right conditions, because it depends on how our brain interprets what is going on around us. However, recognising that we are moving (or have moved) into the more unhelpful fixed mindset can be helpful so that we can decide if we are OK with our decision to quit, or avoid or give up.

In the world of career objectives, our growth mindset strategies might rely on seeking and receiving regular feedback about our performance, demonstrating our capability (doing a good job rather than an OK job) and overcoming unexpected challenges by problem solving.

Technically, if we all embraced a growth mindset 100% of the time, we should confidently declare that we love getting feedback at work, we are totally comfortable with not performing perfectly in our job (because it's an opportunity to grow of course) and we would embrace any obstacles to career success as learning events – which of course is bullshit.

The growth mindset elephant

It would also be naive to think that we have a growth mindset in every circumstance, all the time, particularly if we're going through a challenging time trying to achieve our career aspirations. There's always going to be something that happens to us which causes us to stop in our tracks and think we can't do it. This is what makes us normal functioning humans.

What makes us resilient is realising this has happened, and then engaging the strategies in this book to get back on track, and into a more growth and solution focussed mindset.

This highlights the importance of having clear goals using our GRID coaching framework, without which we run the risk of drifting off into the world of research without really considering what a growth mindset is trying to help us achieve.

I believe having a strong growth mindset also comes with its challenges; it's not all blue sky and fluffy clouds. For example, this way of thinking can result in a restlessness. A sense that there is always more that could be done, skills that could be developed, more achievements to be reached – how do you know when to stop?

The recognition of a growth mindset can lead us to have to consider ourselves more fully, something that not all of us are comfortable doing. In doing so, we might find that there are things that don't serve us, which we need to disconnect from. Unhelpful thought patterns that need to be rewired or the acknowledgement that who we are right now is not going to get us where we want to go.

That we need to "let stuff go" is fundamental to the journey of reshaping and optimising our thinking. This depth of change can be scary, and affronting for some people, and it can result in reshaping not only who we are but the world we live in: our friends and family may not like the new, more resilient version of "us".

If you are <u>totally and utterly convinced</u> that the reason you haven't achieved your career goals is because somebody else hasn't noticed you, because your boss is an idiot or because you've reached as high as you can go, and NOTHING can convince you otherwise then this probably isn't the right book for you.

But if you're curious about cultivating your growth mindset, want to learn about creating self-driven resilience and re-energise your career focus, then welcome. Please go ahead and buy this book because I think you're going to like it.

And remember that businesses/employers are going to like it too, because the thinking goes hand in hand with the trending Solutions Focus at work; the Continuous Improvement frameworks, Lessons Learned workshops and other initiatives which contribute towards enhancing business performance.

You're going to develop killer skills that make you even more attractive to employers, and you're going to get stronger along the way.

How it's going to work

You're already resilient. It's very unlikely that you've been able to get this far in life (whatever point you're at) without creating and using coping strategies, and learning some lessons along the way.

We're going to unpack the strategies you've used, and explore how well they are working for you and we're going to check that your energy isn't just focussed on one or two Resilience Foundations, but that you're checking into all four of them, and continually reviewing how well they are working for you.

The four Foundations for resilience at work are:

1   **Emotional Honesty** – having emotional awareness, compassion and gratitude
2   **Self-Care** – consciously monitoring and acting on spiritual and physical wellness
3   **Connecting** – spending time with social tribes, role models and mentors
4   **Learning** – seeking feedback, looking for evidence, strengths based growth mindset.

To be at your optimal resilience level, you must be dialling up (or dialling down) these four factors. Failing to be emotionally honest can result in avoidance which can build up stress over time, failing to invest in Self-Care can mean we don't recharge our batteries for the pressures of everyday work. Not enough Connecting can leave us feeling isolated and having to face issues alone, and neglecting to look for Learning can result in imagined pressure or repeated patterns.

Figure 3.1 The Resilience Foundations: framework

Coaching moment

Think about the reason you have picked up this book – the thing that's causing you to want to be more resilient at work. Without reading anything at all about resilience (yet), what impact do you think it might have on you to:

1   Be more honest with yourself about the impact that not feeling resilient is having on you?
2   Nurture yourself a little more – investing in activities that give you your energy back?
3   Connect with another person who has faced this, and learn from them or ask them for help?
4   Find some facts to help you check what's true, or research information about what you could do differently?

Learning preferences

Using the coaching approach in this book, you will review your current experience of each Foundation of our resilience framework, explore ideas to develop your resilience and design a personal plan to dial up or dial down in the areas that you most want to influence.

How you implement your personal plan is likely to depend on your learning preference, and so this book has been deliberately designed so there is something for everybody.

There are several different frameworks available, for example VAK or VARK (Visual, Aural, Read/Write, Kinaesthetic), Kolb/Honey and Mumford and Visual/Auditory/Kinaesthetic (or Tactile).

In this book, we are using a combination of Kolb and Honey and Mumford Learning preferences to support our learning journey . . . the aim is to ensure there is something for everybody.

- **Activists**: you typically enjoy learning by doing – you'll likely want to just try your ideas out as soon as possible. Activities that appeal to you are likely to include brainstorming, experimenting, role play, group discussion and problem solving. Right now, you'll probably be thinking, *"Let's just get started!"* (Hold tight we're nearly ready . . . .)
- **Pragmatists**: you naturally prefer to understand how what we learn is going to work in the real world. Activities that appeal to you are likely to include case studies and thinking about the practical applications of what you learn. You'll probably be wondering, *"Show me the case studies that prove it"* (there are examples all through the book, I promise).
- **Reflectors**: you like to think about what you are learning. Activities that appeal to you will likely be reading around the subject and watching others. As you go through the book, you'll be developing ideas and saying, *"Give me some time to plan my approach"* (the self-reflection coaching will give you the space to do this).
- **Theorists**: you largely learn by understanding how what you are learning fits with what you already know. Activities which will appeal to you are likely to include reading around the subject and exploring models and theories. Your key question will likely be, *"Help me understand the principals behind this"* (each section has a Tell me more! which has been created just for you).

From the research, we also know that learning will be enhanced if it's tailored to the way we prefer to explore new concepts, so this book has been designed to appeal at some level to all these different preferences.

At the end of each chapter, there's an opportunity to decide what you will do with what you learn.

This will support something called the learning transfer; the thing that happens when you do something differently, and which helps you know you've spent your money wisely (and haven't just bought a book which you read, and then sits on your shelf while you go back to doing what you always did).

Coaching moment

When was the last time you learned to do something new, and thoroughly enjoyed the experience? (Not that time when you were forced to listen to a lecture about something that seemed to go on forever.)

1   What was the main method that the learning was shared with you?
2   How did you make sure that you were able to do something practical with what you learned?
3   What are you doing differently because of this learning – and what impact is this having on you?

If you're not sure of your learning preference, or if you like to learn in multiple ways (many of us do!) then please go ahead and try the different routes to dial up your Resilience Foundations.

Or be a bit daring and try out a learning approach that doesn't immediately appeal to you. The main thing to remember is that the learning has only worked, if you're doing something differently as a result of reading/watching/reflecting/trying . . . so it's important that you take action as a result of what you explore.

As of 2017, all these learning frameworks are coming under considerable scrutiny by neuroscience researchers who are starting to wonder if perhaps they aren't so helpful after all. The researchers suggest that there's limited evidence to support the existence of specific learning styles, though they agree that we all have learning preferences and recommend that more work should be done in this area . . . watch this space.

Putting your learning preference into a "box", and suggesting that this is going to be the only way, or the best way for you to develop is likely to be restrictive, but there's no doubt that we all learn better under certain conditions.

Building some of the latest thinking into our work together you might consider doing the following:

- **Chunking**: read a chapter at a time, make a plan at the end of each chapter and spend a couple of weeks implementing your plan before moving on. It might take you a few months to work through the book, but you'll be changing as you go along.
- **Talking**: find another person to talk to about what you're learning, what you're doing as a result and the impact that it's having on you. All of the coaching exercises have been designed so you can do them alone, or with a partner.

- **Reflecting**: use the Resilience Reviews that are suggested in the book to write down what you're noticing about yourself; what is changing? What is getting better? What isn't changing? What is getting worse? Simply creating this awareness can be a catalyst to embed your learning even more.

Tell me more!

Read

- Mindset: The new psychology of success. Carol S. Dweck, 2008
- The Agile Learner. James Anderson, 2017
- Honey and Mumford Learning Styles which are based on Kolb: Experiential Learning Cycle. www.businessballs.com/kolblearningstyles.htm

Watch

- www.mindtools.com/mnemlsty.html
- www.youtube.com/watch?v=LNHBMFCzznE

Play

- www.mindsetonline.com (For an online assessment of your current mindset and a measure of whether it's mostly focussed on a Fixed or Growth mindset.)
- http://vark-learn.com/the-vark-questionnaire/ (For a quick assessment of your VARK profile.)

4   Resilience frameworks and Foundations

More than a survival strategy – an opportunity to flourish and grow

Resources in this chapter:
Coaching moments:

- Trending resilience
- Noticing response
- Resilience indicators
- What resilience looks like
- Resilience goals
- Refresher
- Coping strategies
- Resilience quiz

What is this chapter about?

This chapter explores the evolution of the global explosion of interest in resilience and aims to start a conversation about defining what resilience means for you, so that you'll know that you are achieving (or moving towards) your personal resilience goals.

We will investigate the qualities of resilient people, how it is currently impacting you at work and identify the extent to which you are already being resilient in your work and your life.

It's such a tricky topic; not even the academic and mental wellbeing worlds can agree about whether resilience is the ability to cope with and recover from stress, or whether it's something more than that.

Having lived in Christchurch during the rebuild, I believe that it's something more than just recovering . . . it includes finding ways to grow from hardship, so that you are even stronger in the future. If we simply recover from difficulties then how are we becoming more resilient? Surely, we are just coping with the circumstances?

In this book, we'll explore all the different factors that contribute to resilience, and share the stories of those who have travelled a resilient journey . . . I want to let you decide what it means for you.

To begin, let's consider how the concept of resilience came to be, in the first place.

Resilience

ri-zil-yuh ns, ri-zil-ee-uh ns

\<Noun\>

"The capacity to recover quickly from difficulties: toughness"

(Oxford Dictionary)

"The ability to be able to recover readily from illness, depression, adversity, or the like: buoyancy"

(Dictionary.com)

"The ability to recover from setbacks, adapt well to change, and keep going in the face of adversity."

(Harvard Business Review)

A brief history of resilience

The origins of the word "resilience" are found within the Latin word, *resiliens*; a derivative of *resilire* which means, "to spring back, rebound or recoil".

Resilience was originally associated with material science, so quite literally referred to the capacity of materials to go back to their original shape after being distorted.

If we use this analogy and consider resilience as simply a way of being at work ("I am being resilient") then having resilience might be "the ability to rebound from anything that comes our way which takes our career off its original path". Yet we would be the same as before, with the same skills, the same outlook and the same resources. This approach to resilience leaves us with only one possibility; to return to the previous state.

In a world that is naturally filled with disappointments, unexpected challenges and tribulations at work, I'm not sure I would find a single person that would put their hand up in response to me asking, "whose career isn't quite going to plan and has no desire to change how they can handle that?".

The contradiction of resilience: it's desirable and yet we're getting bored with it.

It's a VERY desirable skill to have – from our own perspective and from that of our employer too.

Imagine that you've hired an entire company of resilient people, you could say with certainty that you have confidence that everybody will handle all the ups and downs, ins and outs of business easily.

So, the future of resilience surely lies in finding ways to build a holistic capability across all employees, from the outset? AND a way to make it appealing to people again.

If we look around us we can find evidence of the desirability for being more resilient in a great many places, and not just on a personal level.

For example, it drives the development of resilient crops that thrive despite changing climates, it influences the way we plan our cities to give us the best chance of success and it guides how we operate businesses to help them flourish in difficult circumstances.

Coaching moment: trending resilience

Hop onto Google right now and look up resilience projects in your country or industry of work. It's a hot and trending topic just now.
  Consider:

1   What are the resilience projects that could influence your work in some way?
2   Who are the resilience specialists in your country?
3   How could you tap into what's going on with these projects or specialists so you're connected to the most up to date information for your resilience toolkit all the time? Maybe they've got a newsletter you can sign up to, or they might run local workshops?

If you look up the specialised areas for resilience research right now, the reference points for resilience which you might see include:

No doubt by the time this book is published there will be even more reference points for resilience. That's the beauty of learning – it represents constant growth and evolution.

Perhaps that's the whole point; that the objective should not just be to recover from setbacks, but to grow. If the thing (or things) that doesn't go to plan gives us the opportunity to learn from and grow, then the future possibilities become infinite . . . therefore we are constantly learning more about resilience.

It's no wonder we are a bit overwhelmed with it all then, perhaps we need a resilient approach just to stay the course while we explore the concept of resilience!

Figure 4.1 Resilience "flower"

According to the Web of Science (a programme that collates and evaluates outputs from 7,000+ academic and research institutes) there was a nine-fold increase in the use of the term "resilience" in published items between 1997 and 2015, and the number of people who searched for "resilience" on Google more than doubled between 2004 and 2015.

By the way, if you just did the Coaching moments exercise above, you're now part of these statistics next time they are run.

It has been described as a trend, a fad and a formula.

My approach in writing this book is to suggest that resilience is a word which implies the person doing it, learning about it and growing it has a desire for strength in whatever situation they are in, and it's personal so telling you how to do it just wouldn't work.

I'm sure more of you would volunteer your hands in the air if I asked, "whose career isn't going to plan and wants to learn how they can not only change this, but learn ways of becoming even stronger for the future?"

From my own experiences, I have begun to wonder whether having resilience is more of an opportunity to "Spring Forward" instead of "Spring Back" as per the early definitions. To find a place of strength at work and then keep moving on towards our goals and ambitions, perhaps on a different path or with different tools; to keep evolving, refocussing and getting stronger?

From a scientific perspective, resilience is itself a very complex concept with foundations in psychological studies. It has now become a phrase to be applied to individuals, organisations and communities as we strive to develop our own knowledge and capability to survive and thrive in adversity.

As you might imagine, one of the biggest challenges in researching this book was deciding the parameters of resilience within which to write.

To be clear, our journey here will explore how general concepts for building resilience can be interpreted and applied by people who are specifically seeking more strength in their world of work.

Research about resilience is both complicated and controversial, but the one thing that all research agrees on is that where resilience exists, there is a likelihood that change or uncertainty will be handled in a stronger way and with more successful or desirable outcomes.

I want some of that, so how do I do it?

Resilient characteristics

Resilience has only really been researched since the 1970s and therefore is a relatively new and evolving subject matter in the world of scientific evidence. However, this still gives us almost fifty years of empirical evidence to explore.

Studies started by suggesting that individuals with resilience were totally invincible, thankfully a hypothesis that was challenged swiftly, given the realities of living a life of complete invincibility. Can you imagine it? What a lot of pressure . . .

And what of that moment when you realise that you haven't been born with it; the resilience factor. You are not resilient, nor are you invincible and you are powerless to change this. How depressing.

The 1980s and 1990s brought a new exploration of resilience, which suggested that external factors also had a great influence on our ability to be resilient, as well as the characteristics we naturally possess. This was a view of resilience which included an element of chance, in fact some studies attributed part of a person's ability to be resilience to luck; for example, whether you had a supportive family growing up.

These studies showed that specific traits or dispositions were a major factor in whether somebody was more, or less, resilient but that the impact of not just our family but also our work and our community were also vital in influencing the amount of resilience we possessed, and the extent to which it could be enhanced.

The clinical studies which made these suggestions were principally based on studies of children. Specifically, children who were "thriving" despite growing up in high risk environments which subjected them to poverty, abusive relationships and mentally unwell parents. Despite growing up in these environments, the children demonstrated an extraordinary inner strength, which was attributed to resilience.

The list of characteristics which we should aim to grow or nurture to become more resilient had begun. From this early research, our wish list of attributes included: self-esteem, self-efficacy and autonomy.

Building on these early studies of resilient attributes, more recent research has suggested that the personal qualities associated with resilient people do indeed include self-esteem, self-efficacy and autonomy, but also include other traits like conscientiousness, agreeableness, openness to experience, self-directedness, low rumination, communication, detached coping strategies, problem solving skills and optimism.

Combining these findings with research by neuroscientists about how we can influence our perception of events (for example whether something that happens to us is a traumatic event, or an event which hasn't resulted in what we hoped for, but we can learn from it) and we have some useful studies to draw from.

Even more hopeful is the observation that resilience can be developed, it's not a stable state. Yes, some of us are born with more of it than others, and yes, some of us must overcome significant external influences to develop it – but develop it we can, should we choose to do so.

Genuine resilience versus coping strategies?

The latest thinking about resilience suggests that we all have a "tipping point"; a very personal point in time after which the coping strategies that we normally apply to control the things that stress us out no longer work as well as we need them to.

Stressors at work can mount up, and we can all be resilient to a point – but once our tipping point is reached, we must consciously make choices about how we handle ourselves and rebalance to a more resilient state.

For example, research by Dr Derek Roger presents clear evidence that rumination plays an enormous part in contributing to our resilience; suggesting that most of us will have a physiological response to stressors (for example, our heart beat and blood pressure will change) but that for those who find the stressors most . . . well "stressful" . . . . they are the ones that either worry about beforehand, or dwell on afterwards.

As a result, any coping strategy that we can develop which supports us in better handling this tendency to ruminate (for example, looking for the learning, finding and maintaining a helpful emotional response and Self-Care strategies that create more positive thinking space) will contribute to growing our resilience.

This personal response contributes to creating the challenge of believing there can be a "one size fits all" solution to resilience. Luckily this book is filled with ideas for coping strategies that you can tailor for your own needs.

Quick fix resources that promise you will be more resilient by simply implementing them are not going to be as effective or long lasting as personalising your approach, and then constantly reviewing and adjusting it.

Coaching tales

Kyran and Marta were both included in a leadership development programme which was aimed at growing leadership capability for people not in "traditional" leadership roles. They worked together on their project, often going to meetings and working on outcomes together.

Neither had a team that reported to them, but both were very ambitious at work – constantly looking for ways to grow in their career.

Part of the leadership development programme included a feedback survey, which requested contributions from their peers, their managers and their customers.

In separate meetings, Kyran and Marta reviewed the feedback they received.

Both Kyran and Marta discovered that while they were very well regarded by their peers and their managers, there was a distinct difference in how they were viewed by customers. Almost half of their customers reported that they didn't trust Kyran and Marta as much as they would like.

This came as a great surprise for both Kyran and Marta, and resulted in considerable emotion when it was brought up.

Marta responded by getting very angry indeed. She shared her view that the customers (who were anonymous in the survey) must have colluded to create their response.

She expressed rage that anybody would doubt her, when she was doing all she could to deliver a great outcome for them. Marta concluded that information must be being held back by her customers and as a result it was difficult for her to be able to work with them.

Marta dialled up her Emotional Honesty Resilience Foundation, but in a way which wasn't helpful in that moment. Her personal tipping point had been reached.

In the heat of the moment she wondered why she was bothering and suggested that she might just give up and find a less stressful job somewhere else. Marta left her review meeting in a highly emotional state.

At her next coaching discussion, Marta was still fuming about the feedback that she had received. She shared that it had been keeping her awake at night, and she had been constantly replaying meetings where she thought the feedback had come from, looking for ways to blame her customers for the lack of trust. She was agonising over the situation, rather than exploring the learning for a solution.

In his feedback meeting, Kyran was also very angry to begin with, but within minutes of sharing his anger at the result he started looking for ways to improve things.

He shared that while he had created a great relationship with some of his clients, there were indeed others whom he found more challenging to connect with.

He decided that he would spend some time dialling up his Connecting and Learning Resilience Foundations and reflect on how he had created better relationships. He would then use some of those strategies to change his approach with clients who he wanted to influence.

He also decided to talk to all his customers personally to find out directly what they believed he could do differently to give them a better experience of working together. Rather than focus on the feedback itself, he decided to use it as a launch pad for doing things differently and changing the relationships, so they were more positive.

In the end, Kyran convinced a very reluctant Marta that they should work together to improve their relationships across all suppliers, and the event highlighted two very different responses to the stressor, reinforcing what latest research suggests to us about the very personal nature of resilience.

Reflection: whether a resilience stressor is perceived as an opportunity to grow or a reason to give up is incredibly personal and should not be underestimated. Having a support person to have an emotionally honest conversation with can help us to make more balanced, reframed decisions about our career.

While researching this book and creating the frameworks for our journey I discovered that there was a distinct shortage of academic research specifically focussed on building resilience for job hunting and career success.

As a result, resilience research that relates to more general principals of emotional and psychological resilience in life is used as a baseline for our exploration, combined with organisational resilience research findings.

All my sources are included in the Tell me more! sections of every chapter.

I'd love to encourage more exploration in this area (perhaps if you're reading this book and considering a PhD you might consider exploring this topic?) so that writers in the future of books about career related resilience can refer to more robust direct evidence to support their message.

This short summary doesn't even begin to touch the sides of the wonderful research about building resilience in other areas however; stress related resilience, resilience in children, academic resilience, organisational resilience, emotional and psychological resilience . . . and more!

If what you read in this book interests you, I'd strongly suggest you search out more data to challenge or support the approach I've suggested.

Why do we need to be resilient?

Almost all the research I found about resilience indicated that there are two very specific circumstances which create the need to be resilient:

1   The presence of significant adversity, trauma, tragedy or risk
2   The desire for a positive adaptation of the person who is facing this significant adversity, trauma, tragedy or risk.

In other words, something must happen to you (that isn't very nice) and you have to want to both survive <u>and</u> thrive as a result of it.

What is awesome about this simple definition is that it supposes we can positively adapt to whatever has happened to us; even if we have grown up with trauma and then experience adversity at work we can still learn to rewire our genetic and neural pathways to become more resilient.

However, the simplicity of the definition is also presents us with several challenges:

> What if there were conditions which created the need for your resilience which were not deemed as "significant"– for example a slow growing frustration at not being considered for a requested pay rise in your work over several years?

> What about the need for resilience where the circumstances are entirely more positive with low levels of adversity, trauma, tragedy or risk – for example, if your work requires an enormous concert to be planned which requires a year of planning, excitement and resilience? Or, if you are learning a fantastic new skill, but growing confidence in using the new skill requires patience, commitment and resilience?

> Or, where there is a combination of factors – for example if you work somewhere there is a significant event, like the earthquakes in Christchurch, followed by an intense five-year project of exciting, continuous improvement, like at SCIRT? This resulted in a complex mix of push resilience and pull resilience.

These circumstances are further complicated by studies which suggest that it's very possible for us to have different resilient responses under different circumstances; for example, we might be made redundant at work and find that our resilience levels drop significantly, and yet maintain our resilience levels if we're turned down for a promotion that very same year.

Herein lies one of the main problems with books, tools and resources that tell us to do specific things to grow our resilience, rather than encouraging us to explore what resilience is and make a personal plan to get there.

The requirement for resilience at work comes in a variety of forms ranging from the more obvious sudden redundancy or business takeover, through to the creeping uncertainty of being promised a role in the future which doesn't ever eventuate.

What causes a need for resilience at work is likely to be dependent on a combination of time, life stage and context. What causes significant adversity, trauma, tragedy or risk at work in our twenties might be totally different to that which causes it in our forties or sixties. But the good news is that the resilience strategies we can use are not restricted by our age or experience, they are applicable across all generations.

This gives us a great opportunity to reflect on whether events actually cause stress or whether it's the emotion that we attach to the event that creates the stress response (and therefore the need to dial up our Resilience Foundations)?

It also helps to reinforce that this a book of resilience strategies for EVERYBODY regardless of your age or stage of career. What triggers your need for the tools and resources will be personal to you.

Here are some of the triggers that were shared by HR and Business professionals for the need for resilience in their workplace:

- Job loss
- Threat of job loss
- Manager
- Culture
- Receiving feedback
- Colleagues
- Lack of challenge

Coaching moment: noticing response

We are learning that to be more resilient in these circumstances, we could start by exploring our emotional response to the potential stressful event.

1   What am I thinking or feeling as a response to <insert stressor>?
2   How is what I am thinking or feeling helping me or another person in any way?
3   What could be a more useful way to think or feel about this situation?

Continuing to worry about the situation is neither beneficial, nor proactive and won't solve the problem or generate a solution. Dialling up your Resilience Foundations will.

All too often, if we face circumstances at work like those identified above, we approach professionals in the career related industry to help us move on; we walk away from these situations, or we "hang in there" getting more and more frustrated instead of exploring the possible impact that strengthening our Resilience Foundations could have now or in the future.

We also have a tendency to repeat our patterns too . . . the stressors that we walk away from in one job will likely raise their heads again in our next job so developing resilient strategies to overcome them will be quite literally career changing.

Also, it's only when we are faced with challenge or setbacks that we even find out if we have (or need) resilience; if you're lucky enough to never have anything go wrong then you might never need it.

Thankfully, this book creates the circumstances for you to personalise your resilience journey.

Resilience@work

In our next chapter, we explore the definition of something called VUCA Change and its impact on our workplaces in detail, examining the new (or enhanced) dynamics that are influencing our workplaces, and subsequently creating the pressures which result in obstacles to achieving our career ambitions.

Some of the main VUCA Changes which I believe are contributing to increased curiosity in developing career resilience include:

- **Longer Lives**: if we are working for longer, then it makes sense that we will need to be more resilient to achieve our career goals over a longer period. These days, it's not unusual to have a fifty to sixty year career, sometimes choosing to "re-career" instead of retiring. This also has an impact on the mix of people we work with, for example some companies have up to five generations of employee at the same time – imagine the source of possible friction in the company café as Baby Boomers sip their lattés with Gen X, Gen Y (or Millennials) and Gen Z (or iGen, or Centennials), given the widespread generalisations about how these groups get along (or not). Some companies are even lucky enough to have Traditionalists in the mix too (born pre-1945).
- **Energy Levels**: we just seem busier these days, don't we? Emails, letters and phone calls are no longer the three main sources of incoming information that we need to stay up to date. Now we have additional places to check like social media sites, school related internet updates, business internet sites, internet websites, communication sites. Something as simple as sending a text requires a moment extra to consider whether it should be a text, a Facebook message, a Skype message

or a LinkedIn message. We don't just have one data source for connections, they are multiple. This hyper connectivity and responsiveness can be exhausting. Working out how to find peace despite the noise (rather than peace away from the noise) is a bigger challenge than ever, and it impacts our need to be resilient at work.

- **Workplace Trends**: places that we work in and structures that are in place when we work there have changed and are changing. We have flatter hierarchies with fewer opportunities to progress our career up, global competition from a more mobile workforce, more transient organisations with shorter lifecycles (meaning that they offer a job for life, because they are only likely to last a few years). The average length of time that a Fortune 500 company stays listed has gone from over sixty years to fifteen years; and global market volatility results in change on a daily basis. The growth of flexible working patterns (like nine-day fortnights, part time working, job shares) has been great for diversity but brings its own sets of pressure which can impact our success at work. Workplace disruptors like the gig economy, crowdsourcing, artificial intelligence and machine learning are so new that I'm not sure we've quite got to grips with how they might influence our career progression; perhaps we will be able to explore that in the next version of this book. There has been more of a focus on empowering employees over the years; allowing them to make more decisions and yet with this comes the increased risk of the outcome of these decisions.

- **Self-Interest**: my belief is that we are becoming more selfish. In some ways, we are seeing the darker side of this in the current global political and social unrest. Harnessing the positive side of selfishness and self-interest means that we can take more ownership of growing our own skills, instead of waiting for permission from our employer. I like to believe that we've become more interested in resilience because overall, we're more aware of how much control we have personally over our ability to learn, grow and thrive at work. We have realised that we don't have to be reliant on our employer to provide the "safe" environment within which we work so we don't need to be resilient. In fact, it's highly likely that much of what we need to be resilient about comes from our working environment, so doesn't it make sense for us to take control of what we can to influence our experience for the better?

Do you need to be more resilient at work?

In researching this book, HR and Business professionals from around the world were invited to share what they saw when somebody at work did not seem as resilient as they could be.

This is what they shared:

Figure 4.2 Word cloud: low resilience

So, it seems that any of these factors are going to suggest to the people we work with that we are not at our most resilient, even if we are just having a bad moment.

It's interesting that almost every respondent identified sickness and absence as a clear sign that there is a potential resilience issue. We'll explore this in more detail when we review the impact of the Self-Care Resilience Foundation, but it's worth asking yourself what your health record at work looks like just now.

In considering what we look like when we're not resilient at work, let's be totally honest and acknowledge right now that if you only look, speak and behave this way when you are at work, and things are a totally different picture when you're at home then your job is probably one of the main sources of your resilience problems.

That's great news however, because it gives us a better idea about where to look to start creating ideas and solutions as we go through this book.

Coaching moment: resilience indicators

Reflect on the word cloud of what people at work look like when they aren't at their most resilient, according to HR and Business professionals. Create a column with three rows.

1   Row One: make a note of any of these descriptors that might describe you at work (even just a teeny bit).
2   Row Two: write down all the things that you believe are contributing to this. For example, the impact of your manager, your team, the skills you use/don't use, the culture of your work, the effect of life outside work.
3   Row Three: what impact is this having on you?

Coaching moment: what resilience looks like

Now think about a person (perhaps a friend, or a colleague or even somebody famous) who personifies what you believe resilience looks like.

1   How would you describe what they look like?
2   How would you describe what they sound like?
3   What are the things about them that cause you to believe they are resilient?

Resilience: personalised Part 1

Why do you want it?

Now you've met resilience, and hopefully understand a little bit about where it comes from and what it looks like, so the next place we'll go together is to understand who or what is driving your desire to grow your resilience levels in the first place?

This means that we are checking into the Goal part of our GRID framework. Remember it's going to guide our exploration and help to make sure that the things we do are going to take us closer to what we want to achieve.

Coaching moment: resilience goals

Take a minute to reflect on what caused you to pick up this book in the first place, and how you hope that it's going to help you.
   Consider:

1   What do you believe is currently preventing you from achieving your career ambitions? This might give us a clue about where you could focus your efforts.
2   What would you like to change at work by becoming more resilient?
3   What causes you to believe that you're not already resilient enough in your career?

Understanding what is driving our desire to learn and grow new skills is always an important place to start because it helps us to understand whose agenda we are working towards.

This book is about resilience at work, to achieve our career ambitions . . . and there are always at least two parties in that relationship; you and your employer (which might even be a lot more than one person, especially if you've got multiple managers etc.)

There will also likely be the influence of other people in your life too; your partner, siblings, parents, closest friends etc.

These other "voices" which are likely to be influencing your decision to want to develop Resilience Attributes might include: partners who have shared we "just don't seem ourselves" anymore, children who notice we get cross when we are getting ready to go to work, friends who have started avoiding asking how our job is going.

In applying our GRID coaching framework to our thinking, we should pause for a moment to understand our reason (or reasons) for wanting to develop your resilience in the first place. This represents your own resilience Goal.

My own goals for learning how to grow my resilience were both personal and professional.

- From a personal perspective, I wanted to support my emotional and physical response to experiencing significant earthquakes in New Zealand. I wanted to use them as a catalyst to become stronger whenever I face major obstacles in the future.
- From a professional perspective, I wanted to understand the latest research to better support the teams that I was working within Christchurch, ensuring I could build the latest thinking into my coaching and training.

In defining these reasons, I am now able to understand and track my progress, even though I know that I will never be "perfectly resilient" across all these subjects; at all times.

Resilience: personalised Part 2

What does it look like?

So far, we've heard from academics and researchers about their view on how being resilient is defined, so let's make it personal for our own situation. This helps us to make sure we've got a clearer view of what we're looking for.

The definition for my own interpretation of resilience is this:

> My ability to stay solution focussed and continue to take one step at a time towards the things I really want to achieve in my career; learning and growing from anything that doesn't go to plan on the way.

Because I have this definition, I know that any time I become problem focussed, or stop doing things which take me closer towards what I want from my career ambitions then I need to pause and reflect on the Resilience Foundations, asking myself what I might do differently to get back on track. What could I dial up (or down) to get back on track?

Notice my reference to the clear view of what I want in my career (not what other people want for me), and the acknowledgement that things might not always turn out the way I want them to. This is real world stuff, and the real world rarely provides us with the perfect conditions.

Consider what you have read about resilience so far. How would you describe your definition of resilience?

My story: Noel

Noel was an accountant. He had been employed by his company for almost two years and had never enjoyed himself there. He spent much of his time complaining to his colleagues, he was often off work with illness and he was turned down for promotions and pay increases every year.

And yet, Noel stayed at work. Becoming more and more miserable, and losing confidence day after day. Can you imagine what that's like? He was at an all-time low, and yet he believed that he was being resilient because he was still in his job.

(continued)

(continued)

Working with his coach, and using the GRID framework to explore each of the Foundations for resilience, he made some important discoveries.

Noel was not giving energy to any of the Foundations. Not a single one. Can you imagine what it must have been like for Noel to wake every morning and face going to work?

He confided that the main reason he was doing accounting was because his wife believed this to be a safe career option, one that brought a good steady stream of work and very little risk. This was something he had known for a long time, but had chosen not to share either with her, or anybody at work. He was not fuelling his Emotional Honesty Foundation. He realised that he didn't have his own career goal, he was achieving somebody else's goal for him.

He realised that because he had lost so much confidence at work, he was no longer meeting up with his friends. He was scared that they would notice how down he had become and no longer want to spend time with him.

Which was ironic because they had stopped calling anyway, because he always had an excuse not to meet up. Not only was he avoiding his connections outside work but inside work he was spending time only with those people who were also not enjoying work. They had created a "mutual unappreciation" society.

Self-Care was not even a feature for Noel. Without his external connections, he had given up on his sporting meet-ups, and in fact he realised he had also started eating badly, because he didn't feel good about himself.

Being honest about all of this this was a very powerful moment for Noel, and one that upset him greatly.

When his coach asked him about how much energy he was giving to his Learning Foundation, Noel was confused. He couldn't understand how any sort of learning might help him in growing his resilience to achieve his career goals.

Together with his coach, Noel explored what he might consider learning about to create more Ideas for growing his resilience:

- Feedback about what work he did that was valued (he was still employed, and had been for two years so surely something must be right?)
- Reflection and learning about what he was looking for at work, to help him find his voice again in defining his career ambitions.
- Feedback about where he could grow his skills so that next time a pay rise opportunity came up, he was in a stronger place to apply.
- Information about other roles in the company that were more in line with what he wanted to do, once he had a clearer idea of his ambitions.

Noel decided to start by focussing on learning about his career ambitions. He realised that the daily requirements of his accounting role which were backward looking were what he no longer enjoyed. His real buzz happened when he was future focussed and making recommendations about changing systems and processes.

First, he shared this with his manager. It took a lot of courage to do this, and his first conversation didn't go so well. His manager told him that he wasn't prepared to consider Noel for any other role, because he was only just hanging on in his current one.

At first, this made Noel really angry. He felt like he was being let down by his employer all over again, and was ready to walk away.

His coach helped him pause to think this decision through. He realised that he might not interview so well if he was both angry and lacking confidence, he wasn't sure he would get great references and he decided it would feel like giving up.

So, Noel made an even braver decision. He decided to change who he was at work entirely.

He stopped spending time with the people who he had been hanging out with at work. At first, he spent a lot of time by himself but then he gradually found work colleagues who were more positive.

He also started mountain biking again, something that he hadn't done in over a year. It was very hard for him to go to that first bike ride after so long, but soon he was loving the new energy that it gave him and reconnecting with friends he hadn't spoken to in a long time.

Noel had finally noticed where his energy was going, and had decided that he wanted to dial up his energy across all the Resilience Foundations.

It would be great to be able to share that there is a happy ending to this story, and that Noel now has his future focussed accounting role. Except he's not quite there yet. He hasn't even told his wife that he has plans to redirect his career, but he has shared that he feels like a completely new person.

He has more energy, he's more optimistic, he is making better food choices and he is on the path to a much more resilient career.

Reflection: rebuilding resilience might take quite a bit of time if you've neglected it until today. It might involve making some courageous decisions, taking some scary actions or exploring parts of yourself which you've avoided. But it's likely to be career changing as a result.

One of the recommendations from Positive Psychology is to consider these three questions when faced with something that's not gone to plan:

1   Who is to blame for this? (me or not me?)
2   How long will this last? (always, or just for now?)
3   How much of my life will this affect? (everything or just the immediate stuff?)

For those of us with a pessimistic outlook, and therefore a less resilient approach we may decide that the thing that's not gone to plan is going to ruin our lives or our day forever.

Those of us with a more optimistic, and more resilient outlook will find it easier to maintain perspective.

Interestingly the question about who is to blame depends on the circumstances, for example a pessimist may blame themselves for achieving a poor grade, or blame a teacher for their poor grades, the key is what happens because of this knowledge; an optimist will then look for ways to achieve a better grade regardless of the perceived cause. A pessimist will be more likely to halt their thinking once they have allocated blame. They have found the cause for their low resilience, and can relax.

We'll grow our understanding of this as we travel through the book together.

Reality: how resilient are you already?

It's time to check into your resilience Reality, which is the next step of the GRID coaching framework because we've already identified our Goal.

In doing so, we will explore how resilient you already are, where you've been resilient previously and identify the areas that you most want to change.

Coaching moment: refresher

Let's quickly remind ourselves of what your Goal is for reading this book and growing your resilience at work (Chapter 2).

Let's also refresh our memory of what your personal definition of resilience looks like (Chapter 3).

From the start of the book we implied that resilience is a very personal thing, so we've got a few different ways to explore what being resilient is like for you.

The first thing we'll do is look at the strategies you've used most recently to be resilient;

Coaching moments: coping strategies

Make a note of all the things that you've experienced in the last two months at work which didn't quite go to plan and took you away from achieving your resilience goals. Check your diary, social media posts and emails to find clues if you can't remember. Start noticing your existing resilience.

What happened?	*How did I respond?*	*What helped me to handle this?*

What do you notice about the events that didn't go to plan?

What do you notice about the way that you responded?

What have been your main strategies for handling things that didn't go to plan?

Next, consider the following two quizzes which have been compiled from the latest research about resilient attributes and from HR and Business professional feedback.

They are not psychometric assessments, but are intended to inspire your thinking and guide you to chapters in this book which might support you the best.

Once you've decided which quiz appeals to you the most, you can use the results to decide which chapter is going to be most helpful for you to visit next . . . or just read the book chapter by chapter like a normal book. It's your journey – you decide.

Use the definitions in Table 4.1 to consider the extent that you demonstrate the Resilience Attributes. Take a resilience Selfie. If your answers are Rarely or Never you might consider reading the chapter about growing this Attribute first.

Use the questions in Table 4.2 to consider the extent that you believe the statements to be true. Total up each column and make a note of your total score for the Resilience Foundation. You may decide to read about dialling up the lowest overall scores first.

Table 4.1 Quiz: resilient characteristics

	Attribute	Always	Sometimes	Rarely	Never	Foundation
1	Optimism – I expect that there will be a positive outcome sooner or later from most situations at work.					Emotional Honesty
2	Self-confidence – I have a strong belief in my own capability, and seek regular guidance/ feedback about how I do what I do at work.					Learning
3	Mindfulness – I can recognise my thoughts, emotions and reactions at work, noticing when they are unhelpful and deliberately choosing how to respond.					Self-Care
4	Determined – I am not discouraged by setbacks and am willing to work hard to achieve success.					Learning
5	Courage – I allow myself to be scared in the moment but I use strategies to help me to act despite this.					Emotional Honesty
6	Enterprising - I am good at finding alternative solutions to match the changing circumstances of work if my original plans don't work out.					Learning
7	Considerate – I am thoughtful towards others, consider the impact of my actions and show kindness to other people.					Connecting
8	Connected – I have a strong social network of friends and colleagues, whom I call on for advice, support and ideas.					Connecting

| 9 | Energised – I am excited by my work and passionate about what I do. I feel vibrant. | Self-Care |
| 10 | Anticipating – I regularly look at research for possible changes which might impact my work or my industry. | Learning |

Table 4.2 Quiz: resilient beliefs and actions

Score	Always	Sometimes	Rarely	Never	TOTAL
Emotional Honesty	4	3	2	1	
1 I like to consider different reasons for my emotional responses at work					
2 I believe that it is important to experience a wide range of emotions					
3 I believe that I deserve to enjoy my job					
4 I talk honestly with at least one person about my work					
5 I recognise when my emotions are impacting my work					
6 I know what causes the greatest stress response for me at work					
7 I believe that experiencing a negative emotion is an important message about something which could be improved at work					
8 I am working towards my own career ambitions					
TOTAL					
Self-Care	4	3	2	1	
1 I focus on what I am doing in the moment					
2 Overall, I enjoy going to work each day					
3 I mostly feel like my workload is manageable					

(continued)

Table 4.2 (continued)

Score	Always	Sometimes	Rarely	Never	TOTAL
Self-Care	4	3	2	1	
4 I can switch off easily from my work requirements					
5 I recognise when pressures at work impact my ability to feel like "me"					
6 Overall, I feel good about myself					
7 I regularly take time to recharge from work pressures					
8 I ask for help when I need it					
TOTAL					
Connecting	4	3	2	1	
1 I find it easy to talk to new people about work related topics					
2 There is at least one person at work that I enjoy talking to					
3 I make time to catch up with a friend every day					
4 I believe that having other people who I can talk to about my career ambitions is important					
5 I regularly stay in touch with people I have worked with in previous jobs					
6 My friends know they can rely on me to help them					
7 Conversations with my friends at work are largely focussed on positive topics					
8 I like to do kind things for other people					
TOTAL					
Learning	4	3	2	1	
1 I have reviewed my career to look for lessons I have learned along the way					
2 I like to research or reflect on decisions before I take them					
3 I believe that if there is a problem I can use it to grow my capability					
4 I use feedback or guidance to find ways to grow my capability and confidence at work					

5   My learning plan at work is
    designed to build my resilience and
    achieve my career ambitions
6   If things didn't go to plan I am
    confident that I would still achieve
    my career ambitions eventually
7   I am good at coping with changes
    at work
8   I monitor my industry or role to
    watch for early warning signals or
    possible issues

TOTAL

Coaching moment: resilience quiz

Consider the results of the resilience quiz that you selected.

You may wish to review the results straight away, or you might choose to reflect on them, alone or with another person who knows you well enough to question or agree with your responses.

1   What are the three areas where you scored the highest? These are likely to be your current resilience strengths.
2   Which areas of the resilience quiz are you most concerned about? These are likely to be your current resilience weak spots.
3   How are your resilience strengths and resilience weak spots influencing the achievement of your career ambitions?

These resilience quizzes can form the basis for your journey through this book, and create a snapshot of your perception of your own resilience right now.

You could consider talking about it with a colleague, friend or career coach who may be able to expand your thinking. For example, they might help you to consider whether you have overestimated or underestimated your current resilience in each area.

TIP: A good check can be to name one or two examples for each answer you have given, for example; name who you talk to at work, specify the feedback that you've received, share a courageous decision you have taken, describe something that didn't go to plan which you learned from. This will help you to focus on evidence-based answers, not just what you think you "should" say for the quiz answers (called social desirability bias if you'd like to look it up).

The resilience elephants

There are several elephants in the room to consider as we reflect on what we're learning about our own resilience. Consider which of these are relevant to you, and what impact they might be having:

- **Cause and effect:** because we are all very different, and because company cultures are all very different there are sometimes moments when these clash, creating the conditions for a "perfect resilience storm". Knowing what your personal values are, and being emotionally honest when evaluating how your company is supporting them can make the difference between choosing to leave a company and choosing to stay. Both decisions demonstrate resilience, assuming we have objectively considered (or tried) dialling up or down our Resilience Foundations. If at any time you feel in danger at work, then forcing yourself to be resilient and stick it out is not helpful; resilience at all costs is not the intention of our work together. Keep an eye on resilience indicators; workplaces that offer lots of resilience focussed activities might be awesome companies who are very committed to developing resilience, or might be an indicator that you need to be resilient to work there.

- **So what?!:** what if we really don't care about being resilient? I mean we totally don't give an absolute hoot about it (although I must point out that you're still reading this book so you might care a little bit). What if we are ambitious about our work, frustrated with not achieving those ambitions and don't care about being more resilient? Or we've had a serious ego blow by being given some feedback about our career ambitions, and it's totally knocked our self-confidence to the point where we don't want to consider it at all. My suggestion is this: focus on the actions, not the words. Let go of the word resilience, stop reading this chapter right at this very moment, don't even bother reading the next couple of chapters and simply go to the chapters on Emotional Honesty, Self-Care, Connecting and Learning. Sod reading about resilience, just focus on doing resilience and see what happens.

  - o Commit to doing at least one thing differently because of what you learn about the Foundations of resilience, and come back to me in six months to let me know if you still can't be bothered with resilience.
  - o I'd seriously love to hear from you, because it will help any future editions of this book to be even more robust.

- **The resilience trap:** if you've ever heard about something called sensitisation, you'll know that it refers to an interesting phenomenon. Simply speaking, what if by focussing on a global need to improve our resilience, we are putting ideas into people's heads that there is stuff ahead that we need to be resilient for? An amplification that we need to start scanning our world for things which are potentially going to hurt or derail us? I'd certainly be a bit worried if my manager sat me down and explained that the company was going to start a programme to improve resilience, particularly if it hadn't been a focus previously; I might assume there was something scary coming, like a restructure or multiple redundancies.

How will I know I'm getting more resilient?

There are several different ways we could assess whether the investment you've made in buying this book, reading it and choosing some things to do differently has made a difference to you.

Here are some suggestions:

1   What do you think is changing?
2   What does your employer think is changing?
3   What do your friends and family think is changing?
4   **What do your quiz results tell you?** If you complete the quiz results again in three to four months' time, you should notice that there are changes. You may be dialling up your resilience in one or more Foundations, or dialling down your resilience in one or more Foundations.
5   **What does the research suggest?** You should notice some of these things happening to you; increased energy and positivity, decreased distress, illness and sadness and a better quality of sleep.

We will review these measures through the chapters, and again at the close of the book.

We asked employers to describe what they would see when employees were becoming more resilient; this is what they shared:

- Proactive
- Realistic
- More positive
- Contributing
- Build connections internally
- Build connections externally
- Ideas focussed
- Supportive
- Increased confidence

HR and Business reflect

There were some truly inspiring and hopeful observations about resilience at work from the HR and Business professionals from around the world who contributed their ideas to this book.

I've included some of them here, and I hope that you will have the opportunity to develop your own resilience in companies where people think and behave like this:

> "(We want managers to) give somebody time to talk about something even if they aren't personally able to influence any of the things that cause concern. You are showing (your team) that you care enough to listen".
>
> "You don't have to see the whole staircase, you just need to take the first step forward".

"People are different and do not react the same way to the same advice. It's important for any manager to know the employee and tailor the conversation based on reality and facts".

"If we consider that our levels of resilience are measured in terms of how we respond to risk, then therein begins the first challenge. What I define as a risk, and what you define as a risk are likely to be very different. The only way I can find out is to talk to you, but I need to you to be honest in what you say" .

"Where I work requires extreme resilience. We deal every day with clients who are facing trauma personally. As a result, we have found ways to combine Foundations of resilience in supporting our employees; they have collaborative supervision sessions where they are encouraged to share their learning journeys with each other, their one-to-one supervision purely focusses on emotional honesty. Self-care is one area we'd like to improve, so we're going to ask staff what they want more of at work".

"My company is very flat structured, there are limited opportunities for promotion into traditional hierarchy roles. As a result, we have a secondment system where employees can spend between 3-6 months working with any other team. If they enjoy the secondment we look at redesigning roles to accommodate a more permanent move. We've had very positive feedback about how this helps to prevent resignations, because it's feeding a need to develop at work".

Management corner

Consider having a discussion with your team to review the resilience quiz or what you've learned about resilience in this book so far.

They may prefer to keep some answers private, or share only part of the survey or an area that interests them the most.

They might decide to have this conversation with someone from the HR team, another friend or colleague at work or a career coach instead of you; their manager.

Questions to explore:

1   To what extent do you agree with their self-perception; the scores they chose? Ask for examples to support them if their perception is different to yours.
2   What opportunities might there be for them to access work based learning to support growth in this area?
3   Have they ever developed this area for themselves or seen others grow their ability? If so, what did they do?

Summary

Let's pause to reflect on what we've achieved so far:

1 Background: we've explored some research about resilience at work.
2 Background: we've reviewed the Adaptive Resilience framework, and considered how the framework and the research has influenced the design of Resilient Foundations and Attributes.
3 You've defined why you're wanting to develop resilience at work, and what it will look like; your **Goal**.
4 We've taken a snapshot of your resilience **Reality** by completing one (or both) of the quizzes.
5 The next step is for us to consider some **Ideas** to help you achieve your Goal. We can do this by continuing to read the book, or by choosing to focus on the chapter which is dedicated to influence your quiz results. At the end of each chapter, you will have the opportunity to reflect on what you're learning and commit to **Do** something as a result.

Five vital facts about resilience

1 **Resilience is Personal:** this creates an opportunity to define your own resilience, what it means, how you'll get there and when you will know that you've arrived. This will become your Resilience Goal.
2 **Resilience is Positive:** you do not get to sit still or moan forever. You find ways to explore and challenge the things that are not going the way you'd like them the go. It's an empowering concept that puts you in the driving seat of your response, even if you cannot always change outcomes as much as you'd like.
3 **Resilience is Possible:** academic research suggests that anybody can learn to be more resilient, at any time of their lives. Chances are you have found a need to be more resilient for a reason. It's time to acknowledge that fully.
4 **Resilience is Powerful:** if you have deliberately developed your resilience factor because of reading this book, accessed some of the additional materials and grown your capability, you will be in a very powerful position in the workplace. Employers are on the lookout for people with your skills, and value them highly.
5 **Resilience is a Process:** you don't just read this book, sit back and relax and magically become more resilient. You need to continually check and tweak, dialling the Foundations of resilience up or down as required.

Do: it's time to make a personal plan

Reading this book is not going to make you more resilient.

If you're serious about becoming more resilient and achieving your career ambitions, you need to reflect on what you've learned, how it's going to help you and what you're going to do differently. Then you will need to actually do things differently.

You might complete this reflection about what you've learned alone, or you might talk to somebody about it.

This section about resilience has underlined the importance of . . .
It has given me a better understanding of . . .
What I've learned about myself is . . .
What I'm particularly thankful for is . . .
What I'm going to do immediately as a result is . . .
What I'm going to do over the next twelve months is . . .
The impact this will have is . . .
What could get in the way is . . .
(If this happens I'm going to . . .)
I will know I have succeeded because . . .
I am going to check what I've achieved on . . . (date)
The person who will help me to stay accountable to this plan is:

SCIRT and the Adaptive Resilience framework

LEARNING LESSONS FROM REBUILDING A CITY AFTER THE MOST DESTRUCTIVE EARTHQUAKES IN NEW ZEALAND TO DATE
Resources in this section:

- Adaptive Resilience framework
- SCIRT resilience activities
- Resilience Foundations
- Resilience Attributes

In this section, we will introduce you to the work of Resilient Organisations and SCIRT.

We'll review their work and consider how their tools, methodologies and frameworks have led to the design of the Resilience Foundations and Resilience Attributes which form the basis for this book.

> It's 2011 and you are working in a team of researchers and consultants at Resilient Organisations; a social enterprise based at the University of Canterbury.
>
> You are already deeply involved in understanding what contributes to creating a resilient organisational culture and now you have a unique opportunity to walk side by side with businesses as they confront the reality of recovering from the devastating earthquakes that began in September 2010.
>
> You collaborate with one of these businesses (SCIRT) to consider the question: "What does it take to cope and even flourish in major turbulence and uncertainty?"

The city was (and to some extent still is) a focus point for professional organisations interested in exploring and understanding first-hand, what happens to businesses, to people and to societies when they are faced with extreme uncertainty and trauma.

With over 11,000 aftershocks, the challenge to rebuild and recover in Christchurch (and the subsequent North Canterbury region after additional earthquakes in 2016) has been high on the New Zealand political agenda, with a 2014 report from Deloitte noting dramatic challenges in the region as including; housing shortages, insurance company disputes, transportation issues, drainage and flooding issues.

SCIRT played a fundamental role in the rebuild and recovery of the city, bringing together a competitive collaboration (in the form of an Alliance) of companies into a virtual organisation responsible for operating in unison to achieve the ambitious rebuild goals.

Over NZ$2 billion rebuild of damaged horizontal infrastructure was required through the city; including roads, waste water pipes and fresh water pipes. Nothing like this had ever been achieved in New Zealand before, it was ground breaking and there just weren't enough people in the country with the knowledge, skills and experience to achieve this.

The collaboration included:

- Christchurch City Council
- Canterbury Earthquake Recovery Authority (CERA)
- New Zealand Transport Agency (NZTA)
- Delivery Team: City Care
- Delivery Team: Downer
- Delivery Team: Fletcher Construction
- Delivery Team: Fulton Hogan
- Delivery Team: McConnell Dowell

Many of these organisations also worked with local sub-contracting teams, to achieve the sheer scale of rebuild that was required. At its peak, over 2,000 people worked at or on behalf of SCIRT.

A project of this size and scale had never been experienced before in New Zealand, and it was apparent from the start that a very different approach would be required to support the resilience of a workforce.

Everybody on the project was working in an environment where there would be extreme Volatility, Uncertainty, Complexity and Ambiguity (VUCA) from many sources including:

- The public scrutiny of the residents in a city that wanted its roads and utilities back as quickly as possible.
- A lack of skills and experience for this sort of work within New Zealand.
- Undocumented systems of infrastructure under the ground.
- Government analysis of all decision making at the highest level.

- A desire from the construction industry to lift capability in several business metrics (e.g. leadership, environmental focus, health and safety).
- Ongoing aftershocks for the first three years in particular, many of which were classed as severe (MM7.0+).

In addition to working in this VUCA world at work, many of the SCIRT employees were facing personal challenges outside work that included rebuilding their homes, wrangling insurance claims and coping with their own personal post-traumatic stress, or that of their families.

Coaching tales: Suzie

Suzie was a Geotechnical Engineer and had not long arrived from Scotland to support the rebuild of Christchurch. She was planning to stay for twelve months to support the early planning of the work ahead.

Suzie's work involved climbing into ground trenches in order to drill, sample and check the ratios of soil. The recommendations that she made from her analyses contributed to decisions about whether that particular part of ground was safe to continue working on.

During one of these fact-finding expeditions in 2011, there was a magnitude 5.9 aftershock, followed shortly afterwards by a 6.3. Suzie asked to meet with her coach the following day, and during this discussion became very emotional indeed.

She shared that she had been utterly petrified by the experience and was planning to return to Scotland as soon as possible. Talking through her story her whole body was shaking and she struggled to hold back tears.

The intensity of her Emotional Honesty was such that she decided no amount of discussion about resilience was going to help her. She had had enough.

For her, in that moment, the best decision was for her to return to her previous employer six months earlier than planned.

Suzie sought the support of an Employee Assistance Programme counsellor, and spent several days off work, talking through her response. She realised that the intensity of her response was completely normal, and she developed coping strategies for supporting her physiological response back to a more normal state.

She also decided that remaining in her role was not a possibility, she found it far too stressful. Talking this through with her employer, she was able to reshape her role so that she was more responsible for the measurements and analysis of results, but not the drilling.

Suzie was very lucky that this was a possibility for her. She still returned to Scotland sooner than planned, but in a much more helpful emotional state, and with more resilience than she had ever experienced.

> **Reflection: if your emotional response is extreme, consider how to explore alternative ways to do your job, there may be changes that can be made in the short to medium term while you grow your resilience, or you may need to change your role completely if that isn't possible.**

As an organisation, SCIRT was determined to consciously create a culture to encourage and support both high performance and resilience for all of its employees.

This was partly achieved by deliberately forming a relationship with the Resilient Organisations team, based at Canterbury University.

This decision was both academic and supportive; SCIRT could learn from the Resilient Organisations consultants about how best to create the conditions for resilience, while also sharing the SCIRT story to contribute to further academic research and analysis.

Resilient Organisations

Resilient Organisations is a research and consulting group focussed on helping organisations, industries and economies to thrive in any environment.

Based in Canterbury University, they conduct robust, original research to understand and advance the ability of organisations to anticipate and prepare for, proactively respond to, and recover effectively from disruptions of all kinds.

They define a "Resilient Organisation" as one which learns and grows from a significant adverse experience, often taking the opportunity to emerge stronger and refocussed. These organisations also understand that being resilient is an ongoing process, not an outcome or stable condition that is reached.

Because a Resilient Organisation needs to be self-aware, well led and collaborative with engaged staff, these factors are all good for day to day business, and not just in the event of a disaster.

A group of University of Canterbury researchers, affiliated with Resilient Organisations, are also exploring resilience from the perspective of employees. They are looking at how employees can find ways to thrive in an environment of change. Their ideas are included throughout this book.

The main framework for the SCIRT resilience culture was closely aligned with the Adaptive Resilience framework, created by the University of Canterbury team led by Venkatamaran Nilakant and Bernard Walker.

This Adaptive Resilience framework highlights four major areas of focus that contribute to growing organisational resilience and includes:

1   **Leadership**: the Leadership team is made up of bosses who are regarded by their teams as good at doing the day to day management (like achieving business goals) and who are also compassionate and possess good Emotional Quotient (EQ) skills. This contributes to an environment where staff are empowered and feel trusted at work.

2   **Learning from Experience**: the organisation goes beyond identifying "lessons learned" and makes changes in how it operates because of the lessons learned. The environment creates opportunities to continuously innovate.

3   **Staff Wellbeing and Engagement**: the employee's wellness and engagement are monitored, evaluated and consciously given focus because of initiatives that are deliberately designed into the business. This is much more than an annual engagement survey and an Employee Assistance Programme (EAP) poster in the loo.

4   **Collaboration**: the organisation fosters an internal and external network of strong mutually beneficial relationships and partnerships. There is a willingness and even a drive to collaborate with others to share knowledge and in some cases, resources.

There are several other global research institutes who are also dedicated to growing an understanding of how to deliberately create resilience in organisations. They include:

- The Resilience Research Centre, Canada
- The Wellbeing and Resilience Centre, Australia
- The Resilience Institute, Global collaboration.

Each of these has designed their own measures of resilience, and associated frameworks which are then used to support the work of these organisations.

What is interesting to note is that despite the global nature of the research, the resilience drivers on the frameworks all indicate similar areas of attention:

Figure 4.3 The Adaptive Resilience framework

1   Leaders who do the right things – in the right way.
2   A focus on relationships.
3   An innovative approach to work which focusses on learning.
4   A workforce that is healthy and engaged.

Bringing Adaptive Resilience to life at SCIRT

Achieving success at work when you're using any deliberately designed activity requires a regular check of progress, and this was no different with the use of the Adaptive Resilience framework at SCIRT.

The Adaptive Resilience framework from Resilient Organisations led to the development of a Peak Performance Model, a tool for tracking the measurement of results which was used each month to check into the focus for each team.

Every month, the four Delivery Teams would check where their energy was going at that particular time and consider how it was influencing what their achievement of business results.

Any issues that were flagged from business results (e.g. Key Result Areas) meant that there was the opportunity to consider whether there was a need to "dial up" one of the sections of Peak Performance Model, therefore refocussing Adaptive Resilience activities.

> For example, when the results from the six-monthly wellbeing survey started to show signs of decline, more activities were offered to support the development of employee wellbeing.

It's worth noting that most of the Peak Performance activities to build resilience were largely offered and not mandated. As a result, it became a personal choice about whether employees chose to access the opportunities offered, along with what area of focus they attended. This was to ensure that the Peak Performance framework respected the individuality of the people in the teams at SCIRT, however it also highlights the importance of employees knowing about resilience and understanding when they might need to choose to attend something to help them personally.

Some of the features which were deliberately designed into the SCIRT Peak Performance Plan to dial up the four sections of the Adaptive Resilience framework included:

Table 4.3 Adaptive Resilience at SCIRT

Adaptive Resilience	*SCIRT Initiatives*
Leadership	• Leadership coaching to develop emotional intelligence, including 360-degree reporting • Leadership coaching to support new people leaders • Leadership Wide Angle View Expected programme (not silo approach to problem solving)

(continued)

Table 4.3 (continued)

Adaptive Resilience	SCIRT Initiatives
	• Frontline Crew Leadership programme • Intentional leadership language used by management team • Development initiatives championed by middle and senior managers
Learning from Experience	• Lunch and Learn Fridays • Peer learning forums • Solutioning workshops • Lessons Learned workshops • Learning Legacy was a funded aspect of the programme from early on • My GROWth journey career planning • Strength to Strength change and transition workshops • Fostering relationship with academia and hosting students and visitors to learn about SCIRT (and learn from them) • External audit of Peak Performance Plan • Formal Induction Process at the end of an assignment (like induction at the start of a job but targeted instead on what needs to be let go, passed on and taken forward. It includes a celebration of what has been learned, and how each person has grown from their experience).
Staff Wellbeing and Engagement	• Brain based neuroscience workshops to focus on sustainable peak performance • Wellbeing and engagement six-monthly measures with action plans for each business • Collaboration with the *"All Right?"* Canterbury team of psychologists • Annual Wellbeing Game • Board ownership of a Champion role in this area • Monthly publication written with success, celebration and growth in mind • Prioritising and time management workshops
Collaboration	• Cross-organisation learning and development workshops • Cross-team wellbeing events • Shared office space; not only across SCIRT organisations but associated organisations like Red Cross • "Christchurch first, SCIRT second, home organisation third" shared as mantra from Day One Induction and built into all activities • SCIRT-wide induction used for all SCIRT team members together from sub-contractors on site to senior managers • Specialist leadership groups at every level of the project, bringing together leaders from across the Home Organisations.

Working within the features of the Adaptive Resilience framework for five years sowed the seed for exploring how its core research findings might influence the building of personal resilience to achieve career ambitions.

We noticed that resilient companies don't just focus on one of the Adaptive Resilience factors, they give energy and action to each of the four foundations and continually reviewed the impact and effect on the results. Where there was a lull or slide in one of the factors that showed up on the measures, there resulted a conscious effort to "dial up" the activities in that area.

The result was a holistic and continuous approach to developing organisational resilience.

Further research into the latest ideas about developing resilience led to the discovery that while there are a great many excellent tools and resources for developing resilience in part (many of which are included in this book as ideas in case you want to research them further) there was an opportunity to design a more holistic framework for considering them, so that resilience at work could be developed in a much more personalised way.

In addition, I wanted to recognise that simplifying resilience was required. If we are going through a hard time at work, it would be understandable if personal resources were depleted, so creating a complex model that had to be followed unconditionally would not be helpful.

So, I looked for how the Adaptive Resilience principles compared with current research about related factors like workplace stress, wellbeing and engagement.

Here are the four Resilience Foundations that were developed as a result:

Figure 4.4 The Resilience Foundations: framework (from Chapter 3)

1 **Emotional Honesty:** the ability firstly to recognise and then share genuine emotions with somebody who will listen, empathise and support us into a more helpful state is fundamental to resilience at work and the first step in becoming more resilient. Noticing this, is critical. Without this, our conversations run the risk of on the one hand being relegated to superficial discussions about being "fine" (which can result in the view that no action is required) or emotional conversations that get stuck in drama (which can result in getting stuck in the role of victim). Knowing who we are, what we stand for and where we are going greatly influences our emotional wellbeing.

2 **Self-Care:** finding the energy to stay resilient on the path that we have chosen towards our career ambitions is only possible if we are taking the time to recharge regularly. Dialling up the Self-Care practices for our physical and spiritual wellbeing is very personal, and depends on the needs and drives of the individual. Without Self-Care, we can sometimes more easily give up on career ambitions, because we are too exhausted and depleted to continue.

3 **Connecting:** finding and nurturing positive relationships with colleagues and friends who can support you in your career ambitions contribute directly to our sense of social wellbeing. This influences resilience in both our current and future work because it gives us the opportunity to both offer and receive help and support.

4 **Learning:** if we are not learning from the circumstances that create our need to be resilient, then we are simply coping. Cultivating a mindset of continual personal improvement contributes to our sense of intellectual wellbeing. By seeking regular guidance about our strengths, we build our confidence, and by both learning from the past and keeping an eye on the future our sense of control in uncertain times can be positively influenced.

The Resilient Attributes were developed as a result of reflecting on the qualities required for success in each of the Resilience Foundations, and from my experience of working with clients who were more (or less) successful in their resilience.

I have not tested these attributes with rigorous scientific study, but they have been assessed by academic peer review of this manuscript. They have also been reviewed and supported by the New Zealand Institute of Wellbeing and Resilience, which is currently being established within the city, as further testament to the legacy of Christchurch.

The Resilience Foundations and Attributes

This is how the Resilience Foundations and Attributes compare with the work of Resilient Organisations:

Table 4.4 The Resilience Foundations: Attributes

Resilient Organisations Adaptive Resilience	Resilience Foundation	Resilient Attributes
1 **Leadership – good management skills, strong emotional intelligence and compassionate approach**	**Emotional Honesty – emotional awareness, compassion and gratitude. Emotional wellbeing**	• Optimistic • Courageous
2 **Staff wellbeing and engagement – monitor, evaluate and address issues**	**Self-Care – consciously monitoring and ensuring spiritual and physical wellbeing. Includes stress response. Spiritual and Physical wellbeing**	• Mindful • Energised
3 **Collaboration – internal and external relationships of mutual benefits and partnerships**	**Connecting – clear membership of tribes, role models and mentors. Social wellbeing**	• Connected • Considerate
4 **Learning from Experience – a continuous improvement culture with evidence of what has changed as a result**	**Learning – seeking feedback, tailoring development plans, strengths based and growth mindset. Intellectual wellbeing**	• Self-confident • Determined • Enterprising • Anticipating

We learned that developing resilience isn't simply about finding a cheerleader, somebody who can root for us, applaud our successes and give us a boost when we are down.

And becoming more resilient isn't simply a case of sucking it up, toughing it out or trying harder and longer.

It's also more than simply going to a yoga class, practising gratitude or using mindfulness apps.

While these options can be very helpful and contribute greatly to our coping strategies the growth of resilience comes from all four Foundations and must include an element of learning.

Developing resilience comes from a personal combination of four Foundations which can be dialled up or down as the need arises – but only if we are conscious of what they are, and how they are impacting us.

Considering resilience in this way enables us to objectively reflect on our experience at work, and whether our resilience levels might be influenced by dialling up (or down) one of the four Resilience Foundations by calling up our Resilient Attributes to play.

Coaching tales: Rowan

Rowan was a team leader in a small roading crew. He wasn't enjoying his work very much at all because he didn't believe he had the skills to be a leader.

As a result, he had decided to focus his energy on Self-Care, particularly physical Self-Care. Constantly turning up late or leaving early because of gym visits he was "sent" for coaching by his manager.

His manager was secretly hoping that coaching conversations might help him work out what his career ambitions were, because giving him feedback about his tardiness didn't seem to be working, and his manager did not want to start the process of termination – he believed that Rowan was an awesome employee.

Using the GRID coaching framework, Rowan realised that his Goal at work was to develop confidence in his capabilities – so he would need to dial up his Learning Foundation; seeking feedback on his skills to help him work out where to focus his development. He also decided that he should be more honest about how he felt in his role, and used his coaching conversations to prepare for that.

Reflection: if we are unable to be honest about our emotions with a manager, we may need to consider who else will listen, and who we can be honest sharing our work experience with.

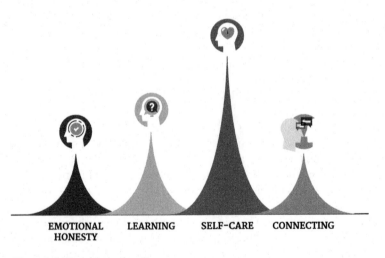

Figure 4.5 Coaching tales: Rowan

Coaching tales: Beth

Beth had just started a new job and was absolutely loving it. All her time was spent talking to other parts of the business, connecting with customers and asking questions about what was going well (or otherwise). She supplemented this by researching the industry best practice approaches for doing her job. Even when she wasn't at work, she was busy thinking about new ways of doing her job better.

Beth was energised by her job, but could feel that something wasn't quite right. She knew her approach wasn't going to be sustainable, and wanted to explore possible things to change.

Using the GRID coaching framework, she realised that her Goal was to create a more centred approach to her job, where she could balance her work related excitement with her life outside work. Even though she was energised about her work, she wasn't finding time to find peace, and that resulted in her feeling not quite like herself.

She decided that she would need to dial down either her Connecting or Learning focus to create some time so that she could dial up her Self-Care.

Reflection: we can be resilient in the short term by spending all our energy in a limited number of Foundations, but that long term resilience requires us to play with all four dials.

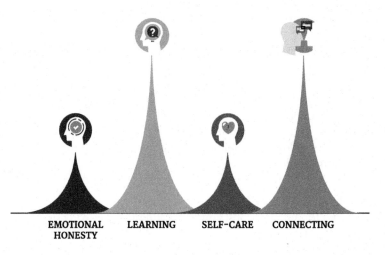

EMOTIONAL   LEARNING   SELF-CARE   CONNECTING
HONESTY

Figure 4.6 Coaching tales: Beth

Coaching moment

Consider what your Resilience Profile might look like using the four Resilience Foundations.

1   Which Foundation(s) do you think are getting most of your focus right now?
2   Which Foundation(s) do you think are being neglected?
3   What impact do you think this is having on your ability to achieve your career ambitions at work?

Some organisations, like SCIRT, take their responsibility to create the right environment for resilience at work very seriously. They deliberately design actions to grow the resilience of their employees, they provide the environment to cultivate resilience and they develop tools and resources to support this.

Some organisations don't.

This book has been designed to explore how we can all take responsibility for growing our own resilience at any time, regardless of what our company is doing . . . and regardless of the support we get from our manager or team leader.

This book aims to give us the tools and resources to do this ourselves.

Coaching moments

Current job

Consider your own organisation (or one that you would very much like to work at).

1   What have you already learned about resilience that you would you love to see implemented at your work?
2   Who could you talk about this with?
3   What role would you potentially like to play in designing or implementing these ideas?

Future job

In applying for any new jobs, consider asking the following questions during the interview process.

The questions will help you to consider whether your potential new employer is as committed as you are to developing resilience.

1   What development have you specifically offered to your leaders in the last twelve months to grow their emotional intelligence?
2   How is learning shared across the organisation?
3   How do you encourage collaboration across the business and outside the business?
4   What wellbeing activities have you encouraged employees to take part in over last six months?

A learning legacy

From the moment that the great value in sharing the lessons learned along the way was realised, there was a commitment to supporting the design and implementation of a project called the SCIRT Learning Legacy.

This resulted in the SCIRT Learning Legacy website filled with free resources and tools to support organisations and communities worldwide, particularly those in high hazard zones.

This SCIRT Learning Legacy contributed to inspiring the book you're reading now.

Tell me more!

Read

- Understanding Uncertainty and Reducing Vulnerability: Lessons from resilient thinking. F. Berkes, 2007. http://research-legacy.arch.tamu.edu/epsru/Course_Readings/Ldev671MARS689/LDEV671_Readings/Berkes_understandinguncertainty_nathaz.pdf
- Loss, Trauma and Human Resilience: Have we underestimated the human capacity to thrive after extremely adverse events? G. A. Bonanno, 2004. www.ncbi.nlm.nih.gov/pubmed/14736317
- Vulnerable but Invincible: A longitudinal study of resilient children and youth. E. Werner and R. Smith, 1982 and 1989
- Resilience: The big picture – top themes and trends. E. Lovell, A. Bahadur, T. Tanner and H. Morsi. The Overseas Development Institute. www.odi.org/sites/odi.org.uk/files/resource-documents/10626.pdf
- www.challengeofchange.co.nz (Dr Derek Roger and his team bring together psychology, psychometrics and neuroscience to influence change at work.)
- Coaching for Leadership Resilience: An integrated approach. Carmelina Lawton Smith, 2017
- How People Learn to be Resilient. Maria Konnikova, 2016
- The Relationship Between Personality Traits and Psychological Resilience. Grace Fayombo, 2010

- Ordinary Magic: Lessons from research and resilience in human development. Ann Maasten, 2009
- Handbook of Resilience in Children. Emmy Werner, 1971
- The Resilience Scale. Gail Wagnild and Heather Young, 1993
- Building Resilience in the Workplace. Chartered Institute of Personnel and Development (UK), 2011
- The Resilience Dividend. Judith Rodin, 2014
- The Resilience Institute and The Hardiness Institute
- Secrets of Resilient People. John Lees, 2014
- Option B: Facing adversity, building resilience and finding joy. Adam Grant and Sheryl Sandberg, 2017
- Grit: The power of passion and perseverance. Angela Duckworth, 2016
- The Resilience Factor: 7 keys to finding your inner strength and overcoming life's hurdles. Karen Reivich and Andrew Shatte, 2002
- The Road to Resilience. The American Psychological Association. www.apa.org/helpcenter/road-resilience.aspx
- www.wellbeingandresilience.com/resilience (The Centre for Wellbeing and Resilience.)

Watch

- TED Talk: The Fringe Benefits of Failure. J. K. Rowling
- Positively Resilient: www.youtube.com/watch?v=-eWpyoGfRg0
- The science of becoming more resilient: www.youtube.com/watch?v=AEWnTjgGVcw
- Change your brain and resilience: www.youtube.com/watch?v=q7XE9pYnC5E
- www.ted.com/talks/angela_lee_duckworth_grit_the_power_of_passion_and_perseverance

Play

- Quiz: Personal Adaptability Inventory. Audra Proctor. www.changefirst.com
- Quiz: University of Penn State offers several online assessments to support your understanding of what your start point is. www.authentichappiness.sas.upenn.edu/testcenter

SCIRT

Throughout the five-year project there was a website which kept Christchurch residents constantly updated on progress.

This has now become the Learning Legacy website, where tools, resources and lessons learned are shared for other organisations who would like to learn from the journey.

- https://scirtlearninglegacy.org.nz/ (The Learning Legacy Site.)
- https://scirtlearninglegacy.org.nz/story/peak-performance-coaching-scirt (Information about the Peak Performance coaching team.)

Resilient Organisations

Resilient Organisations, Christchurch, New Zealand, offers a fresh perspective on complex challenges of working in a world that is filled with disruption.

- www.resorgs.org.nz/ (The Resilient Organisations website.)
- www.resorgs.org.nz/images/stories/pdfs/scirt_case_study.pdf (The case study of SCIRT.)

The New Zealand Institute of Wellbeing and Resilience

Dr Lucy Hone and Dr Denise Quinlan are the Founders of the New Zealand Institute of Wellbeing and Resilience. Their academic research currently informs some of the latest thinking around the world regarding the escalating levels of wellbeing issues at work, in education and the community. I have been working with them to explore the wellbeing and resilience research for this book, and I am delighted to be joining their journey as a trusted member of their team.

- www.nziwr.co.nz

Resilience frameworks and Foundations

GRID	**Here are some questions for you to consider, as you reflect on what you have learned in this chapter. They have been designed to help you decide how to use what you have read. You may wish to consider the questions alone, with a friend or with your manager at work.**
GOAL	• What will be different when you are more resilient than you are right now?
	• What are the main reasons that you want to develop resilience?
	• When have you felt resilient at work? What was different to now?
	• What are some of the clues that you are not at your most resilient now – what are you seeing or feeling?
	• Who do you know that typifies resilience at work? Explore.
REALITY	• What impact is this having on you?
	• What strategies have you used in the past to develop your resilience at work (or in life) to achieve your goals?
	• How much energy are you currently giving right now to the four Foundations of resilience? Emotional Honesty? Self-Care? Connecting? Learning?

(continued)

(continued)

- During a time when you felt more resilient than now, how was your focus on these four Foundations of resilience different?
- What might you need to do more of to become more resilient?
- What might you need to let go of to become more resilient?

IDEAS

- What have you already learned about resilience which you could try out?
- How could you give more energy to Emotional Honesty? Self-Care? Connecting? Learning?
- Who do you know that seems to be more resilient at work and what could you learn from them?
- If you made a teeny change to become more resilient what could that be?
- What are some of the bigger changes which you could make?
- Where could you go to find out more about building resilience strategies?

DO

- What are you going to do immediately?
- What do you need to plan to do over the next twelve months or longer term?
- Who could provide you with support to become more resilient?
- How could your employer or manager potentially support you?
- What might prevent you from achieving this and if this happens, what will you do to overcome it?
- How will you know you're doing the right thing? What will be different?

5   The world of VUCA Change

Resources in this chapter:

- Identifying sources of pressure at work
- VUCA Change
- Strategies for VUCA success
- Emoji Island
- VUCA Watch

What is this chapter about?

One of the main influencers on our need for resilience at work is that of change.

Our boss changes; and they have a very different working style to our previous boss, the legislation changes, and we need to use different processes or the job we want to apply for changes and we no longer have the knowledge, skills and experience that are needed.

This chapter introduces a framework for considering change in the workplace and helps us to consider the strategies we already have for both anticipating and navigating change.

Because we are growing our resilience (and therefore finding ways to not just survive change but use it as a catalyst for personal growth) we will be exploring how you might really lean into the things at work which change.

Noticing change

If you were to take a few moments to reflect on things that have changed in your life since yesterday, what would you notice?

Perhaps there would be some barely perceptible changes - Your body is a little bit older? Your hair is a little bit longer? The flowers in your garden a little more beautiful?

Maybe there would be some more noticeable changes to those very same things – a tattoo? A haircut? Some new landscaping?

Our world is constantly altering, changing and shifting in both subtle and obvious ways simultaneously. Some of this we have control over, and some of this we have no control over.

This is not exactly an earth-shattering revelation.

We all know that everything around us constantly changes, so let's introduce some more unusual thinking into our reflections:

What if all change was not created equal?

Coaching moment

Think about the last six months of your life **AND** your work. Consider the reality of changes that you have experienced – whether big or small, life changing or inconsequential, complete or still in progress. How is your job different? How have you already changed and grown?

- What do you observe as having gained during this time?
- What do you observe as having lost or let go during this time?
- How do your experiences differ between planned and unplanned change?
- What have your coping strategies included so far – the things that have kept you going or helped you through?
- Who has supported you during these changes?

Sources of pressure at work

An online survey revealed some of the main sources of pressure at work as including:

- Top down pressure
- Policy changes
- Manager support
- Relationships at work
- Overlooked for promotion
- Not considered for new job
- Money issues
- Fear of the unknown
- Need more qualifications
- Life pressures
- Fear
- Fatigue
- Not enjoying job
- No obvious next step on the ladder
- Waiting for a miracle
- Don't know what I want

- Not enough feedback
- Limiting self-beliefs
- Time management issues
- Too much work
- Uncertain industry
- Idea blockers

Not all of these sources of pressure will lead to stress at work, for some people these things ignite creativity or energy. Some people will simply see these things as frustrations or challenges to overcome. The source of pressure becomes a workplace stressor (and therefore a possible place to develop resilience) when we perceive it as something we cannot overcome, or we fixate on it negatively.

Coaching moment

Take a moment to think about what your sources of pressure are for you in the workplace. Notice whether any of them are on the list above and add extra ones that haven't been noted.

1   Consider how long these pressures have been a part of your work experience: a short time? A long time? Present in each role you have had?
2   Think about when you have worked and NOT experienced these pressures in your job. What was different about this time? How were you thinking or being differently?
3   How could you use these observations to help you do more than just survive at work – what ideas are you developing for changes that you could make?

Introducing VUCA Change

The idea of change as being made up of different components originated in the US Military during the 1990s. General George Casey introduced the idea of sub-categories within change including; Volatility, Uncertainty, Complexity and Ambiguity to better equip and train military staff.

The application of military learning to the world of business is fairly common; from ways to be more decisive through to instilling ultimate trust so it's not surprising that the world of business has looked for VUCA to expand its thinking about navigating change.

The VUCA framework is effectively built on two principals; how much understanding or knowledge we have about something, and how well we can predict the outcome of our actions.

In breaking down change like this, we can not only identify whether there are times when we flourish (and therefore work out what sort of change we love), but we can also consider our wider coping strategies.

Here are some examples of how VUCA might look in your workplace:

VUCA	Definition	Examples at work
Volatile	Something totally out of the blue Unpredictable and/or turbulent Rapid, unexpected or unstable change	Company goes bust Redundancy Random interruptions
Uncertain	No obvious cause and effect Lack of reliability Unclear impact	No feedback about performance Job insecurity Unpredictable leaders
Complex	Complicated or Intricate circumstances Overwhelming information Confusing possibilities	Multiple stakeholders Too much information Red tape preventing innovation
Ambiguous	Multiple interpretations Lack of clarity or precedent Vague information	Confusion from reporting lines Unclear career development Unclear information

According to the research about VUCA, if we experience these VUCA Changes at work here are some of the outcomes we might see:

VUCA	Definition	Possible Outcomes
Volatile	Something totally out of the blue Unpredictable and/or turbulent Rapid, unexpected or unstable change	Emotional outbursts Unpredictable behaviours Stand-offs Poorly informed decision making
Uncertain	No obvious cause and effect Lack of reliability Unclear impact	Doubt and hesitation Frustration "Analysis paralysis"
Complex	Complicated or intricate circumstances Overwhelming information Confusing possibilities	Confusion Misinformation (perceived or real) Action without understanding
Ambiguous	Multiple interpretations Lack of clarity or precedent Vague information	Time wasting Resistance to ris. "Chinese Whispers" (also known as "Russian Scandal" or "Telephone")

Suddenly, we can more easily start to recognise our own personal response to change (and we might even begin to recognise the responses of other people in our team, which can help us to realise that responses to change can be very different).

Once we've done this, we can begin to prioritise how we're going to handle our response, helping us into a more helpful state, by using the Resilience Foundations to help us.

Coaching moment

Reflect on the stressors that you have identified at work (the reasons that you need to be resilient) and consider where they might sit within the VUCA framework.

1   Where are your main areas of stress right now? Are they Volatile? Complex? Uncertain? Ambiguous?
2   Are there any elements of VUCA where you are not experiencing stress?
3   For the areas where you are not experiencing stress, what do you think you are doing differently?

Examples of VUCA at work

VUCA	Definition	Examples
Volatile	Something totally out of the blue. Unpredictable and/or turbulent. Rapid or unstable change	Ruben was enjoying his job as a successful team leader in a retail organisation when he was unexpectedly offered a shareholder role in a new start-up company. The role conflicted with his current work because it was with a competitor. He resigned from his role without really understanding what his new role expected of him because he was so excited.
Uncertain	No obvious cause and effect. Lack of reliability	Karen wants to reconnect with possible work leads as she approaches the end of her employment contract but has been told the contract might be extended. She has been told this for the last three months and now has just twenty days left on her contract. She hasn't done anything despite knowing that her contract is nearly over.

(continued)

(continued)

VUCA	Definition	Examples
Complex	Complicated or intricate circumstances Overwhelming information	Rick would like more enjoyment in his role as an engineer and was on the verge of resigning, however he is also part way through completing a leadership diploma, is moving home and expecting a baby with his partner. He feels totally trapped and is getting more stressed every day.
Ambiguous	Multiple interpretations Lack of clarity or precedent	Tracy accepted a role at a national airline eight years ago. Every year she discusses her desire and potential to progress into a more senior role at her formal appraisal, but still believes she has no clear information about how to actually achieve this. She is now very negative and frequently shares her frustrations with her team.

Your VUCA challenges

Make a note of some of the things that are happening to you which fall into the VUCA framework.

VUCA	Definition	Your Experience
Volatile	Something totally out of the blue Unpredictable and/or turbulent Rapid or unstable change	
Uncertain	No obvious cause and effect Lack of reliability	
Complex	Complicated or intricate circumstances Overwhelming information	
Ambiguous	Multiple interpretations Lack of clarity or precedent	

Strategies for VUCA success

During the SCIRT project, we started to notice strategies that people were using to help them when they faced a VUCA situation.

If something totally unexpected and Volatile happened; EVEN if it was a positive unexpected occurrence, some people in the team had a bit of a meltdown. The main thing that kept them from over reacting and believing the sky to be falling was to remind themselves of what they ultimately wanted to achieve – their **Vision**.

Another person was facing a situation which was especially Uncertain. One road requiring attention had no plans at all to highlight where existing infrastructure was laid (like telephone and internet cables) so the team asked HEAPS of questions of the underground companies until they had created more **Understanding**.

One meeting we attended was incredibly high in Complexity; with multiple stakeholder and no clear guidelines on the reason for the meeting. The strategy for this situation was to talk to as many people as possible who were involved – therefore increasing understanding more of their ideas and decisions and building **Communication and Collaboration** with them.

Where Ambiguity was the issue, we found that not only did we benefit from increasing our communication and asking more questions (the same as Uncertainty and Complexity), but we also researched what has gone before (and worked) and then presented possible solutions to explore how well they meet the needs of the circumstances. We made **Assumptions** and then checked them out.

With this approach, we re-designed VUCA for ourselves so that whenever we were faced with change which caused a sense of anxiety, unease, nervousness or any other unhelpful response we looked for opportunities to explore:

- Vision
- Understanding
- Communication/Collaboration
- Assumption checking

We are keeping these principles in mind as we move through the book – constantly referring back to our goals, bigger picture or vision . . . asking ourselves questions to create understanding and communication and questioning the assumptions that we have made about our circumstances by challenging our thoughts.

Your VUCA strategies

Each of us already has wisdom and resources to thrive and grow in Volatile, Unexpected, Complex and Ambiguous change during our career.

We know this because you've already likely used your wisdom and resources to thrive and grow in your life outside your career.

Whether you are just starting out from school, adjusting the direction of your career journey or approaching your later years in life you can draw on a whole range of techniques and resources to support you and this book will develop even more for your bag of tools. They can be used whether you are just starting your career, or whether you are entering the later years of your career and they can be used within your current place of work or to support you while you look for a new job.

Of course, the reality (and we learned this from our chapter about resilience) is that for some of us it will be harder to overcome VUCA Change than for others. We may have additional environmental, or physical factors to overcome, as well as the mental hurdle of the change itself.

If you find that your own strategies aren't quite working for you, then you might want to consider additional support, whether from a career coach, a counsellor or other mental health professional who can support your journey.

The good news is that there's currently a global trend towards acknowledging this; the reality that while we can all grow our resilience, for some it might take additional support. The examples being set by public figures including Princes William and Harry, Sheryl Sandberg and Stephen Fry have all contributed greatly to encouraging honest discussion about this previously sensitive topic.

This approach contributes directly towards the Emotional Honesty Foundation for resilience, which is explored in Chapter 6.

Coaching moment

For at least one week, keep a diary of the things that happen to you in your work, and in your life. Choose which category you would like to put each event in (e.g. something unexpected you might decide to place in the Volatile row). Then use the framework below to start noticing your strategies.

VUCA	Your experience: what happened	What you were thinking	How you behaved: your actions	What you did that helped you
Volatile				
Uncertain				
Complex				
Ambiguous				

Now that we've got a clearer understanding of the things at work that might be causing our stress or pressure, and therefore creating a need to be resilient, we can begin to explore some simple steps to address them.

VUCA	Definition	Possible solution
Volatile	Something totally out of the blue Unpredictable and/or turbulent Rapid, unexpected or unstable change	**Stay focussed on the Vision**: clean up/ update your social media profile to make sure it all matches e.g. your LinkedIn profile and CV; ensure your networks are robust and your interview technique is strong in case you need to find a new way to achieve your goals.
Uncertain	No obvious cause and effect Lack of reliability Unclear impact	**Create understanding**: ask lots of open questions from your team, your manager, your customers . . . anybody who can help you find some answers.
Complex	Complicated or intricate circumstances Overwhelming information Confusing possibilities	**Communicate and Collaborate more**: consider the information that you believe is missing and create questions to help you fill in as many gaps as possible. Talk to others about this.
Ambiguous	Multiple interpretations Lack of clarity or precedent Vague information	**Check assumptions**: ask more questions and experiment to see what works. By trying something and checking if it's right you are likely to begin clearing the haze.

Coaching moment

What are the other tools and resources that might be able to help you at work? For example, does your employer have information websites? Newsletters or updates?

The world of Change has the potential to present any number of scenarios to us every day at work. Table 5.1 provides some of the circumstances that can contribute to our need to be more resilient, as identified by contributors to this book.

VUCA Changes at work

According to a report by the World Economic Forum (The Future of Jobs and Skills), almost 65% of the jobs that students who are at school now will be doing in the future don't even exist yet . . . how incredible is that?!

And for some of us, how potentially terrifying.

Table 5.1 VUCA strategies

	Definition	Possible career scenarios	Three critical questions to consider	What to avoid	Tools and resources
V	**Volatile** – rapid change and unpredictability, turbulent environment, unexpected outcomes Remember your Vision	• Unexpected job offers • Sudden redundancy • Undesirable impact of industry change (e.g. financial crash) • Sudden change of culture (e.g. hostile takeover)	1 What do I need to do to reconnect with my Bigger Picture? 2 How can I remain calm so that I can make a considered decision about my next action? 3 What other ways could I achieve my goals, despite what has just happened?	• Panic • Acting without thinking • Running away • Fight, flight or freeze	Career Vision Board Career Mission ResilienceCheck in Reconnect with values Name and normalise emotions
U	**Uncertain** – lack of reliability, no clear cause and effect, high potential for surprise Seek more Understanding	• Multiple rejections from job applications • No clear path to achieve the job you really want • Limited guidance to support achieving your career goals	1 How could I find out about possible actions by looking at different teams/organisations? 2 What questions could help me to have more certainty about this? 3 Who could answer my questions?	• Giving up • Resigning without reaching out to understand • Blaming others for lack of information	Look for feedback/ evidence at every stage Be honest about lack of preparation/mistakes Reflect on what you're doing and learning Research what's in other organisations/roles

C Complex – complicated or intricate, multiple and inter-related forces, overwhelming volume of information. Build your Collaborations	• Multiple stakeholders or clients at work • Not being fulfilled by work but being too busy to do anything about it • Global team structure • Distress caused by workplace	1 Who do I know who could help me work this out? 2 Who else has experienced this and how did they handle it? 3 How could my manager or mentor help me to unravel this?	• Getting overwhelmed by detail • Overlooking simple short term strategies • Trying to solve the problem alone	Temperature check for career every six months Online forums to discuss issues Best practice reviews in journals
A Ambiguous – multitude of options and outcomes, lack of clarity, more than one interpretation. Become more Agile	• Many possible career paths to choose from • Not sure what is required for a pay rise • Requirements of role unclear • New policy/procedure roll out • Performance at work is unclear	1 What's the smallest step I could take towards achieving my goals regardless? 2 How can I "test and check" to create more clarity? 3 Who might know some of the answers?	• Total inaction or resistance • Just doing what other people think you should do • Making up a story about what is causing ambiguity	Career decision matrix Test and check evidence Seek more feedback Ask open questions Experiment and learn from what doesn't go to plan Summarising what's expected

Workplaces have changed considerably within the last thirty years. If you were to search for roles which have disappeared from our world during this time they might include things like:

1   Switchboard operator
2   Dictaphone operator
3   Typing pools
4   Bowling alley pinsetters
5   Street sweeper
6   Bus conductor

On the flip side, we could consider some of the jobs available today that were probably unthinkable in the 1990s:

1   Social media analyst
2   App developer
3   Professional gamer
4   Data mining
5   Cloud computing
6   Uber driver

If you had suggested to a teenager back in the 1990s that you were scared for their future because jobs that they would be doing don't exist, so you can't help them and you feel helpless . . . that would have no doubt caused considerable angst. If that same teenager is now working as a professional gamer, or developing the latest app, I'm sure they would wave away your concerns with a glint in their eye.

There absolutely will be continued change and evolution; just as there always has and jobs will continue to both disappear and be created along the way.

However, it's very unlikely that this will happen overnight despite what dramatic news reports suggest . . . (none of the jobs above ceased to exist overnight) in fact only the Volatile element of VUCA Change is likely to take us completely by surprise (for example, our company goes out of business overnight or our boss fires us out of the blue), and often if we reflect a little there are subtle signs that this might be on the cards (for example; declining profits, fewer projects or financial troubles).

By dialling up our Learning Resilience Foundations and considering our role, our company and our industry every three to six months we are likely more easily to notice the signs that our job is at risk or disappearing and we can do something about it. We are less likely to sleepwalk into finding that our role or organisation no longer exists.

Coaching moment

Take a few minutes to think about your own workplace. Consider all the jobs you have had (or if you are early in your career, the subjects you have studied).

What are the jobs (or subjects) which have declined or disappeared?

What are the new jobs (or subjects) which have evolved or appeared?

1   What excites you about the changes that you have noticed?
2   What concerns you about the changes that you have noticed?
3   How could you use these observations to influence your resilience? (for example, could you look for opportunities to upskill into something you are unsure of which seems to be getting popular? Could you learn what's happening overseas to see if you can predict some of the possible outcomes?)

Thirty years of change

When you think about work in general; the job you have, the skills you're using, the changes you know about (or the ones you don't know about) what comes to mind?

Coaching moment

Look at the picture of Emoji Island and think about how you feel at work right now.

1   Which emotions/emoji do you most identify with right now? What do you think is contributing to feeling like this?
2   Which emotions/emoji would you prefer to be more like? What is the difference between the two?
3   What will need to happen for you to begin the transition from the emotion/emoji you feel like now to the emotion/emoji you would prefer to become?

(continued)

(continued)

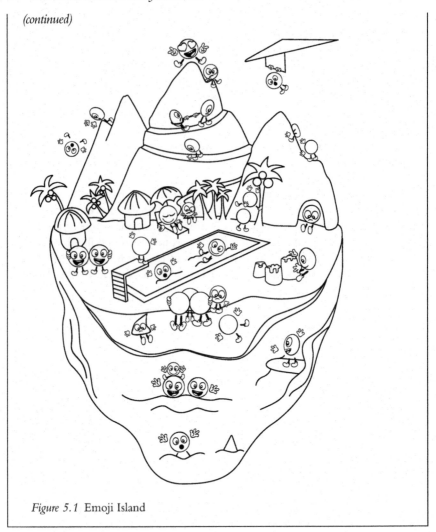

Figure 5.1 Emoji Island

In the 1990s, academic institutes were teaching us that the following areas were likely to experience rapid or significant change in the coming decade:

- Technological change
- Shifting skills requirements
- Responsive organisations
- Business productivity
- Diversity
- Participative leadership styles
- Flexible careers

It would seem they were pretty much spot on, though how do these categories compare with our world of work today?

There is little doubt that we are unbelievably more technically connected and enabled than we were thirty years ago, which has had an interesting effect on when, where and how we can work. On the one hand, it's brought us the ability to work pretty much any place and any time – but on the other hand it's created a significant challenge for defining the transition between when we work and when we don't.

In Deloitte's report "Rewriting the Rules for the Digital Age" (2017 Global Human Capital Trends) there are revised categories for us to consider focussing our attention. These are areas where significant likely change has been identified and they include:

- Technological change
- Shifting skills requirements
- Agile organisations
- Business productivity
- Diversity
- Emotionally intelligent leadership
- Careers and learning

If we compare this latest report with those academic findings from thirty years ago we might notice several interesting things:

- There is considerable similarity between the areas of work that were identified as likely to cause change in the 1990s and those of today.
- The role of technology, shifting skills, diversity and business productivity requirements have stayed the same. We are, and always will be, impacted by technology, need to continually update our skills in a way that's personal to our unique requirements and we must ultimately deliver results that lead to business success.
- There is now even more interest in the potential for careers and learning to influence how we handle and navigate change. That our organisations are shifting gives us the opportunity to pursue previously unknown career options.

Another interesting observation made by the Deloitte team was that overall, individuals tend to keep up with the pace of change better than businesses. They suggest that on closer examination of stress sources at work, we might find that business practice, policy or procedure that is associated with change is the source of stress rather than the change itself.

This is great, because it serves to highlight even more strongly that by focussing on enabling ourselves to have a more helpful response to the thing that's stressing us out at work, then we will be able to grow even more resilient.

The Deloitte team also suggest that because many organisations are structured to support a Silo Mindset (e.g. finance team sits together, HR team sits together, project team sits together) this may undermine the potential for organisations to be more connected and collaborative, thus undermining this Resilience Foundation. It's worth asking yourself how you could overcome this if it's an issue for you . . . no need to ask everybody to move their desks around, it could be as simple as getting to know people in the other teams.

The WAY we do work has also changed over the years . . . consider the following:

Figure 5.2 Word cloud: the way we work

Some of these changes might lead to better work options for you, and some may lead to worse options. None of them are guaranteed within your workplace, but it's certainly worth being aware that they exist in case there are ways to make them work for both you and your employer.

The rise of the Results Only Work Environment within this context is interesting, since it effectively reduces the need to be "at" work (as in very traditional workplace structures) and calls for delivery of work on a results basis.

This is what consultants and contractors have been traditionally used for, but now it's growing with the increased use of interim or temporary workers like Giggers and those working in Alliances and they make up a much larger part of the company. The pressures at work will likely shift but may present in different forms even with all that freedom and flexibility.

Coaching tales: Becky

Becky was incredibly stressed about the volatility of her journey to work in the morning. Sometimes she could arrive by the scheduled 8:30am start time, but because her commute involved travelling through a very congested zone she was often up to thirty minutes late and very flustered.

Realising this was not a good way to start her day, she decided to have an honest conversation with her manager. Her vision remained to work a full day, and to ensure that she could start and finish by her agreed times.

In reviewing this with her manager, they realised that she had the opportunity to start her working day at home – she would check her emails, return phone calls and begin any work which didn't require her presence in the office, leaving home by 7:45am.

Becky's commute went from 1–1 ½ hours to just 45 minutes with this simple change. She was also much less stressed when she arrived at work, and her commitment to work soared.

Reflection: identifying the points of VUCA friction and then creating a plan to address them can be hugely beneficial.

Coaching moment

Reflect on the way you <u>currently</u> do your job (perhaps from the list above or another option).

1   What are the benefits to you of working in this way?
2   If you cannot think of any benefits, what would be the benefits to you of working in a different way? What would be the benefits to your business?
3   What would be the risks of changing the way you work, to you? Your business?

You may decide to have a conversation with your HR team or your manager about what you have reflected on here, or you may decide to simply consider this way of working at some point in the future.

If you were to explore the skills which will likely still be required in our future world of work, you would find that you are developing them by working through this book.

Analytical and problem solving skills are developed by growing our ability to ask and consider good questions. By using the GRID framework and exploring our own thoughts and possibilities, rather than expecting somebody else to tell us what to do we are stepping into futureproofing our analytical capabilities.

Our focus on connections will supercharge our confidence in building relationships, which is going to be critical to support the way we work with different types of employee – we will likely not be working in the same team, sitting in the same area of the office, so being able to build and cultivate friendships at work will likely make a difference – we are all going to have more opportunity to collaborate in order to achieve results, rather than wait for a boss to tell us what to do.

Constantly looking for ways to grow is fundamental to a self-coaching mindset, which is based on the belief that there are always ways for us to grow and learn, should we choose to do so. Noticing when something isn't going to plan, and then deciding to lean into it further to unpack it, explore it and work out how to change it is going to contribute to you standing out from the crowd of other employees who are still waiting for their fairy godmother to fix it.

Coaching moment

Your job or industry	Ten years ago?	Today?	Ten years in the future?
What were the most sought after skills?			
How did you use technology, and what systems were "hot"?			
What were the biggest challenges for the job or industry?			
What was the working environment like?			
What was trendy?			
What were the key drivers for change?			

VUCA *watch*

Book a critical meeting into your diary right now; just half hour reviews, every three to six months, of the following questions to help you stay in touch with what's going on in your industry and your job.

It won't guarantee that you will be certain of what's around the corner, but it will help you to start to notice trends.

Coaching moment

Below are questions to ask yourself every three to six months to stay ahead of what might be going on in your industry or work. If you have any concerns about what you find, you could talk to your manager or your HR team to explore them.

1   What are the career strategists saying about my role, my company or my industry? (Check out the resources in the Tell me more! section.)
2   How much feedback have I had about my performance at work? (If the answer is "very little", use the resources of Chapter 9, Learning, to find out more.)
3   How has the value of my organisation changed since my last review? (Visit pages like those identified in the Tell me more! section to find out more about market share, market ranking etc.)
4   What are people saying about my company? (Check out places like www.glassdoor.com, customer surveys or simply google your organisation to see what comes up as their latest news.)
5   What is the pipeline of work for my role? Team? Company?
6   What could you do to protect your career for the future (e.g. cross skilling, transferable skills, becoming an A performer, multiple income streams, flexible location)?

The watchlist

Of course, the world where we live (and therefore where we work) is rapidly changing, so this isn't an exhaustive list . . . but if you're working in any of the areas outlined below, it would be a really good idea to check into the latest research every three to six months to see whether you need to make more drastic changes.

1   **Power industry**: massive changes expected in an industry under constant pressure from both supply (availability of resources) and demand (desires of consumers). We are likely to see a decline in the need for some skills and possibly even a shift to more locally provided power sources. However, there will be a rise in need for skills using newer or more unusual energy sources.
2   **Printing**: already revolutionised by the growth of online reading, the industry is being further shaken by the explosion of 3D printing, which is already being used by aircraft manufacturers, by vets to support animal surgery and even by everyday folks like us to bring our selfies to life! As a result, despite threatening jobs in the traditional areas of printing, there is

likely to be a significant need for skills to repair and service them, along with the designers and architects of the systems themselves.

3   **Car industry**: the rapid rise in technology enabling driverless cars, along with vehicles that no longer use petrol or diesel, will likely result in an enormous shift to this industry. This will undoubtedly have a knock-on impact to anybody in a role which services this, including taxi drivers, bus drivers, truck drivers through to less obvious areas like repairs and possibly even medical professionals as accident rates (hopefully) decline. However, there will likely be a rise in related areas like engineers to service the new vehicles, traffic designers to revise roads and ways to monitor movements.

4   **Education**: previously considered as a stalwart in predicable employment, this industry is one of the most innovative, presumably because of the very nature in which it operates (learning and growth). The surge of online, high quality and often free learning from open coursewear options like Massive Open Online Course (MOOC) and Massachusetts Institute of Technology (MIT) will likely result in the declining need for teachers and related professionals. However, there will likely be a rise in the need for coaches to embed learning, and designers to create the materials.

5   **Bots:** the 2004 film about life in a world of robots ("I, Robot") seemed to be onto something when we look around at the phenomenal growth in the use of robots to support our work. Drones are being used for planning, planting and monitoring in the agricultural sector, for warehousing and sourcing in retail and even for bricklaying in the construction industry. New skills are being sought with roles that are able to "drive" them.

The VUCA elephants

It's all very well exploring the Volatile, Uncertain, Complex and Ambiguous world that we work in, but what if some of us are facing these scenarios:

Multiple challenges

Handling change at work with resilience is often hard enough, without adding to it by also needing to deal with changes in our private life too.

It absolutely, completely and utterly can be done; which is the whole point of writing this book. In Christchurch, we have plenty of stories where normal everyday people have handled the demands of their job while simultaneously rebuilding of their home and supporting their family.

Some of these people found it easier than others, some of these people grew stronger, and therefore more resilient as a result (now living in better homes, or with new skills).

However, the fact remains that if you have layer upon layer of challenge and change, things will be harder for you. This does not mean you've failed, nor does it mean you cannot be resilient – it simply means you may need to use a different strategy. If you dial up all of the Resilience Foundations in this book (you are emotionally honest, you look after yourself, you lean into your connections and look for ways to learn from what you're experiencing) and you're still feeling stuck – then it's likely a sign that you should find a health professional to support you.

Talk to your GP, access your Employee Assistance Programme, visit a counsellor . . . do something. Doing nothing means that are likely to have to go with whatever the situation evolves – doing something means that you will at least be able to have more control over what happens.

Careful what you wish for

Ask any career professional for the main reasons that people decide to leave their job and one of the top contenders is usually, "a micro manager".

A major trend over the last thirty years has been the growth of "employee led" initiatives at work, for example employee led performance conversations, innovations and learning, thus overriding some of the micro management and putting us, the employees, very much in the driving seat.

The rise of the concept of Holacracy at work very much plays a part in this, with organisations challenging the rigid and hierarchical structures (and never-changing organisational charts that result from this). Introducing this level of flexibility creates a new format for us to work in.

The upside of this is that we can all play a more active role in contributing to our experience at work, but the downside is that it takes more work on our part; we have to take some ideas to the conversations. So, if we want less micro management and more opportunity for self-driven success, we need to be prepared to step into the void and provide information and solutions.

Growth is optional

You can of course choose to be the person that has worked in the organisation for twenty years and become part of the furniture. There's a certain sort of comfort to this place and there's absolutely no reason why you should become the "office Eeyore" (moaning and complaining about things that change) just because you've worked somewhere for a long time – in fact, it's quite possible to stay in a job for a really long time and simply enjoy the ride.

Bear in mind that it's likely that your colleagues will expect you to "be" a certain way, and this may make it even harder for you to change and grow, should you decide to do so.

Tell me more!

Read

- Rewriting the Rules for the Digital Age. 2017 Human Capital Trends. Deloitte. (A survey of more than 10,000 HR and Business leaders across 140 countries contributed to this cutting-edge report which explores the potential impact of transformation and disruption at work.)
- Who Moved my Cheese? Dr Spencer Johnston, 1998

- The Individual, Work and Organisation. Robin Fincham and Peter Rhodes, 1992
- Switch: How to change things when change is hard. Chip Heath and Can Heath, 2010
- Transitions: Making sense of life's changes. William Bridges, 2004
- Disruptive Technologies: Advances that will transform life, business and the global economy. www.mckinsey.com/business-functions/digital-mckinsey/our-insights/disruptive-technologies
- The Most Adaptive Companies. Boston Consulting Group, 2012

Websites

- Stay as current as possible with your industry performance:
    o www.bloomberg.com
    o www.fastcompany.com
    o www.fortune.com (Best Companies)
    o Stock exchange sites like: FTSE, NYSE, Market Watch
    o www.standardandpoors.com

- For numbers, facts and trends shaping our world: Pew Research Centre. www.pewresearch.org/
- Radical ideas for the future of 3D modelling and printing: www.thing iverse.com

---

Coaching moment

As you read about what's going on in your industry ask yourself the following questions:

1   How does this information make me feel?
2   How might this information affect my job?
3   Who could I talk to at work to explore what I have learned?

Food for thought?

- Did you know, in 2028 this might happen, www.youtube.com/watch?v=QpEFjWbXog0
- David Autor considers if automation will take away all our jobs, www.ted.com/talks/david_autor_why_are_there_still_so_many_jobs
- Andrew McAffee considers what future jobs might look like, www.youtube.com/watch?v=cXQrbxD9_Ng

Do: it's time to write your story (Action Plan)

This chapter about **VUCA Change** has underlined the importance of . . .
It has given me a better understanding of . . .
What I've learned about myself is . . .
What I'm particularly thankful for is . . .
What I'm going to do as a result is . . .
The impact this will have is . . .
What could get in the way is . . .
   (If this happens I'm going to . . .)
I will know I have succeeded because . . .
I am going to check what I've achieved on . . . (date)
The person who will help me to stay accountable to this plan is:

Part III

The Resilience Foundations

6   Emotional Honesty

The heart of growing more resilient is
to be honest with yourself from the start
and to expect that any negative emotions
you notice are simply a message that there
is possibility for change

Resources in this chapter:

- Emotional Word List
- GRID Emotional Honesty
- TELL Emotional Honesty
- Coaching moments:
  - Workplace stressors
  - Ambitious audit
  - Challenging thoughts
  - Unusual Ideas

What is this chapter about?

This chapter is about the first of our Resilience Foundations: Emotional Honesty. It includes growing an understanding of our emotional awareness, and a conscious focus on compassion and gratitude. The resources are specifically aimed at increasing our optimism and courage.

First, we'll review our definition of Emotional Honesty that is being used in this book, exploring its definitions and what it means.

Then we'll look at what Emotional Honesty means to you, the reasons you want to dial it up, the effect it's having on your resilience at work and your overall Goals for changing it.

After that, we'll review your Reality of being emotionally honest, with yourself, your workplace etc. As we consider Ideas to develop your Emotional Honesty, we'll dip our toes into the worlds of Positive Psychology, Neuroscience and Neurolinguistics.

Finally, you'll create a personalised plan of what you're going to do with what we learn. You might decide to focus on dialling up your Emotional Honesty for yourself, or you might decide to share what you learn with another person.

We've already learned that brains, minds and emotions are incredibly complex and personal things to explore, and I want to respect the incredible knowledge and capability of the researchers and academics that are dedicating their work to finding out about them. As a result, I want to be clear from the start of this chapter that this just the simplified tip of the iceberg.

What I hope to achieve is to ignite a desire for you to find out more (hopefully what you find will be the latest work that is even more current than the information you read in my book).

Put quite simply, the opportunity for us in developing the Emotional Honesty Foundation is that we're going to allow ourselves to experience more emotions from the whole spectrum available to us, roll them around for a while to see what they are like and what happens to us when we experience them, then decide if they are helpful or unhelpful with achieving the thing that we're hoping to achieve at work.

If you find that doing the exercises in this chapter is too hard, and that your emotional response is so intense that you are unable to remain rational then it is strongly recommended that you seek the advice and support of a mental wellbeing professional who can help you.

What is Emotional Honesty?

To be perfectly honest, I don't really buy into this "resilience" hype. It's just a totally unrealistic concept that we would never be sad or angry; surely we will just become fake by pretending to be positive all the time?

This perfectly timed question was asked of a professor at Auckland University as this book was going to print.

It sums up brilliantly some of the reservations and objections to the idea of resilience that we have already considered during our exploration of the Resilience Revolution.

It also gives us a great launch pad for exploring the research and considering our own thoughts, beliefs and definitions of Emotional Honesty.

In response to this question, the professor invited his student to consider the approach of an élite athlete training for an event like the Olympic Games or an extreme marathon.

He asked this question in return, "does your observation therefore mean that athletic resilience requires that we are never tired or injured? That we pretend to be at our best at all times?"

Resilience doesn't avoid dark places.

Far from it, the very nature of resilience suggests that we must encounter obstacles, difficulties and issues to have a need to examine our resilience in the first place.

This concept of Emotional Honesty forms one Foundation from our resilience framework.

The élite athlete must absolutely embrace injury, endure exhaustion and suffer self-doubt.

They dream of an enormous goal, and the work it will take to get there is simply a part of their journey.

They know that there will be sore muscles, aching hearts and burning lungs. They also know that they may not achieve a gold medal or win their race, but this does not make their goal any less worth striving for.

In the same way, job hunting and career ambitions that we have for ourselves become our equivalent of that very élite athletic dream.

Our journey towards it will likely be filled with moments of challenge, obstacle and hardship . . . but it is equally likely to be filled with moments of enjoyment, self-esteem and pride.

Whether we achieve our absolute vision, or a revised version because of unforeseen circumstances, we will be able to hold ourselves with dignity because we know that we did everything that we possibly could, and we didn't give up on the way.

Every day at work, we are likely to experience something that hasn't gone to plan, and you've already reflected on how you have handled the things that have happened to you in the last six months in our chapter about VUCA Change.

So, what if we have an opportunity to make some choices about how we handle the problems, issues and hard times that come our way as we strive to achieve our career ambitions?

For example, imagine that something has gone wrong and we have been knocked off the path we hoped for our career; maybe we asked for an internal promotion and didn't get it.

One response option to this could be that we brush it off, consider that it totally doesn't worry us and our inner voice subsequently tells us that we are being resilient.

This may very well be the case, particularly if we haven't done anything specific other than ask for an internal promotion.

If this was the case, then we likely haven't challenged ourselves in any other way other than to decide to be brave (or cheeky, or hopeful), put our hand up in the air and say, "I'd like to get a promotion please".

But how likely a scenario is this?

What's more likely is that either we brush off the rejection and SAY it doesn't worry us to the people involved in the decision making . . . but then we tell everybody else who will listen how disappointed we are.

Or, we have a conversation internally about how undervalued we are at work, start wondering if we are being discriminated against or start doubting whether we really do have the skills to succeed in our job.

So much of our sense of self is tied up into what we do that this rejection for a role can feel very much like a personal rejection of who we are.

How then, can we use our Emotional Honesty Foundation to help us?

The science of emotional wellness

Emotional wellness describes the extent to which we notice our thoughts, feelings and behaviours – and then, whether we perceive them as positive or negative and what we choose to do with that observation.

It goes beyond the idea that being emotionally well means that we can "handle stress effectively" or be "happy" and encourages us to consider that all emotional responses have their place in helping us to become more resilient.

Culturally defined "unhelpful" emotions can serve as indicators that there is something not right, and therefore create the powerful opportunity to explore what could be changed to improve our experience. They can create a place of power.

These "unhelpful" emotions can also be a perfectly normal and human response to the ups and downs of a lifetime of work.

I've included "unhelpful" emotions in parentheses, because it's usually down to interpretation about whether they are perceived as negative – in our context we are only going to consider emotions as either helpful or unhelpful depending on what we want to achieve. They can be influenced by both our personal values and our culture.

Coaching tales: Sabine

Sabine moved to New Zealand from Germany to support the rebuild of Christchurch. She had not long graduated with a Master's degree, and was looking forward to spending two years in a new country refining her skills.

Sabine's manager, David, was taking part in the Peak Performance Coaching initiative, and therefore met with a Leadership Coach every month. During one conversation, David expressed significant concern about Sabine and asked whether he could discuss her in his coaching session instead of himself.

He had recently caught up with Sabine to discuss her career aspirations on the project, and enquired how she was settling into New Zealand. Sabine had shared that she felt very lonely and homesick, which had surprised David greatly.

He was embarrassed to say that he hadn't known what to say at the time, because her Emotional Honesty had thrown him, and he wanted to explore how to handle this conversation in the future. He wanted to be a supportive manager, but he also didn't want to cross any personal/professional boundaries.

David concluded that expecting Sabine to be positive and settled in so quickly was potentially unrealistic, and based on his own expectations. It was certainly possible, but in this case, had not happened immediately.

He decided that he wanted to follow up with her, to find out if there was anything he could do to support her.

At the next coaching session, David shared that Sabine had been very surprised and a little affronted by his follow-up discussion about her homesickness.

She shared that she believed her experience to be fully expected, since this was the first time she had ever lived away from her family and friends from childhood. She did not feel a need to do anything to change this sense of homesickness or loneliness, and simply trusted that it would resolve over time as she met new friends and took up hobbies.

> **Reflection: emotions are open to interpretation both by those who experience them directly and those who indirectly experience them. They may be interpreted differently across generation and culture. If the person experiencing the emotion is not adversely concerned about their feelings, there may be no need to persuade them to turn around their emotions into a more helpful state. This might be a different story however, if Sabine's homesickness and loneliness was harming her work or her colleagues.**

The origins of emotional wellness began life as the study of emotional illness.

Traditionally, the science of psychology focussed on a "disease model" of emotional wellness within a clinical setting, and it was the goal of psychologists to identify abnormal behaviours and resulting mental illnesses.

This approach has resulted in enormous successes for both understanding and influencing some of the most widely experienced mental illnesses like depression, anxiety and stress which were previously considered incurable.

The humanistic movement in psychology of the mid twentieth century (influenced by the work of psychologists like Carl Rogers and Abraham Maslow) to some extent challenged the traditional psychological approach, by suggesting that the existence in humans of self-awareness and mindfulness contributed to helping us make conscious choices about our reactions to life events.

They suggested that we can intentionally choose what or who we would like to be, and make decisions which take us closer to that goal through challenging and driving our thoughts, words and actions.

Psychology, disrupted

To some extent this humanistic challenge paved the way for one of the most radical of challenges to psychology in the early 2000s when the work of Dr Martin Seligman came to the fore: Positive Psychology.

Seligman suggested that instead of focussing on the science of emotional disease and alleviating what is negative in our lives, psychology had an opportunity to explore the science of emotional strength. So began the Positive Psychology movement.

This is the scientific exploration of positive aspects of human life, such as happiness, wellbeing and flourishing. In our sporting world, we often learn the most from the teams or individuals who are the most successful – there is very little emphasis on how to understand what those teams at the bottom of the league are doing, and very much a focus on what we can learn from those who are flying high.

It makes perfect sense then, that we might gain useful insight from understanding what it is about people who are living amazing lives (and loving their lives). How do they do it, what are their secrets and what can we learn from them?

The founding belief of positive psychologists is that humans largely want to lead meaningful and fulfilled lives. They don't want to be miserable, stressed and dreading that alarm going off on a Monday morning. But they totally acknowledge that the darker side of emotion is not just a reality, it's actually good for the soul – we must be balanced, not just focussed on positive emotions.

Positive Psychology believes that humans actually **want** to understand and nurture what is good about themselves and find ways to improve our experiences of work, love and life. That seems like a grand idea to me.

The Positive Psychology Centre at Penn State University is currently one of the most active in this area, and is home to Dr Seligman himself. The science and the research currently focusses on three main areas:

1   **Understanding positive emotions:** the extent to which we are content with what has happened to us in life and work, feel happy in the "now" and have hope for the future.
2   **Understanding individual emotions:** this research focusses on the impact that our Values and Strengths have upon the extent that we can live a "good" life.
3   **Understanding positive organisations:** this is the study of how we behave when we are in a group, a workplace or a community.

Evidence wise, this is an extremely new area of psychology, which of course has its sceptics, because it is science. Scientists are always looking for ways to prove or disprove what they identify from their research, that's quite the point. It's a large part of their job.

I believe the sceptics make our conclusions stronger.

In this case some of the claims include that it's a happy science for the rich, a self-help option wrapped in pseudo-science and that it's blinding us to real issues in our world.

Having worked with its principles for five years I've found personally that there are parts of Positive Psychology that are useful for anybody, the science is undeniable and it could make a massive difference to helping us embrace and find solutions for the real issues in our world.

Their conclusion that we must all be cheerful, outgoing, goal-driven and status-seeking extraverts is a bit bonkers if you ask me. Keep reading the book, try out the exercises and let me know what you think.

Enter, Neuroscience

If Positive Psychology is the science of understanding how we might consciously choose to seek optimism and lean into our Strengths, then Neuroscience is the tool for x-raying what happens inside us when we do this; exploring the conditions it causes and the changes that happen to our body.

The University of Pennsylvania, USA, is leading the way within this specialised area combining the two fields of understanding, with their Positive Neuroscience Project, established in 2008. Still a very new science, but my goodness what an amazing opportunity to connect with what they are already learning about how to benefit from their findings.

One of the most exciting things for our resilience project is that the neuroscience findings have unequivocally challenged the idea that we "can't teach an old dog new tricks".

Their findings conclude that our brain can totally reorganise itself by creating new neural connections (and dispensing with older ones that are no longer helpful). This totally supports the suggestion that a fixed mindset can be challenged, that we can choose to change how we respond emotionally to external stressors, that we can learn new ways to connect at work and that we can dial up our learning anytime.

> When a new sports product gets released – promising stronger muscles, faster spring times, leaner tissue mass – there are plenty of us who don't think twice about jumping on board to reap the benefits, in fact many don't even stop to check it's a good idea based in scientific research.
>
> Imagine how our lives (goodness, perhaps even our world) might change if we jumped onto the positive psychology, emotional intelligence and neuroscience trains and went for a ride to find out more?
>
> Thankfully, there are global collaborations who are absolutely committed to doing just this, and exploring how we might harness this knowledge and begin to more positively influence life changing things like conflict resolution, which might eventually impact enormous things, like future wars.

The last of the Big Three: Emotional Intelligence (EQ)

Sitting rather comfortably alongside Positive Psychology and Neuroscience is the concept of Emotional Intelligence (known as EQ). In 1996, Dan Goleman wrote a rather interesting book about this, thus popularising some academic research by two psychologists called John Mayer and Peter Salovey.

All emotions are helpful – they bring us a message about how we are experiencing the things that are happening around us. They let us know if our situation is causing a positive or not so positive environment for us.

In a nutshell, emotionally intelligent people can recognise their own emotional response (they have a wide range of emotional vocabulary) and then intentionally use what they notice to support their desired outcomes. They then deliberately use their thoughts and behaviour to guide their emotions, rather than letting their emotions dictate their thinking and behaviour.

See where we're going with this?

Remember that emotionally intelligent leaders are one of the four cornerstones of Resilient Organisations Adaptive Leadership Framework, and so we have translated it out of their leadership context and into our more general world of work for this Foundation.

"Brains are hot" or just "neuro-bollocks"?

The fascination with understanding what goes on inside our heads is what led to the explosion of interest in Neuroscience.

Capturing what happens inside our brain (the physical organ inside our head) and exploring how the thoughts, feelings, perceptions, emotions, memories, neural responses etc. that occur within the brain as life around us occurs, is fascinating.

There is no one, single definition for how this happens, so for this book we'll consider that the brain is the organ which acquires information and which provides the neural responses which occur in response to the lens through which we see our world.

> *Our mind creates the lens through which we filter what we observe and therefore interprets what it sees, resulting in the neurochemical responses to what it perceives to be true.*

Neuroscience explores this and more; also capturing the nervous system and with it the network of neurons responsible for creating those thoughts, feelings and actions.

Neuroscience elephants

Like all trending areas of research, there are sceptics so let's consider some of the possible issues with the work of Neuroscience before we decide how to embrace it to support our resilience at work.

- Brain Maps show us which areas of our brain are working the hardest; they highlight increased oxygen consumption. This tells us where in the brain is working – but not what it's actually doing (or telling us . . . the inner voice which leads to thought).

- Brain Maps don't help us to identify whether we choose the area that lights up, or whether it lights up by itself.
- Brain Maps can't yet take into consideration the wider environmental influences that cause the response, so any findings are currently limited to the lab.

While we don't want to oversimplify the work of Neuroscience, we also don't want to miss the contributions that it might make to helping us understand more about Emotional Honesty.

Like the evolution of understanding DNA and all the retrospective opportunities that has brought to our world, along with its as yet unknown power for impacting the future, the possibilities for expanding the science of understanding our brain is incredible. We can only see as much as our equipment can currently tell us . . . but I'm going to be watching this space.

Goal: what do you want to achieve?

Emotional Honesty@work

According to the Centre for Disease Control and Prevention along with the World Health Organisation, almost a quarter of us view parts of our job as our number one stressor. Given that changing organisational culture can take a while, and therefore unless we change employers these things might not change any time soon; wouldn't it be helpful to explore alternative ways to respond to these stressors?

A survey to understand the main areas at work where we find ourselves experiencing significant stressors led to the following examples:

Figure 6.1 Word cloud: stressors at work

It is interesting to notice that all the things that were shared are external to us. We attach meaning to what happens.

Even the reference to Grief (it was noted as the grief of patients and owners by a vet – not of the vet herself). It's also interesting to note that what creates this sense of pressure for some might result in an entirely different emotional response for others.

> For example, stifling innovation is hugely frustrating for those of us who thrive on growth and development, but hugely reassuring for those of us who desire stability and certainty.
>
> Unclear policies can result in uncertainty about possible outcomes for some of us, and for others it creates an energising environment for creating clarity.

Exploring this gives us a great opportunity to consider how something that is happening to us externally can cause an emotional response internally, and recognise that our emotional response might not be the only response available.

Coaching moment

Consider the things at work that have been noted by other people as contributing to their lack of Emotional Honesty at work.

1   What are the things that resonate with you?
2   What are the other areas where you are holding back your Emotional Honesty?
3   What impact is this having on you?

If there was one thing that you would like to be more emotionally honest about, what would it be?

What will it feel when you are able to be more honest about this? What impact will it have on you? How might it change your relationship with others? (Remember, you're not actually telling anybody yet, just considering how it might be.)

What might the risks be with this Emotional Honesty? The thing(s) that are holding you back?

What will you need to stop doing, or let go of to overcome this?

Anything that is preventing us from achieving our career ambitions, and resulting in an undesirable emotional response for us is likely to be noted on our list, so it gives us a clue that if we had a different experience of those things, we might be more resilient (or we might not need to worry about our resilience in the first place).

Beginning to consider the different areas where you aren't being emotionally honest can be hugely powerful and can create a sense that you are at least being honest with yourself about their impact. We will use the remainder of this chapter together to look more deeply at the emotional response you are having and consider what you might do with what you notice, along with a consideration of whether you might want to be more emotionally honest with anybody else too (and how).

Reality: how emotionally honest are you already?

Using what we've learned so far about Emotional Honesty, let's explore what is happening for you. There are two steps to this process; firstly, being emotionally honest with yourself, and then considering how to use that information to be emotionally honest with another person.

Most of us have a default safe word.

By this, I mean a word that deflects any requirement to really talk about feelings with another person. Start to notice your own safe word, it might be "good", or "fine", or "ok" . . . whatever it is, it's likely to be very bland, not very meaningful and discourage further exploration by the conversation.

This is perfectly normal and creates more time in the conversation to talk about more meaningful things like the weather, or what's happening in the current "soap du jour".

However, it loses its helpfulness if it's not a very honest response and the impact of not being honest is that we somehow lose a little bit of ourselves.

Like when your manager asks how your day is going and you want to say:

> *"Like hell actually. I just got shouted at by a customer, my computer isn't working properly, you haven't given me a raise in years, I hate the way you email me instead of talking to me and I got given a cappuccino when I asked for a latte".*

So, you say:

> *"Good" or "fine" or "OK".*

There are lots of reasons why we avoid Emotional Honesty; cultural expectations, family habits, privacy preferences, the level of trust or rapport we have with our manager . . . but over time this avoidance can result in a whole heap of unhelpful outcomes, ranging from repressed emotions through to physical outcomes.

I wonder if one of the main reasons we avoid Emotional Honesty at work is because we're worried about what happens if our employer discovers we are human, with a whole range of unhelpful thoughts and feelings as well as helpful ones – but we might lose our job if we have unhelpful ones.

The Rational Behaviour Therapy of Dr Maxie Maultsby is hugely helpful in this space; she asserts that humans have an incurable error making tendency, and that every single human being is fallible. This is further enhanced by Brené Brown's exploration of vulnerability, and the power that we can all find when we relax into this and embrace our fallibility and vulnerability as inevitable and a potential source of learning.

The reality for some is that our employer might very well sack us from our job, especially if we have unhelpful emotions a lot, for a long time or our unhelpful emotions get in the way of our work or the work of others. Performance issues and incapacity are a very real reason for potential dismissal – though formal performance improvement plans to support our development are usually implemented first to make us aware of our unhelpful emotions and help to support us through them.

At the risk of being incredibly controversial, I do believe that if we suffer from any or all of the above (unhelpful emotions a lot, for a long time or our unhelpful emotions get in the way of our work or the work of others) then we do have a responsibility to talk to our employer about it, so they can help us.

Perhaps they will need to work with us to make changes to our job so we have fewer unhelpful emotions, perhaps we will need a different job entirely, perhaps we will need some extra support from specialists who can work through our mental wellbeing issues with us.

Of course, we might have a terrible employer who considers these support options for about five seconds and then terminates our contract, which of course means that we might find ourselves forced to find a new employer. Although that doesn't entirely sound like such a bad thing if this is how they have treated you. I say this in jest of course, but it certainly is worthy of consideration.

Dialling up our Emotional Honesty takes courage. We may even decide that we just want to dial up our Emotional Honesty for ourselves (without telling anybody else what we learn) or for those we love outside work. Both of these options are absolutely fine.

One way to dial up our Emotional Honesty is to begin using a wider range of words to describe our emotions. One way to do this is with an Emotional Word List.

Coaching tales: Ben

Attending a Psychology of Change workshop at SCIRT, Ben reflected on the concept of the Emotional Word List. He had been invited to consider what he felt about leaving the project, and returning to Business as Usual in his Home Organisation.

> *"This is all very well, but I'm an engineer"* he said. *"All I want to understand is whether I am happy or sad. I do not care to learn about anything in between".*

Then Ben looked at the Emotional Word List, and realised that there were a whole lot of other emotions that were playing out for him as he approached the end of his contract. He explored how these emotional responses compared to responses he'd had to situations involving change in the past, looking for patterns and finding coping strategies.

By the end of the workshop, Ben had decided to take the Emotional Word List home to discuss with his children, who were both about to start a new school. He decided that widening their emotional inventory and the ability to talk about feelings would be another legacy from the SCIRT project.

Reflection: for some people, exploring wider emotions can be perceived as a waste of time, or overwhelming. Feelings can be dismissed and ignored or suppressed, but there is always the opportunity to bring them into a richer discussion about experience.

Emotional Word List

There are a great many emotional word lists available for us to use. Because they are designed for a variety of circumstances, they each have a very different look and feel.

The reason this Emotional Word List is being used is because I believe it is more balanced than those commercially available.

There are more equal amounts of "positive" and "negative" emotional options. In addition, having a soft, neutral and extreme emotional response helps us to create more context around the emotion that we are discussing.

It was designed with a North Canterbury Counselling Service, and has been tested for face validity but has not been subjected to the rigorous statistical testing which might be associated with emotional assessments. As a result, you may wish to select your own Emotional Word List instead.

Designed by Kathryn Jackson, with support from North Canterbury Counselling Services.

Table 6.1 Emotional Word List

Soft State	Affection Fondness Amiable Warmth Appreciation Close	Grateful Thankful Glad Optimistic Interested Pleased	Peaceful Relaxed Acceptance Content Fortunate Sense of Belonging	Confident Dynamic Compelling Impressive Free Self-assured	Annoyed Cross Cranky Impatient Critical Antagonistic	Puzzled Hesitant Uneasy Doubtful Apprehensive Cautious Intrigued Vigilant Concerned	Jaded Gloomy Let down Pessimistic Disappointed Remorseful Apathetic	Nauseated Objectionable Reluctance Criticism Boredom
Neutral State	Love Passion Tender Admiration Respect Attracted	Joy Cheerful Friendly Kind Playful Fulfilled Positive Alive	Safe OK Calm Open Secure Trust Protected	Powerful Proud Strong Capable Credible Robust Effective	Anger Hurt Bitter Resentful Exasperated Mad Irritable	Fear Afraid Anxious Worried Scared Alarmed Suspicious Confused	Sadness Empty Sorrowful Tearful Woeful Upset Miserable Lonely Guilty Miserable	Disgust Dislike Distaste Antipathy Displeasure Contempt
Intense State	Lust Yearning Ecstasy Adoration Infatuation Worship Devotion	Ecstatic Excited Thrilled Elated Enraptured	Impervious Shielded Sheltered Immune Defended	Intense Obsessive Forceful Controlling Forcible Zealous Rebellious	Enraged Aggravated Outraged Infuriated Vengeful Seething Furious Aggressive	Terrified Horrified Petrified Panicked Paralysed Threatened Helpless	Grief-stricken Worthless Hopeless Despairing Devastated Depressed Rejected Overcome	Loathing Hatred Revulsion Repugnance Hatefulness Horror Dread

Coaching moment

Review the things that you just identified as directly contributing to areas where you aren't being emotionally honest at work. You might also want to refer to exercises you have done in earlier chapters too. You may choose to do this exercise with somebody, or reflect alone.

Create a table with three columns:

1   **"My Emotional Honesty stressors at work are . . ."** What are the main things that are influencing you?
2   **"Right now, I feel . . ."** What are the emotions that these things cause you to feel? How extreme are these feelings?
3   **"This makes me . . ."** What impact are these emotions having on you?

By unpacking the emotions onto the table and looking at them a bit more objectively we are creating an opportunity for power and strength. We can begin to understand how our emotions are being created, and therefore how we might be able to influence them.

We are also using our words to help us remember that we may have a choice in how we respond these stressors. Right now, this is how you are feeling – and you may choose to stay feeling that way about things. Or you may choose to change to a more helpful emotional state.

If your emotional responses are to the right of the Emotional Word List (the more unhelpful emotions derived from Anger, Fear, Disgust and Sadness), particularly where we are in an unhealthy environment, then the response of your body is likely to be higher in chemicals like adrenalin and cortisol.

This does not make them a bad place to be, nor does it mean we have to quickly turn things around and become all happy again. Your emotions are a message to you about the world that you have found yourself in. They are a gift to be explored.

If your emotional responses are to the left of the list (more helpful emotions derived from Love, Joy, Safe and Powerful), then the response of your body is likely to be higher in dopamine, oxytocin, serotonin and endorphins.

You are literally, as well as metaphorically, going to feel different.

Our brains can't distinguish between real or imagined threats when they are responding. Some things that we do which might give us a clue that Adrenalin or Cortisol are in charge of our thinking process are:

- We're more likely to generalise by saying things like "this always happens . . ." or "they never . . ."
- We are more pessimistic and look for the reasons that something will not work, or why addressing something will be too hard.
- Our thinking can go around and around in circles as we try to solve what we believe is unsolvable; we'll stare at the page for hours, we'll frustrate ourselves and others with not finding the answer.

Having elevated levels of adrenalin can interfere with our ability to think clearly and act confidently, so there's a double whammy of finding ourselves in an unhelpful headspace, and then not able to clearly think a way through. Over time, this response can become an automatic response and changing this takes time and practice.

One way to achieve this is to look for ways of increasing our oxytocin levels. In encouraging you to consider the positive impact that stronger resilience might have on you and in asking you questions during our Coaching moments together (instead of telling you what to do to become resilient) I'm encouraging you to have ideas . . . which creates oxytocin . . . which should start to decrease your cortisol levels.

All these hormones are required for a successfully functioning human being. They are all beneficial under the right circumstances and are the chemical messages that tell us what is happening in our world.

Coaching tales: Joanna

Joanna had been employed by the government for fifteen years and had a clear vision for her career there. She had worked hard to achieve the things that she wanted, and was now working in a team which was dedicated to supporting the education industry.

Following the Christchurch earthquakes, Joanna's entire office had to relocate to temporary premises, and now five years later they were planning to move back into the CBD. This caused huge personal challenge for Joanna who had been very impacted personally and emotionally by the earthquakes.

She was not looking forward to moving back into a high-rise office, nor to a CBD that had changed beyond recognition and reminded her of a time when she was very frightened.

Luckily for Joanna, her employer recognised that this might be a factor for her team, so they invested in providing Resilience training for all team members. Her employer wanted to demonstrate their commitment to listening to the concerns of their team, and helping every person find and access the resources they needed for continued career success.

At the end of the training, Joanna shared that the Emotional Word List had been one of her most powerful moments. She had realised that the sadness, grief and fear that she felt were normal emotions because of experiencing an abnormal event. She realised that she was not experiencing an extreme emotional response after all, but a response that would serve her well in staying emotionally honest. She decided that to grow her resilience she would dial up her Learning Foundation and find out more about how the office was built, the specifications, standards and materials.

Instead of leaving her employer for one that was sited in a low rise, non-CBD building, Joanna was able to return to her motivating and successful career with the government.

Reflection: emotions are there for a reason – they give us a message that we can choose to listen to. Once we are sure that their message is factual, we can take steps to find a way to a more helpful emotional state.

Know yourself

Another way we can create a strong reality for Emotional Honesty is in knowing who we are at work in the first place. When we know who we are, we can become more conscious when we don't feel like ourselves (for example, when we experience a rogue emotion), and this will in turn give us a clue that something at work isn't right.

This doesn't mean we must go all philosophical about absolutely everything (unless we want to), it just means having a good understanding of what we love about work and why we do it.

When we have a strong internal sense of self we are less susceptible to being buffeted by external influences, like receiving feedback about your work. Your sense of self will have internal focus, rather than relying on another person telling you where they believe you are strong, or lacking.

Coaching moment

Reflect on your career to date, or if it's been a short career think about your hopes for the future.

1   What sort of skills or talents do you love to use at work?
2   What sort of employer are you passionate about working for?
3   What kind of manager gets the best work from you?
4   What environment do you thrive in?
5   When did you last enjoy team activities? What were they?
6   When was the last time you "lost track of time" at work? What were you doing?

If you don't know the answer to these questions, then I'd highly suggest you check out some of the resources in the Tell me more! section of this chapter to grow your understanding of your career ambitions. Remember that this isn't a book to help you create career goals, it's a book to remind you about how you can stay strong while you get to where you want to go.

Another way you can reflect on who you truly are is with the help of psychometric assessments. Many organisations use these to support their hiring decisions or to combine with professional development once you've been hired.

Some of the more popular career related ones include Fuel50, Meyers-Briggs, DISC, Belbin Team types and Strengthfinder. These assessments have got a great role to play in helping us understand who we are, and how this might be influencing our resilience.

Their scientific robustness is periodically challenged by academics; however, they are great conversation starters to help us consider the "so what" of our self on our approach to building resilience. The power of "seeing ourselves" in black and white can help us to consider more objectively who we bring to work, and how that compares to who we really are, and who we want to be.

They can help us to consider things like: so, what impact might my profile have on my need for resilience at work? So, what could I do to lean into my profile strengths? So, what are my options for overcoming my profile weak spots?

- For example, very strongly introverted preferences may need to explore ways to connect in an authentic way which doesn't inadvertently create an extreme stress response.
- For example, naturally detail focussed people may find that where they don't have sufficient information about a decision this causes significant distress which becomes a cause of pressure at work.
- For example, people who are not in a role which truly aligns to their natural profile (or who don't have effective coping strategies in place) may find this is a considerable cause of pressure at work (having to "be" somebody they aren't).

If you've ever done one of these assessments (e.g. during a recruitment process or development programme), ask the company if you can see the results to help you grow. Some companies use them during a recruitment process; if you are not subsequently offered the job you might find that you're able to access the data about your results to help you build a picture of who you are.

If your organisation is very committed to supporting achievement of career ambition, there is a super tool that is called Fuel50. It is "career path software, which enables leaders to engage and motivate their teams, and empowers employees to have a visible career pathway within the organisation". It can be bought by individuals and it can be adapted and rolled out across entire organisations.

I am not incentivised in any way to mention this, I'm just a big believer in sharing good ideas, and their Online Career Centre is the best I've ever come across. Don't just take my word for it, check it out for yourself and consider it against the other online tools which might be relevant for you.

An awesome free resource which can support your thinking about who you are that is less career specific is the Values In Action (VIA) Signature Strengths

Survey. For fifteen minutes of your time, you can learn about the character strengths that you already possess which will support you in your quest for more resilience.

As an example, my "Top Five" are Curiosity, Zest, Honesty, Kindness and Social Intelligence – so I'm in my happy place right now; exploring and learning about how to strengthen resilience and then enthusiastically sharing what I've learned with you, in the hope that it will help you in some way become stronger too.

I know that any time I need to dial up my resilience levels, and emotional wellness I can lean into these strengths, and use them to top up my four Resilience Foundations.

I am also conscious that my "Bottom Three" are Bravery, Spirituality and Appreciation of Beauty and Excellence. Remember these are not weaknesses, they are lesser strengths which don't feel like you. These likely play a strong role in the lack of attention I give to my own spiritual wellbeing (something I have to very consciously dial up with the help of a diary reminder!), and why I'm very glad I have a publisher to ensure the pages that you're reading look great and reach the exceptional standards I would like them to.

We can use our strengths to develop our lesser strengths should we wish to do so, for example I might ask myself for ways to embrace my curiosity and discover ways to become more brave – ironic really given the courage that it's taken for me to write this book.

Coaching moment

Reflect on any personal assessments you have done about who you are. At the very least you should be able to use your free Signature Strengths results.

1   If you were leaning further into who you really are to achieve your career ambitions what could you do?
2   What ideas could you incorporate from the latest research about your psychometric personality?
3   Who do you know with a similar profile, and what tools and resources have they used to help them?

My story: Pete

Pete was a member of a team at a council in New Zealand. He had been in the team for many years, and was an experienced member of the roading crew.

(continued)

(continued)

Pete's manager was learning about how to build resilience at work and encouraged the whole team to use the Fuel50 tool, specifically to explore Motivators at Work. The thinking behind this was that once everybody had a clearer idea of what motivated them at work, they would be able to look for more opportunities to get it, therefore building their enjoyment and their resilience in their work.

Pete realised that one of the main things that motivated him was the challenge of growing people and that he wanted to become a manager. One day, he wanted to lead the very team he was currently a part of.

Sharing this with his manager was only part of the story. Pete realised that he also needed to share that emotionally this was a pretty big deal for him. He was nervous about how to make the transition between being "one of the boys" to stepping into a leadership role, and whether he had the skills to do this.

Discussing this fully with his boss was therefore critical to make sure Pete had the support he needed to achieve his career goals.

During the discussion, Pete and his manager agreed a training plan that would enable him to build confidence in leadership skills. They also found ways that Pete could start taking on more leadership responsibilities, and discussed the possibility of a mentor who had transitioned from being part of the team into a more senior role.

Reflection: working out what we really enjoy and then looking for ways to achieve this can result in creating stressful circumstances for ourselves. This might accidentally create the very stressors that we are trying to overcome. If we can be emotionally honest about this we can often find ways to build coping strategies to help us overcome our stressors.

Fight, flight or freeze?

We scan our environment five times a second, checking against a threat–reward continuum. Our brains have evolved to alert us to and minimise threat and maximise reward and our emotions are the internal chemical signal of whether we are perceiving a threat or a reward.

In our very distant past, we might have been looking for a predator that might eat us . . . today, maybe a colleague that we don't get on with or a manager that we believe is out to get us.

Research suggests that when the predominant chemical reaction in our body in this state is adrenalin, we can get a buzz, or a high; and it's actually a little bit addictive.

This makes sense, because our body is programmed to fight, take flight or freeze when we perceive there to be a danger.

This can be helpful to a certain point, because it can give us the injection of energy we need to focus or deliver, but we all have a tipping point after which it becomes unhelpful.

When you reach that tipping point you can consider a couple of things:

1 **Get rid of some of the things you're doing:** talk to your boss about revising deadlines, sharing workload, dial down the Resilience Foundations you don't need, stop talking to people that bring you down.
2 **Get better at handling what you're doing:** dial up the Resilience Foundations that you need, learn how to re-prioritise what you're handling, improve your boundary setting, ask more questions, seek mental support.

But we've got to be emotionally honest with ourselves that we've reached our own personal tipping point.

When we are in an extreme state of "fight, flight or freeze" our adrenalin and cortisol levels are elevated and this can get in the way of our ability to think clearly, or to learn from what we are experiencing (unless it's learning never to find ourselves in this situation ever again!).

We might quite literally need to wait until our neurochemicals rebalance before we can work out how we want to handle ourselves (or find somebody to help us think through what we could do), which is why you should always wait a day before sending that emotionally worded email!

In contrast, when we have higher levels of dopamine, oxytocin, serotonin and endorphins in our body which are caused by the more helpful emotions on the left of the Emotional Word List (our very own personal DOSE of positivity) this reinforces new learning, supports the development of new connections within our brain and helps to cement new ideas.

The work of Barb Fredrickson, from the University of California finds that when we are in this more positive state, our emotions signal it is safe for us to "approach and learn", and so creating this more helpful state is critical as the first step to walking the path to achieving our career ambitions.

Extreme states

When you reflect on the Emotional Word List exercise we just did, how extreme are your current emotional responses overall?

No doubt you've worked with somebody who had extreme emotional reactions at work.

Regardless of whether it's an extreme positive or an extreme negative response, it's rarely dignified or comfortable to watch.

- The one who cries whenever they have a deep and meaningful conversation.
- The one who explodes in meetings.
- The one who always thinks that every decision the managers take is a conspiracy against them.
- The one who bounces around all the time with overexcitement.
- The one who snaps at you any time you ask a question.

Coaching moment

Take another look at the Emotional Word List, and focus entirely on the intense state descriptions. Think about a time when you were in an intense state of emotion, whether it was a helpful or unhelpful emotion.

1   How did the intense state feel within your body? Where did you experience the emotion?
2   What did you do when you experienced this intense state?
3   How did you manage to dial down this intense state of emotion?

Coaching tales: Bevan

Bevan was a team leader in an electrical organisation, and was taking part in a coaching programme as a result of being on a development course.

In between training workshops, he met a coach to talk about what he had learned, how he was using his new skills and the impact it was having.

One of the main challenges for Bevan was Michael, the IT Guy. Michael's role meant that he was always out and about on the office floor, helping people with minor IT concerns, setting up computers, resolving outages.

The concern about working with Michael was that he was very prone to explosive outbursts. Not just a quick swear, but a real full on toddler-type tantrum when IT systems went wrong.

Bevan had been Michael's manager for almost five years (yes, this had been going on that long . . . can you imagine what it was like working in that company, and the reputation Michael had created for himself?) and had been avoiding the discussion for all this time.

It reached a tipping point when the company moved back into their rebuilt offices, because instead of just a floor of around ten people the whole company (about thirty-five people) were now in the open plan space. This was a problem that needed to be tackled.

One of Bevan's leadership workshops focussed on having feedback discussions, and a coaching framework that he learned there seemed perfect to support his discussion with Michael. It took a lot of courage, but it resulted in creating a shared understanding of the frustrations that Michael really had, and the emotional outbursts that this created.

Using the framework, Bevan shared a specific example of one of Michael's outbursts, and explained the impact it had on the people around him. This required a LOT of courage, both from Bevan in starting the discussion, and from Michael in choosing to be honest.

It turned out that Michael had joined the company very shortly after a disgruntled IT professional had decided to leave, so there was a legacy of issues relating to software choices, server providers and reporting systems that he had no influence over.

Michael shared that since he joined, he had discussed his concerns numerous times with the Operations Manager, and made suggestions for new and more reliable solutions, but his conversations seemed to fall on deaf ears.

Because Michael really enjoyed working at the company, he didn't want to leave but he found himself feeling trapped in a job where there were significant frustrations which caused emotional anguish.

Finding somebody who would listen to him was career changing for Michael. Together with Bevan they created a plan to find ways of influencing the Operations Manager into considering new IT solutions. They dialled up Michael's Learning Foundation (he researched information and learned how to write business cases), and Bevan lent his support to the three-way discussion. The company has not made big changes yet, but has made some short term fixes in the meantime, while longer term solutions are discussed.

Michael shared that without this emotionally honest conversation, he might have "lost the plot" at work; for him, finding his voice was critical.

Reflection: Emotional Honesty can be a critical Foundation for Resilience. Michael could have invested energy in dialling up his Self-Care, Learning and Connections, but never achieved the change he wanted to.

In Bevan's Coaching tale, we can see an example of how a compassionate manager was able to support Michael in understanding and then influencing his extreme emotional response. What if you are not as lucky as Michael, and your manager is not equipped (or not interested) in supporting you?

How are you going to talk to somebody with Emotional Honesty, and without extreme responses? This of course assumes that you decide to share what you are learning with somebody, which you might decide against. Totally your decision.

Learning about frameworks to help us practice Emotional Honesty can be helpful to consider, and the one that Bevan used is called the TELL framework.

It is widely taught to managers who are learning about sharing feedback if they are required to have performance reviews. So, you're about to learn some management secrets, which might come in pretty handy if your career ambitions include becoming a manager someday.

TELL stands for:

- **Tell:** give a specific example of what happened
- **Explain:** share the impact or effect of what happened
- **Listen:** ask for understanding, explore what caused the specific example to occur, create possible solutions together
- **Let them know:** create consequences or next steps, agree when to review progress.

Given that one of the changes we are facing at work (highlighted in our chapter on VUCA Change) is the likely transformation of how we receive feedback about our performance at work, we might find that we get less structured or specific feedback in the future. Some companies are opting out of formal processes, preferring more "in the moment" discussions.

Imagine if you could use the TELL framework to share information about what's causing your need to be resilient, along with some ideas for what you would like to see change. Therefore, driving your own feedback processes along the way. Double whammy.

Here's your opportunity to explore what "in the moment" discussions about your emotional response to things that are causing stress at work, and therefore impacting your resilience.

If we prepare what we'd like to say in advance, it's less likely (though not guaranteed) to be as difficult or extreme to discuss. This should help us to think through what we want to say, as well as going into the discussion with some ideas about possible outcomes we would like.

There is no guarantee that you will get what you're looking for, and of course you will need to think very carefully about whether you have this conversation in the first place, as well as what you would like to say – but that shouldn't stop us considering it as an Idea.

Coaching tales

Veronica works at a regional radio station, where she joined as a graduate in the sales and marketing team.

Over a period of two years she has been taking on more responsibility, and now manages significantly more accounts than she used to. She also does some of the promotional activities and delivers training relating to sales.

Veronica wanted to use her coaching conversations to practice interview technique because she felt totally overlooked at work and wanted to find a new job. Even more than this, she believed she was being taken advantage of, and this conflicted significantly with her personal values.

Because this was her first job, Veronica couldn't review her career lifeline exercise to reflect on the approach that she was taking to managing her Emotional Honesty, but she did recognise that at home and in her flat share there were things that happened which made her feel a similar way. In these situations, she feared creating a bad feeling in the flat, which caused her to avoid having the discussions, and repress her Emotional Honesty further.

She confided that the reason she didn't say anything was because she feared being sacked. Which was ironic in a way considering she wanted to use her coaching conversations to find a new job.

When we used the TELL framework to explore what Veronica might like to say, she was surprised at how simply it helped her to see possible way of being more emotionally honest at work. This is what she wrote:

- **Tell:** We have now had four reviews of my performance since I started working here, and in each review, I am told I am performing well, am rewarded with new responsibilities and am turned down for additional pay or working hours.
- **Explain:** As a result, I feel resentful because it seems like you are asking me to do more and more, but you are not recognising that my work has changed significantly since I joined. I also feel conflicted because while I am very proud to work here, I feel trapped in a job that I am not enjoying.
- **Listen:** Please could you let me know a bit more about the reasons that I am being turned down for promotion so that I can address them? I'd also like to create some ideas for how we might resolve this in the future, for example, are there qualifications I need or better information about the sales targets I am achieving, or market information about what other people in my role are being paid?
- **Let them know:** I'd like to have a monthly discussion with you about this, and would love to have agreed a solution by the end of June.

Reflection: being emotionally honest takes courage because there are risks and always the possibility that you will be turned down or rejected. Planning what you would like to say, staying solution focussed and being open to the likelihood of a positive outcome can help to reduce the risks.

Another way that you could prepare your emotionally honest conversation is by using our GRID coaching framework to support your planning.

Remember the GRID acronym stands for;

- Goal: what you'd like to achieve
- Reality: what's happening right now

- Ideas: what you could do
- Do: what you will do

As an example, if Veronica was to use GRID to have the same evidence-based conversation she might prepare something like this:

- **Goal:** my goal at work is to continue doing what I am currently doing, because I love it . . . but I'd also like to be sure that I'm being fairly recognised and rewarded for the contribution that I make.
- **Reality:** in reality, over the last couple of years I have added several new areas of responsibility to my additional role, including promotional activities and training. Did you know that in the last six months I've brought NZ$20,000 worth of advertising to our radio station, and trained fourteen people in the latest sales techniques that I learned at university?
- **Ideas:** I'd love to consider some ideas with you for how I can make sure I'm seriously considered for a pay review, for example how about I look at the increase in sales achievements since I ran the training course? I could also talk to our HR person to find out more about my job description and pay scales, so I can make sure I have all the required knowledge, skills and abilities. What else do you think I could I do?
- **Do:** OK, so we've talked about possible things for me to do, what is going to make the biggest difference to your ability to consider my goal of being fairly recognised and rewarded for my work? I really do love working here, and I'm determined to find a good outcome here.

My story: go with flowers

Working with a client, we considered how to have a difficult conversation with somebody outside work to help him prepare for one he needed to have in work.

Together we wondered how to create the best environment for a positive, helpful conversation and his conclusion was that he would "go with flowers".

For him, this meant taking an offering; a gesture of goodwill to indicate that there was an intention of working together to create a favourable outcome.

My client decided that using a preparation tool like the TELL or GRID framework would represent arriving with flowers because it would signal he had done some preparatory thinking, and brought a solution focussed approach . . . not a problem to dump on the managers desk or be angry about.

He wishes to remain anonymous, but I'd like to thank him for his wonderful analogy.

Ambitious audit

An even more holistic way to the Emotional Honesty Foundation is to consider how you are currently feeling about each of these critical areas of your work.

This will help you to create a more balanced view of your feelings at work, rather than just focussing on the things that you believe are the stressors.

1 **Learning and development:** e.g. career progression, training, new skills
2 **Feedback and guidance:** e.g. how often you get information about your strengths and areas for development, and how helpful it is
3 **Financials:** e.g. salary, bonus, retirement benefits
4 **Non-financials:** e.g. holidays, employee discounts, company car
5 **The organization:** e.g. its values, culture, branding
6 **What you do:** e.g. the skills, knowledge and experience you use in your job right now
7 **Life balance:** e.g. hours worked, business travel, boundaries
8 **Your team:** e.g. immediate team, wider team, socialising
9 **Your clients:** e.g. internal and external relationships
10 **Your manager:** e.g. leadership style, how valued you feel.

Coaching moment

For each of the ten areas above, either choose a word from the Emotions Word List to describe how you feel about them or allocate a score of 1–5 depending on how happy you are with their current state.

Look at the words you have chosen to describe how you feel about these areas of your work (or the numbers you have assigned). Your plan is not to share your emotions with anybody at this point, only to recognise, name and acknowledge them. Consider these questions:

1 What are the areas at work which are creating the most helpful emotional states for you?
2 What are the areas at work which are creating the least helpful emotional states for you?
3 If nothing changes about the things which are creating the least helpful emotional states for you, what is likely to happen?

Learning to catch our emotional response like this can be super helpful. We are raising our consciousness, and therefore Emotional Honesty with ourselves.

Remember, the situation doesn't make you feel a certain way, the thoughts and beliefs that you attach to that situation make you feel that way.

There are a couple of ways this might look in the workplace:

- **Subconscious**: your emotional response might be automatic because of habit or something that has happened before. As an example, you get asked to do something extra at work today (this is on top of everything extra that you're already doing), your immediate thought is, "this is such bullshit, this always happens to me, no wonder I'm always stressed out", which leads to an emotional response of anger and frustration. Over time, whenever you are asked to do something extra at work, your automatic emotional response could become anger or frustration.
- **Transmitted**: we might accidentally "catch" the emotions of the people who we work with; this is called emotional contagion. This is where it's super important to have an idea of your baseline emotions – the words that describe how you feel "normally" so you can tell if what you're experiencing is different and consider the cause, so you can check whether what your emotions are telling you is truly what you believe, or whether you have picked up on the verbal or non-verbal cues of those around you. As an example, your company announces redundancies are imminent. Several team members have been through a restructure previously and were traumatised by the incident. Their emotional response is to panic and share how utterly terrified they are by the uncertainty. You had previously been anxious that redundancy might cause some issues, but now you become terrified too by the prospect. Your emotional response has been amped up.

Ideas: what could you do to dial up Emotional Honesty?

We've already started to gather a few ideas about what we might do along the way, because the Coaching moments have been deliberately designed to help you think in a Solutions Focussed way.

Remember that our emotional response can be a choice about the thing that stimulated it; the source of pressure which we perceive as stress. When we are conscious of the process that's happening we can choose if we want to learn to change.

It's why we can overcome our fear of speaking in public or heights and it's a reason for the continued success of anger management programmes, for example.

Here are some more ideas for you to consider:

Challenging your emotional response

Fact or fiction?

One way that we can challenge our emotional response is to check if it is the truth. Considering other possibilities, for example, if we are given some feedback about our performance which causes us to feel hurt or worthless, our boss might indeed be out to get us.

Table 6.2 Thinking traps

Thinking Trap	What it looks like	Remind yourself	Ask yourself
Exaggerating	If this happens it's a complete disaster, it's all going to go wrong.	It may not be a disaster at all – it could be a warning or a gift.	If it really does go totally wrong, how could I make it through?
Tunnel vision	There's only one way out of this.	Creating possibilities can help us to come unstuck.	Where could I go to find more ideas about this?
Personalising	It's totally my fault.	There may have been other contributing factors.	What else might have contributed to making this happen?
Externalising	It's nothing to do with me, all their fault.	There may have been something that I said or did which contributed to things.	How might I have contributed to making this happen?
Mind reading	They must be thinking ABC.	Perhaps I need to ask them about this.	What questions could help me more fully understand?
Jumping to conclusions	If it's X then Y is guaranteed to happen.	There may be other outcomes; I should slow down to consider them.	What else could happen instead?
All or nothing	Either I must leave and take a lower paid job or I have to stay here and have a terrible career.	There are always at least two options for every situation (action/no action).	How could I explore other options too?
Thoughts versus likelihood	If I think it then it will happen.	Just thinking about something doesn't always make it so.	What is the likelihood that it will really happen?
If it feels true it must be true	I feel unsure therefore I must be incapable.	There may be other contributing factors.	Where is the evidence to support this?

There's every possibility of course, that another reason might be the driver behind the conversation for example, they might want to prevent us making a mistake they made, or they might think we have great potential and want to support us, or they might be the brave person that cares enough about us to share what others are thinking.

You are right whether you are an optimist, pessimist, risk averse or a fatalist. You are right because this is the reality that you've created for yourself and it can be a reason why it's sometimes hard to imagine how other people can think differently to you. To see things from their Reality.

Just be curious and see whether the meanings you have attached are helpful or not. If not, consider other ways of seeing things by considering how Thinking Traps might be playing their part in interpreting what's going on:

Coaching tales: Kim

Kim was heading on holiday and it was the final two weeks before she departed. Kim worked in the communications team and prided herself on being very organised at work. She had invested considerable time designing a spreadsheet of all the activities that were likely to happen in her absence, along with ideas about who in the team could work on them, or answer press queries.

Working late into the night she sent a message to her team letting them know that this was something she was doing, and where she planned to save it in case they needed to access it.

The next day, Kim was inundated with emails and phone calls asking her to finish off jobs, finalise advertising and submit invoicing requests. She blew an absolute gasket. When invited to consider her emotional response she shared that she felt outraged by her team. She was furious that her colleagues were deliberately stressing her out before she went on holiday, and as a result she wouldn't have time to finish everything and then she would go on her holidays so stressed she wouldn't be able to enjoy herself. Wow.

Working with a coach, Kim began reflecting on the power of her Anger response towards her team. She considered what she normally did before holidays, and realised that she always used this approach, and it always resulted in the same increase in workload at the last minute. She even shared that she "knew" her email would lead to this, but she still sent it anyway.

With support from her coach, she considered other reasons for the increased demands from her team like; knowing she would do a great job, believing she was able to handle it, trusting her implicitly.

Kim also realised that she was secretly a little bit proud and energised by the teams' response, because for her it meant that her team really needed her, and her skills were clearly valued.

Having an objective conversation about her emotional response led to several decisions for Kim; she would ask for help or volunteers to cover the outstanding workload before she left, she would put her out of office on a few days before leaving and she would switch off all technology at 5pm every night in the run up to her departure.

Reflection: when we become conscious of our emotional responses, and where we know we have directly influenced them we can choose whether to continue the decisions that typically lead up to the emotion.

Coaching moment

Choose one of the things that is causing your belief that you need to dial up your Emotional Honesty.

1   What do you think is happening in your workplace to cause this?
2   What might an alternative reason be?
3   What else could be influencing this to happen?
4   Keep asking yourself this question until you have run out of possibilities. Consider asking somebody to help you create possibilities.

Saddling up

This is a true story.

After the Christchurch earthquakes, my husband and I went for a walk around the lagoon near where we lived. We needed some time together and we needed some sunshine. The aftershocks were still too big to risk riding our horses, so we led them instead – it felt good to be out again being doing something "normal".

Along the path, we came across a man who was clearly a little bit bonkers, and very drunk. He was dressed as a cowboy and had a holster round his waist with a pretend gun in one side and a bottle of Jack Daniels in the other. Pausing to talk to us, he handed us a laminated beer mat and explained that he had been sent by the cowboys to the people of Christchurch to share this message. We chatted a while, checked he was going to be OK, and then parted ways.

On the card he gave us were printed these words:

"*Courage is being scared to death, but saddling up anyway" John Wayne.*

I still have that laminated card. It sits in pride of place at the heart of our home because the card, and the memory of receiving the card represents a moment in time that is every Resilience Foundation rolled into one. The Emotional Honesty of acknowledging that it's OK to be scared to death, the importance of Self-Care activities like time with our horses, the power of reaching out to Connect with others like our cowboy reminded us and the importance of Learning from others who have trodden this path before, or who want to share their lessons. And of being strong enough to keep showing up.

Resilience finds us in curious ways. Stay open to noticing your own moment of empowerment.

Sunny side up

Another way that we can encourage our emotional state into a more helpful place is to practice some of the tools of Positive Psychology. Things that can help us to develop a more optimistic and hopeful view of the world. For example:

- **Gratitude focus:** a client at SCIRT designed a chart for the wall where he hung his coat. At the end of the day, he drew a face to represent the day that he had spent and made a couple of bullet points about why he drew the face. Over a couple of weeks, he noticed that when he drew a smiling face and wrote the things that had contributed to having a good work day, he slept better. He also felt much more positive starting the next day, and noticed he felt stronger overall. He became more conscious about the things that were impacting his moods at work, and he started to see patterns that he hadn't realised were there. This home-made mood tracker was a form of gratitude journal that Positive Psychology recommends we consider to consciously grow our awareness of the lovely things that happen to us every day. When we notice just Three Good Things, by writing them down (ideally including as much detail as possible), noting how they make us feel and reviewing them over time, we begin to experience more positive emotions and increased wellbeing overall. How long you choose to continue is up to you, but at least two weeks should create a noticeable shift. Keep going for as long as you find it helpful.
- **Finding or creating laughter:** spending time with optimistic, joyous and positive friends and colleagues can contribute to totally turning around our emotions at work. If you've accidentally got caught up within the office gossip network (those people that exist in every company who love to talk at length about negative stuff) then it's time to consider your options. These Office Dementors can be hugely damaging to our emotions, our confidence and our hope for the future. If you've accidentally got one as your best friend (or if you've managed to become one yourself) then this might be a bit tricky for you, try for just a couple of weeks as an experiment to see how it influences your emotional state. If you don't have anybody at work who seems to fit the requirements for optimistic, joyous and positive, then make sure you are recharging your energy every day at home with people who fit this description. You might also want to consider designing an escape strategy too, if it really is dire in your workplace. Remember that when we are emotionally honest, we might decide that the most resilient path is to find a new place where we can thrive.

Coaching tales: Rouben

Rouben worked in the design team of a medical project which included three complementary external organisations. It was a new collaboration to explore the potential for more projects like this in the future, so it was under the spotlight frequently in all four companies.

Rouben wanted coaching to grow his professional brand at work, because he felt that he had not quite been able to find his voice to share his ambitions – he felt he had been "drifting". He saw this project as a way to be a bit brave and find some courage to achieve his career ambition, which was to work with leading edge medical technology.

One morning, a member of one of the other organisations talked over him during an important meeting and the idea Rouben had been discussing was passed over. Understandably, he was outraged because he believed this kept happening to him. Later that same day, another person from the meeting called Rouben to ask him for support with finalising a design they were working on together. Rouben found himself saying that he was too busy to help and quickly hung up.

Discussing this in his coaching session, Rouben concluded a few very important things.

Firstly, that he would be more conscious in meetings of when he felt strongly enough that his voice should be heard. He decided to find ways of staying strong if another person interrupted him. Secondly, he decided to discuss the morning with the person who interrupted, to share the impact it had on him and dial up his Emotional Honesty. He realised that the other person might just have been in a state of extreme excitement in his haste to share the new idea and may not have even realised what happened. Rouben also realised that his excuse for being busy was simply a way of expressing his disappointment, and he could help his colleague after all. He called back shortly after his coaching session.

Reflection: achieving career ambitions can require us to be brave and step outside our comfortable places, whether we are using new skills or finding new words. Being conscious of the impact that other people have on our emotions – and then the extent that we "pay it forward" – can be hugely powerful because we can choose to break the cycle. In fact, a 2015 study by Tel Aviv University found this to be the exact case; causing a decrease in performance and a tendency to repeat the behaviour with another person.

Labelling emotions

We've already started to use this technique by identifying and writing down the words from our Emotional Word List. In using the list, we are likely to be enhancing the words we have available to identify and describe what we are feeling.

Our life is full of rich and vibrant emotions which create the roller coaster of everyday, so for us to summarise them into a shorthand of just a few descriptions potentially sells ourselves short. We are likely to experience multiple emotions, sometimes at the same time – so understanding that we are not just feeling anger but also fear can help us to decide whether it is fair for us to lash out.

My story: Luciano

Luciano had made the incredibly courageous decision to quit his role as a corporate employee and start his own business.

In doing so, he found that he really needed to dial up his Resilience Foundations very differently from his corporate days, starting with a very conscious focus in his Connections Foundation, so that as much time as possible was spent meeting potential clients and understanding their needs so he could steer his business accordingly.

He found new and innovative ways of doing this when he realised that there weren't enough hours in the day, by combining some of his Self-Care activities (like sports activities) with building his Connections. This was a personal challenge for Luciano who would have preferred to dial up his Learning Foundation; spending his time researching his products and developing marketing products.

Within a year, he had created momentum and had a steady stream of opportunities.

One day, Luciano was surprised by a comment from an unexpectedly disappointed client. The comment left him reeling, and he described the feeling as "the rug being swept from under his feet". He immediately began to doubt his decision to start his business, and question whether he had the strength and resilience to persevere with his plans.

Luciano reflected on this with his coach and became aware that Emotional Honesty was not a Foundation he had given any time to at all during his career. He wanted to brush off the comment, dismissing it as a misunderstanding caused by a client with unrealistic expectations and pretend it never happened.

Instead, he decided to use the Emotional Word List to explore the discussion, and decided that the meeting had left him uneasy, suspicious and let down. Realising this was monumental for Luciano, particularly because this was one of his favourite clients. Recognising this was not a helpful emotional response, he was now able to reflect on how to use these emotions as a powerful catalyst for change.

He has already reviewed business processes to ensure that the issue doesn't happen again, and he's refocussed his awareness on spending time with clients who energise and uplift him to consciously shift his emotional state into a more helpful place. He also plans to rebuild the relationship with his favourite client, now that he can be more objective about what happened.

He shared, "I am feeling clearer and as a result calmer and more comfortable with the situation" because of dialling up his Emotional Honesty.

Reflection: there is much power in simply labelling the emotional responses that you have. It can help us to regulate them more effectively and therefore choose how we continue to respond to them.

Accepting emotions

Another strategy for challenging our emotions is to simply accept them. This was a particularly difficult one for me to get my head around personally, because my "go to" place is to try to work out how to get back into a more helpful state as soon as possible.

This was just not possible with the experience of the trauma from the Christchurch earthquakes, which turned out to be about three years of relentless aftershocks, some so enormous they had people running for cover all over again. Imagine living like that. For the first year, they were coming about every thirty minutes. It was a very similar experience to walking on a boat in a very stormy sea, except you were walking on the ground.

Our mind is incredible. It convinces us of what it believes to be real – and knowing this is one of the reasons that sporting professionals visualise their success before they even kick a ball or hit a run.

The dark side of this visualisation skill is that it can send us interesting and incorrect stories too; I know that I will never again be able to hear the dull rumble of a train approaching without my blood going cold and holding my breath.

This was the sound we heard in the city whenever an enormous aftershock was approaching. Except I know that it's OK to respond like this. It's a perfectly normal response and I don't have to find a more helpful thought to override it. I simply have to let it be, and then look for what is true, now and in the moment.

I know that I just need to ask myself whether in this moment right now, we are having another enormous earthquake or whether the ground is in fact, still.

Often just realising that our reactions are within normal and expected parameters can help us to create a sense of control again. The Emotional Word List can help us to consider this.

My story: Janelle

Janelle worked for a government ministry in a role which required her to broker relationships and grow collaborations. Her clients came from a rich and diverse background, ranging from welfare recipients through to government employees who worked with the Prime Minister of New Zealand. Overall, she loved her job and had a very clear idea about what her career ambitions were; to continue influencing government decision making about welfare beneficiaries.

For the most part, she achieved this very successfully, as evidenced by regular stakeholder feedback and commendations. An avid learner, she came to each of our coaching sessions with examples of resources she had come across that contributed to her understanding of building relationships.

Her commitment to Self-Care was admirable given the high stress and pressure that was associated with her role. She regularly took time out for her physical fitness, finished work every Friday for a "5pm massage" and, during the time we worked together, also took up yoga.

It appeared that she was the textbook example of how to develop and maintain resilience in a highly pressurised and uncertain work environment, particularly if we use our Resilience framework to benchmark her focus.

However, there was one area where she really struggled. Another team leader whom she had known for many years and worked alongside had a very different working style and the two frequently rubbed each other up the wrong way. As a result, her team had a very strained relationship with his team, which in turn was starting to influence business outcomes.

From the start, she recognised this was an issue but constantly brushed off the effect that it was having – sharing that she believed it to be her responsibility to shield her team from the politics of this relationship.

Instead, we focussed on how she had built such successful relationships with other areas of the business, and in reflecting on how she did this Janelle realised that she felt more like herself in those successful relationships; she felt more honest.

She realised that the challenges she had working with this difficult team leader had begun years ago, and the legacy of those challenges were impacting her ability to be "real" in her relationship with him. She felt frustrated that their relationship had never moved beyond the issues of the past.

Rather than confronting him about this, she decided to use our emotionally honest conversation as an opportunity to explore how to be more like herself during future interactions with him. She focussed on bringing her relationship building strengths in the same way that she would with new clients.

> Reflection: Emotional Honesty does not have to be shared to be useful, it can simply be observed and used as a catalyst for change. In addition, we may already be as resilient as we need to be to do our job, but for Janelle dialling this Emotional Honesty up a notch resulted in totally revised relationship with her old colleague.

Emotional Honesty elephants

There are some things about Emotional Honesty that don't get said very often, but they need acknowledging so we are role modelling our honesty.

Terrible employers

Luckily, there are more organisations who are trying to find ways of better understanding and working with the people they employ than there are organisations who don't care a hoot.

Moving to New Zealand in the early 2000s was very interesting, in that despite the incredible standard of living here, with mind-blowing scenery, the friendliest people I've ever come across in my travels and the opportunity for outdoor living like I've always dreamed of – the approach of employers left something to be desired.

Overall, there wasn't the same appetite or perceived need to even consider how to keep employees happy as I had become used to in Europe and the USA. There was a tendency to believe that if people were being paid and went on occasional training courses then they shouldn't expect much more. This approach didn't make them bad employers, it just created conditions which would make it harder for resilience to thrive. It was the norm, and other than a few standout exceptions there were no role models to contend this approach.

Thankfully this is changing very rapidly because there is so much growing evidence to challenge this thinking, and because employees are asking for more. Even in the last five years there has been an enormous growth in the commitment of New Zealand companies to find out more about the story behind who works for them, leading to more honest (and hopefully connected) conversations at work.

However, let's acknowledge that there are truly terrible employers out there in the world. Astounding stories about mistreatment, abuse and exploitation from both companies and managers always find their way into the global Human Resource Consulting commentaries that I research. I've also worked with clients who share stories that take my breath away.

The impact of being emotionally honest if you work for an employer like this could be devastating, especially if you not only realise how upset or frightened you are but you tell yourself that there is no way out.

The likelihood is that being emotionally honest with an employer in these companies could quite honestly end up with you losing your job, or worse.

If this sounds like you, please find somebody to work with you, and support you – maybe a friend, maybe a counsellor from a support agency, maybe even a career advisor from a school you've been to in the past who will support you. There will always be an option and it doesn't have to cost a lot of money, it may even be free . . . just find somebody and realise you are not alone.

You deserve more from work, and I hope that the continued pressure that is being applied globally to organisations in every sector to shift their approaches finds its way to your place of work.

In the meantime, you can choose to learn the Foundations of resilience despite them, and you can find new ways to thrive despite your extra challenging circumstances.

Mind reading

There are far too many people at work, from all generations and diverse backgrounds, who would like something to be different, but believe that their employer should be able to mind-read what is required to resolve their situation.

When nobody at work addresses the things that stress them, or when they shout and shout about things being wrong and broken, then sit back waiting for it all to be fixed and it isn't, they find themselves feeling outraged or rejected and behave accordingly.

We all have the potential to be more honest with ourselves about the impact our stressors are having on us, and then make decisions about what to do with that knowledge:

- We can explore ways of rethinking our emotional response into a more helpful and optimistic state.
- We can have a conversation with somebody about our emotional response and, together, look for ways of changing the circumstances at work.
- We can look for another employer who will listen to and meet our needs.

Remember that we are not simply handing our stressors to our employer to be solved.

In fact, some workplace pressure which causes stress can be entirely outside your or their control; for example, if you work in a medical emergency team, or your company goes bankrupt.

Chances are you've already tried handing your stress to your employer and it didn't make a difference (or you wouldn't be reading this book).

You are working out how you feel, and what you'd like to change – and then you're creating some ideas to share in order to get there.

Coaching moment

Think about something that you are expecting your employer to mind-read about you at work right now. Perhaps you want them to realise that you'd like more money, or for your manager to see that you are working late because you're so busy or communicate more clearly about something.

1   What do you imagine they are thinking about this issue?
2   What are the consequences of you imagining this?
3   What could you do instead to resolve this?

You can't (or won't) play nicely

Sharing how you feel with somebody and the impact it's having requires huge courage. It also requires some commitment to making sure that the conversation stays focussed on your hopes for the future and doesn't disintegrate into a series of accusations and finger pointing, with either you or your manager walking out at the end.

Sometimes if we have never had this sort of conversation before, there is a potential for feedback to surface which hasn't been shared (when we create the environment for honest discussion, that's usually what we get in return) so we need to find ways to make sure that you know what you'd like to say, and have a plan for hitting the "pause" button on the meeting if it starts heading south.

Practising what you want to say can be hugely helpful.

As can using the GRID or TELL frameworks that we have reviewed during the early part of this chapter.

If there's a lot of emotional stuff that you decide to share, consider breaking it into bite sized chunks over the course of a few months. Taking one step at a time is always better than doing nothing.

Agree a plan for calling the meeting to a halt if it takes a turn that was unexpected, but remember that you are using Solutions Based feedback frameworks, so you are setting up the environment to have a positive discussion.

The F-word

Another major Emotional Honesty elephant is the F-word (the impact of our sense of being valued at work; our Financial value). That conversation that we never have with our manager about the impact our pay rate has on how we feel at work . . . so we keep things hidden, and trust can spiral down.

The great news is that there are heaps of resources out there to help us decide if our emotional response to feeling valued is true or false.

In the blink of an eye we can look up approximate pay rates for most of the jobs in the world (albeit for some more obscure ones we might have to use a bit of poetic licence considering similar roles, rather than identical ones).

- Always create an idea of the minimum, mid-point and maximum value for your role.
- Using this range of values, reflect on all the feedback you've had about your work, along with any training and development you've done. This will give you an indication (even if it's a very rough idea) of whether you are a weak, average or strong performer overall in your role.
- The two bits of information can then be combined, ideally if you're an average performer you should expect to see your pay rate is near to the mid-point.

Of course, the world isn't always ideal, so what on earth could you do if you don't like what you see?

Well, it depends on the overall goal for your choice of employment (remember, we go to the Goal on our GRID framework before we create Ideas).

For example, if your pay rate is lower than you would like, but you absolutely love the flexibility that you get at work, or the team are amazing and your manager is very supportive then you might decide that you're OK with the rate being lower.

Or, if your pay rate is lower than you would like, but there are very limited alternative employment options for you, you might decide to discuss how to develop skills in your role which could lead you into another better paid role in the company.

Or, if your pay rate is lower than you would like, and it's way (way) lower than the market rate, you might not reasonably expect an enormous rise immediately. You might need to be very open to a discussion about planned increases.

And through all this deliberating, you might find out that the reason your pay rate is lower is because you're not performing at the level you need in your role.

Which might trigger strong emotional responses from a place of anger, fear or sadness. And that's a totally reasonable emotional response, because you haven't been told about it until now, except now you know so you can do something about it. If you want.

Luckily, you've just read a chapter about how to do that.

Coaching tales

Sally was a real estate agent who worked in a successful franchise. She worked very hard and spent a lot of time ensuring she was continually up to date on the latest legislations and market data.

Sally was very connected to a great many people in her sales patch, both those in business and those who she had bought (and sold) on behalf of. Both her Learning and Connecting Foundations were being well energised.

Sally's biggest challenge was that she had made a significant career change to work as a real estate agent, and greatly missed the camaraderie and buzz of working in a corporate office. She felt that the real estate role she was in prevented her from doing this, because of the competitive nature of the business.

Exploring her emotional response to this, she realised that it was really getting her down. She had started to withdraw from her social life because of feeling more and more isolated. She believed that she was grieving for the lively and vibrant office life she had enjoyed pre-career change.

She realised that although she enjoyed the independence and flexibility of her new industry, the social life was very important to her. Instead of talking this through with her regional manager she decided to do something about it herself.

Sally had decided to dial up her Emotional Honesty, realised what was causing her work stress and stepped into making something happen. She focussed on becoming more active in the social life of her children's school, organising fundraisers, taking part in sporting events and running quiz nights.

Absolutely nothing has changed in her workplace, but she feels much more alive with the social connections that she has re-created outside work, where she finds the social vitality that she needed.

Reflection: work doesn't always provide for every emotional need to be met. By being honest about what is missing we may need to look outside work for ways to address it.

Optimistic mindset

One interesting thing about emotion is that it can be catching, so if we constantly play stories of doom and gloom to ourselves (particularly if those stories do not empower us by suggesting action) then we can totally undermine our sense of hope.

One way to experience this would be to choose the most negative news stories imaginable and spend a week reading them. News stories typically don't include a call to action, or ideas for doing something to help turnaround the circumstances you have just read about (although with the growth of online donation like "Give a little" we are seeing some change).

Typical news stories simply present information (usually sad, scary, depressing stories), which we then read and because of our brains being hard wired to look for danger, we can end up amplifying or over exaggerating the things that we read.

Dr Graham Davey (UK) has extensively researched the psychological effects and finds that we run the risk of exacerbating or contributing to our sense of stress, anxiety or depression. Reading new stories that emphasise suffering and distressing emotions can change our overall mood to one that is more sad, anxious or threatening.

We learned about the neurological impact this has on our body in our Emotional Honesty chapter (e.g. increased levels of adrenalin and cortisol) so we know this is likely to put us in a state of "fight, flight or freeze".

Some situations at work are absolutely unthinkable. If you are on a minimum wage, working three jobs and living in poverty then the fact that you're even reading this book speaks volumes about how strong you are.

And reading news stories about how people in similar horror circumstances have no way out is not going to help.

Until news stories become more solution focussed and also include options like "if you are facing circumstances like this, click here for ideas to help you", then the advice of the resilience experts is to avoid reading them.

Also, don't spend your time wallowing in the shared grief and hurt of others in your circumstances. Your "fight, flight or freeze" response is unlikely to be helpful and may even cause you to believe that there is nothing that you can do to change things, you will learn to be helpless in your situation.

Instead, find stories of hope and inspiration; find people in your community or tribe who have faced down what you are facing, who have dialled up their Resilience Foundations and who have thrived.

Wise Founder shares a few examples to get you started:

- Steve Jobs got fired from his own company.
- JK Rowling lived on welfare.
- Richard Branson has dyslexia.
- Oprah Winfrey was told she was "unfit for TV".
- Jim Carrey used to be homeless.

Coaching moment

Find a current news article about your job or your industry (just type your industry or your job into Google and then "latest news or latest trends").

1   What are the trends or themes that you find yourself reading?
2   What are the stories which excite you? How could you use your excitement to support your Resilience Foundations? (Could you reach out and connect with the authors? Could you learn anything from the materials which are discussed?)
3   What are the stories which concern you? How could you find out more information about these concerns?

My story: Leon

Leon was incredibly frustrated at work. Working in the hospitality industry he had hoped to find a way to use his creative talents but he kept being asked to reproduce the same sort of products. There were limited options in his home town for using his skills so he felt completely trapped and was disconnecting further and further from his work.

He was sent for coaching by his employer who didn't want to lose him but could tell that he was not happy. Leon had been courageous enough to share his frustrations with his manager but didn't know how to create Ideas for what to do about his situation.

Working with his coach, and using his love of art, he decided to paint a picture of what his resilience looked like at that point in time, and what he hoped it might look like into the future.

His picture helped him to discuss his emotional response to feeling trapped at work and gave him new words to consider for how to change things. Using his art also helped the conversation to stay focussed on his picture for the future, and he was able to see possibilities that he hadn't considered previously. He shared that he felt re-energised as a result of spending a short amount of time dreaming about "what could be possible".

Reflection: finding emotional words doesn't have to be about writing lists. You can use your Strengths to explore what you'd like to achieve. You might paint a picture like Leon, or write a story about your life in a year, or build a model that represents what you would like; make the journey your own.

Coaching tales: Kevin

Kevin was a consultant who worked incredibly long hours. It was normal for Kevin to answer his phone late into the night, send emails in the early hours and ask his team to respond to his questions over the weekend.

Kevin was "sent" for coaching by a manager who wanted him to change his behaviour but not the exceptional business results that he was getting.

At first, this decision was challenged by his coach, who invited the manager to consider whether having an emotionally honest feedback conversation might be more suitable. Kevin's manager was new to the company and didn't feel that he had developed enough trust in his team relationships, for a conversation of this nature and asked for an objective review of the situation.

(continued)

(continued)

Kevin started his coaching sessions by talking about his Reality. He shared the impact that his long hours working style was having on his wife and family, and on the sense that he was getting from his own team (he was astute enough to realise they were not happy with his weekend calls). He noticed immediately that he needed to dial up his Self-Care Foundation.

In reflecting on the purpose for his extreme working style (his Goal for his career ambitions) he confessed that his motives were to be noticed by one of his employer's clients as being exceptionally driven at work.

Kevin also confessed that he hadn't thought about the impact of this on his team members, he had been so consumed by delivering. Kevin realised that his commitment to excellence was driving his behaviour, but his obsessive approach to delivering this had wider consequences that he had not considered.

Reflection: sometimes it is not our resilience that needs to be considered, but the impact of our behaviour on the resilience of others.

This is all very well

What if you don't want to share. You don't want to be emotionally honest because you're a private person and what you feel is none of anybody's business. Can you still develop resilience at work?

Absolutely.

First, you will be in the know. The Coaching moments, tools and resources of this chapter have been deliberately designed to help you become more conscious of what feels like you, and what feels just a bit (or a lot) wrong.

When that happens, you can simply use the GRID framework in your head. Start with your Reality, because that's where your emotions live. They are what you experience right now. Then check into your Goal, and then go around the GRID framework. For example;

- **(Reality:** what are the emotions that you have noticed you're experiencing?)
- **Goal:** how do the emotions that you are experiencing compare with the emotions that you would like to experience? What would you like to change, or experience more of?
- **Reality:** how could you prioritise your current emotions, and then look for ways to change them to a more helpful state?
- **Ideas:** what ideas do you have about things that could influence your emotions to a more helpful state? What role could you play? What role could your employer play?
- **Do:** what are you going to do? The quickest route to achieve your Goal? The easiest route to achieve your Goal?

It will no doubt feel pretty clunky to begin with, as it does developing any new skill, but over time you will become more comfortable with recognising and influencing your emotions.

Because you're a human, you won't be able to influence them every time and indeed nor should you because remember that we are becoming more emotionally aware and emotionally honest, not simply positive all the time.

Coaching moment

Jane Pike is a New Zealand based Mind Skills coach who specialises in creating confidence, mental strength, focus and clarity.

Her "move towards" statements can help us to create short sentences about what we want to move towards, so that we focus on the process of "becoming something new" and don't get too hung up about the clunky "in between" time, when we are not quite at the level of helpful thinking that we would like to be.

Perhaps you could remind yourself:

- I am not stuck, I am moving towards change.
- I am not tired, I am moving towards energy.
- I am not overlooked at work, I am moving towards being noticed.
- I have not reached my peak, I am moving towards learning more.
- I am not afraid, I am moving towards finding strength.
- Create three more statements for yourself about what you are moving towards.

Coaching tales: Peter

Peter had worked with his employer, a national airline, for just over three years and had been turned down for a promotion he applied for. His career spanned over fifteen years in the industry working as an engineer and he was progressively losing confidence in his ability.

He approached a career coach to talk through his situation and discuss strategies for applying for another job somewhere new. He was very surprised when his coach encouraged him to look back into his past for clues about what might be affecting his confidence, instead of supporting him by building his CV and interview confidence.

What he noticed was that in his very first job out of school he received some feedback from his manager about being overconfident. His manager told him straight out that he would "never get promoted with the

(continued)

(continued)

attitude he had, because he was too demanding". The effect on Peter at the time was minimal (or so he thought); Peter brushed the comment off as "typical bullshit management".

Since that moment in his career, Peter avoided all discussion about how he was performing at work. He showed up for performance reviews, signed reviews and appraisals and kept his head down low.

Not only was he damaging his professional brand (and therefore harming his possible consideration for future promotion and very likely contributing to his lack of promotions), he was also avoiding finding out where his real strengths and areas for development could be.

With the support of a career coach, he began looking for more guidance about his work and his confidence soared.

Reflection: experiences early in our career can create beliefs that do not serve us. Where something is preventing your career ambitions, consider it fully and wonder how ideas that are attached to it were formed.

Coaching moment

An unusual Idea to consider (but remember, we are creating ideas so there are only unusual ideas, no such thing as a silly idea) is to consider watching a movie or reading a novel about resilience. Consider the following questions:

1   Which character do you most identify with, and why?
2   What do you notice about how they use the Foundations of Emotional Honesty, Self–Care, Connections and Learning to stay or grow resilience?
3   What strategies or tools did you notice that they used to develop or thrive despite their circumstances?

Some movies and novels to consider might include:

- "The Pursuit of Happyness"
- "Groundhog Day"
- "The Shawshank Redemption"
- "Contact"
- "It's a Wonderful Life"
- "Rocky Balboa"

- "Jerry Maguire"
- "Amazing Grace"
- "Room"
- "Rising Strong"
- "Unbroken".

Management corner

Finding the space to acknowledge that you care as a manager is one of the most powerful things you could do in your role. Go beyond just asking, "how are you doing?" and ask more specific questions which invite thought and consideration.

You may need to give your team time to think about what they want to say, and it might take them a little time before they are totally truthful.

Try these simple questions:

- "What's gone well for you today/this week?"
- "What's not going so well just now?"
- "How can I help you?"

Tell me more!

Assessments

- Fuel50 Career Path Software
- Strong Interest Inventory
- VIA Signature Strengths
- Myers–Briggs
- DISC behavioural profile
- Strengthfinder

Career planning resources

- Any book by John Lees. How to Get a Job You Love; Secrets of Resilient People; Career Reboot; Career Roadmap; Just the Job
- What Colour is Your Parachute? Dick Bolles, 2018
- The Pathfinder. Nicholas Lore, 2012
- Career Match. Shoya Zichy and Ann Bidou, 2007

Read

- Womens' Wellness Wisdom: Exhausted to energized – Rushing Woman's Syndrome. Dr Libby Weaver, 2018
- Adrenaline Junkie. Serotonin Seekers. Matt Church. www.mattchurch.com/chemistryofsuccess/
- Stress Less. Sarah Laurie, 2015
- Drive: The surprising truth about what motivates us. Daniel Pink, 2011
- Emotional Intelligence. Daniel Goleman, 2006
- Emotional Resilience. Mental Help.net. Mills and Dombeck, 2005
- Bright-Sided: How the relentless promotion of positive thinking has undermined America. Barbara Ehrenreich, 2009
- Work Without Stress. Derek Roger and Nick Petrie, 2016
- https://greatergood.berkeley.edu/ (The Greater Good Science Centre.)
- www.theworrybug.co.nz (Specialised tools and resources to grow resilience in children.)
- www.positive.news/
- How to Win Friends and Influence People. Dale Carnegie, 1998

Watch

- TED Talk: The New Era of Positive Psychology. Martin Seligman
- TED Talk: The Power of Vulnerability. Brené Brown
- www.ted.com/talks/david_anderson_your_brain_is_more_than_a_bag_of_chemicals
- www.ted.com/talks/kelly_mcgonigal_how_to_make_stress_your_friend
- www.ted.com/talks/guy_winch_the_case_for_emotional_hygiene
- www.youtube.com/watch?v=zPy0xnymGR0

Play

- Emotion Wheel, Robert Plutchik
- Parrot Emotion Tree
- EARL Emotional Classification
- www.authentichappiness.sas.upenn.edu/testcenter

Five vital facts: Emotional Honesty

1 **It's all in your head:** and it can stay there if you prefer. All the information we have reflected on in this chapter can stay a secret that only you are aware of. You have tools for consciously reshaping your emotions into a more helpful place, and you don't need to tell anybody how you're doing it, unless you'd like them to help you.

2 **It's black and white:** to be human, we must experience the full spectrum of emotions. We cannot decide only to live in one half or the other. To become more emotionally honest, we will need to bravely check out what it feels to be in a wider state of emotional being, and then we can become more aware of

where our home is, and if it's helpful. It can also help us to increase our emotional intelligence by considering what other people might be feeling, which can also be done if our response is a helpful emotional state – we might consider what unhelpful emotional states other people might be feeling, and why.

3   **You feel what you feed:** The emotions you feed are the ones you will feel, if you constantly read stories which leave you feeling helpless, or resentful and talk to people whose world view is negative, then guess which emotions you will predominantly experience? You don't have to stop reading the news completely, or meeting old friends that are stuck in their ways, but you do need to notice the effect they have on you if you want to build your Emotional Honesty Foundation.

4   **Preparation is key:** for the most helpful, emotionally honest conversations about your career achievements, you will need to take some time to review what you've learned and what you want to say. Luckily there are some ideas in this chapter to help you.

5   **You can turn things around:** noticing that you are in an unhelpful emotional place can be a gift. The emotions send you a message about how you are experiencing something at work; they can help you identify patterns, tune into something that's not right and make stronger decisions based on your values. Once you've noticed an unhelpful emotion, you can use the tools and resources in this chapter to support you into a more helpful state.

Figure 6.2 Emotional Honesty "flower": what people say

Do: it's time to write your story (Action Plan)

There are some situations at work that we can change if we have an honest conversation with somebody who can help us. There are some situations at work that we cannot change. For the situations we cannot change, you have now been empowered with some tools to help you if you choose to change how you react to them.

Whether you choose to focus what you do on being more emotionally honest with yourself, or sharing that Emotional Honesty with another person, is entirely your choice.

Remember, if working through the resources causes you concern, if you find yourself stuck or feeling worse than when you began, you should seek the support of a professional. The tools and resources presented here are very widely used, researched and highly successful, but if this is all very new or frightening for you, there are people who would really like to help you.

This chapter about Emotional Honesty has underlined the importance of . . .
It has given me a better understanding of . . .
What I've learned about myself is . . .
What I'm particularly thankful for is . . .
What I'm going to do immediately as a result is . . .
What I'm going to do over the next twelve months is . . .
The impact this will have is . . .
What could get in the way is . . .
(If this happens I'm going to . . .)
I will know I have succeeded because . . .
I am going to check what I've achieved on . . . (date)
The person who will help me to stay accountable to this plan is:

Emotional Honesty

GRID	Here are some questions for you to consider as you reflect on what you have learned in this chapter. They have been designed to help you decide how to use what you have read. **You may wish to consider the questions alone, with a friend or with your manager at work.**
GOAL	• What are the things that you would like to be more honest about at work?
	• Who do you need to be more honest about these things with?
	• When have you been able to be more honest about how your work was making you feel?
	• What do you think will be different about your work if you could be totally honest about your emotions?

- How will your work experience be better if you are more emotionally honest?
- What are the words to describe the emotions that you would like to experience at work?
- What is causing you to feel that you are not currently being emotionally honest (the rogue emotion)?

REALITY
- What impact is this having on you at work? Outside work?
- What is stopping you from being more honest about your emotions at work?
- How are the words to describe your emotions at work different now to what you would like them to be?
- How are your Values and Strengths influencing your emotional state?
- What is causing the intense state emotions that are troubling you the most?

IDEAS
- What would be the risks of being more honest about your emotions?
- What would be the advantages of being more honest about your emotions?
- What would be a brave thing to do right now?
- How could you use your Values and Strengths to become even more emotionally resilient?
- How could you use what you have learned in this chapter to change your emotional state to a more helpful one at work?
- Where could you go to find even more information to help you?
- What are the Thinking Traps that you might have fallen into?
- What is likely to happen if you do nothing and are you OK with that outcome?

DO
- Who will you talk to about this?
- What are you going to do because of your reflections?
- What are the tools and resources at work that can support you?
- How could your employer or manager potentially help you?
- What might prevent you from achieving your goals and if this happens, what will you do to overcome it?
- How will you know you're doing the right thing? What will be different?

7 Self-Care

A critical part of resilience, not something to do if there's time

Resources in this chapter:
Coaching moments:

- Previous strategies
- Noticing stressors
- Controlling pressure
- Self-Care strategies
- Your life story
- Personal Stress Plan
- Signature Strengths and PERMA+
- Five Ways to Wellbeing
- Organisational Currency.

What is this chapter about?

This chapter starts by exploring what Self-Care means, and how it might be useful for supporting resilience at work. We will understand more about how workplace stressors can give us an opportunity to grow even stronger, and therefore become more resilient for the future.

We will explore your own current Self-Care focus, and the impact it's having on your resilience and then we will investigate some of the latest thinking about ways we can improve our physical and spiritual wellbeing to become stronger and handle workplace stressors more effectively.

You'll finish by designing your own Self-Care strategies – focussing on the actions that you can choose to take which help you to maintain your optimum physical and spiritual wellness.

In doing so, you create the circumstances for your ability to stay healthy, recharge your batteries or consciously manage known health issues to help you grow resilient at work.

Part of the challenge with our exploration of the concept of Self-Care is that everybody has a different interpretation of what "being well" and achieving good Self-Care looks like.

If we simply make a list of things you should do to attend to your wellbeing, we would run the risk of disrespecting or neglecting the social, cultural or personal elements that are important to you.

We would also miss the opportunity to review what you already do to look after yourself, along with the lessons that you've learned from focussing on Self-Care in previous times of your life, which might be useful to you now.

As a result, it's important for us first to examine your own definition of physical and spiritual Self-Care at work, and then look at the Self-Care strategies you already have in place and how well they are working for you. You can then decide if Self-Care is an area that you would like to dial up to grow your own resilience at work.

Emotional Wellness also plays a part in Self-Care, but we explored that in our chapter on Emotional Honesty, because it is a separate Foundation for resilience.

What is Self-Care at work?

"We are absolutely committed to supporting the wellbeing of our employees. We have discounted rates available at a local gym, a fresh fruit bowl delivered on a Monday and an Employee Assistance Programme that my team can contact whenever they need to". Construction Project Manager.

When we have a strong sense of wellbeing, we feel good and generally happy with the way our life is going. We tend to experience wellbeing when we are both physically and mentally well, when we are spiritually aware and connected (this doesn't have to be in a purely religious sense, it can mean aligned with nature, or with a sense of "being") and we feel like our life has purpose.

Our wellbeing will fluctuate over our lifetime, it is virtually impossible to imagine a full life lived which has been in a state of total wellbeing at all times . . . and one person's wellbeing cannot be compared with another, since their life experiences will be totally unique.

So, if wellbeing is so fundamental to enjoying life and work why am I using the term Self-Care instead of wellbeing?

One word. Accountability.

Our place of work can to some extent provide us with the tools and the environment to support our wellbeing, and many of them (like our construction project above) provide the rudimentary things to enable this.

Some employers provide way more than this, for example, on site fitness facilities or mental wellbeing programmes.

A few employers don't even begin to step up to support their employees – in fact some workplaces directly cause issues with employee wellbeing, but more on that later.

The fundamental difference is in how we choose to use the tools which are provided for us.

Imagine you work for on the construction project identified in our opening statement.

- Do you join the gym? Do you even go to the gym? Regularly? How is it working and helping you to address your wellbeing goals?
- Did you choose the fruit? If not, what stopped you? What did you eat instead? How did it impact your feeling of wellbeing?
- Do you recognise when you need EAP support? Have you called them? Have you visited EAP? What are you doing as a result? How is it influencing your wellbeing at work?

For years, employers have researched and implemented the causes and indicators of wellbeing at work and many have implemented different work practices or offered support as a result.

For some this approach even becomes a source of competitive advantage (check out Glassdoor.com and other employee led reviews of work, like Best Companies or Great Place to Work) – we want to work somewhere that takes our health seriously and we are quick to criticise organisations that don't provide good conditions for us to work.

Yet still the rate of sickness, absence and mental issues reported at workplaces continues to grow.

The perception that employee wellbeing is increasingly important in the workplace, as companies recognise that it can influence how much energy we bring to work (and therefore how much work we might get done), can surely result in positive outcomes; employees that want more support for their wellbeing so they can feel great, and employers that understand the business implications of providing that support, but whose responsibility is wellbeing at work?

It's interesting that we seem to believe that we are entering a time where employers are taking the wellbeing of their employees more seriously (for example the rise in a focus on mindfulness, proactively managing absence data and talking about mental health) and yet employers in the nineteenth century regularly adopted a highly corporate, paternalistic approach to support every aspect of their workers' lives – sometimes to an extreme degree, for example Cadbury, Bourneville Village.

During the 1900s the company was seen as revolutionary for providing pensions, serving meals at lunch, employing full time doctors, physical examinations and apparently even compulsory exercise.

Fast forward to our modern workplaces, and there tend to be many more employee led approaches to wellbeing; indeed, imagine what the response would be to employers who introduced compulsory exercise programmes – which raises the question about where responsibility for wellbeing lies.

No doubt, the research into optimal ways for employers to design, measure and influence wellbeing at work will continue to evolve, particularly because workplaces are looking at costs of:

- US$300 billion/year as a result of accidents, absenteeism, turnover, diminished productivity, medical/legal/insurance costs and compensation awards (source: American Institute of Stress, 2016)
- €20 billion/year as a result of stress related illness (source: the European Agency for Safety and Health at Work, 2014)
- Aus$14.81 billion/year as a result of presenteeism and absenteeism (source: Medibank, 2017)
- NZ$1.5 billion/year due to workplace absence (source: Wellness in the Workplace Survey Report, BusinessNZ and Southern Cross Health Society, 2017)

In the meantime, this chapter will encourage you to support your own wellbeing; what Self-Care strategies are you already using? How well are they working and what else could you do?

Professor Cary Cooper, CBE, (Chartered Institute of Personnel and Development (CIPD) President, 2017) defines this beautifully: "It's the employer's job to create an environment where employees can make healthy lifestyle choices, but employees must take responsibility for their own health and wellbeing".

He illustrates this by referring to the Business in the Community Workwell Model, which highlights the benefits for both business AND employees when they focus on wellbeing at work.

Physical wellbeing at work

Our discussion about physical wellbeing at work refers to these key areas:

- Our nutrition choices (food, alcohol, drugs)
- How we build movement into our day (muscular strength, cardiovascular and/or flexibility)
- Whether we take advantage of health-related benefits (e.g. discounted medical checks)
- Whether we take our holidays
- How well we breathe

Physical wellbeing at work is also massively influenced by the quality of sleep we get while not at work, and there are some useful links about this in the Tell me more! section.

Spiritual wellbeing at work

Our discussion about spiritual wellbeing at work refers to these areas:

- The extent that we use mindfulness or meditation techniques
- Our connectedness with nature
- Our sense that what we are doing is making a difference to the world
- Spiritual practice in accordance with beliefs (e.g. religion or faith).

When we are doing activities that take us closer to our career ambitions, and implementing strategies for overcoming obstacles we are using energy – sometimes a lot of energy.

Energy must be replenished or it gradually erodes over time.

Sometimes the simplest thing that we can do to rebuild our energy is to make time for what we know gives us energy once more.

It's not a "nice thing to do when you've got time", it's a fundamental requirement for resilience.

If you aren't replenishing then you are depleting, and it will be simply a question of time before your supplies run out and your coping strategies fail you.

Emotional Honesty forms the platform for realising when we are not feeling at our best, and then we can explore the extent to which we are dialling up our Resilience Foundations. If we find that Self-Care is lacking, we can reflect on what to do and then take action.

Goal: what do you want to achieve?

Using the GRID approach, we can work out what it's like when you have your Self-Care focus at the level which creates optimum wellbeing for you at work.

This will give you something to aim for; a goal which will help you to decide whether action you choose to take is likely to take you closer to the goal or further away from your goal.

For example, if you know that your optimum wellbeing includes a daily run, and you are facing a whole week of intensive deadlines you can choose to build a daily run into your diary or you can choose not to, but recognise that you may not be at your most resilient to deliver the work required.

Coaching moment: previous strategies

Think about the last time when you felt like your physical and spiritual wellbeing was in a really great place.

Your work energised you, and despite spinning multiple plates of responsibility or doing lots of things at work you were in control and feeling fine.

1   What were your strategies for physical wellbeing?
2   What were your strategies for spiritual wellbeing?
3   How are they different to the strategies you are using right now?

If there was one thing that you could do to get you closer to that feeling again, what would it be?

What will it feel like when you get there? How did it feel when you were in that place before?

What will you need to stop doing, or let go of, to achieve this?

If you honestly can't think of a time when your physical and spiritual wellbeing was in a great place, then use an example of a time when it was better than it is right now (and if it's never been in anything but a terrible state, then you may need to consider talking to a wellbeing at work professional who can support you).

An engaging career

The Human Potential Centre at the University of Auckland is on a mission to enhance the physical health and mental wellbeing of communities across New Zealand.

They have found that happier employees are more likely to demonstrate superior work performance, less likely to leave their current job, more positively evaluated by colleagues, reach higher sales targets, enjoy better physical health and take less time off work than less happy peers (remember our exploration of DOSE earlier? These are the employees who are buzzing with Dopamine, Oxytocin, Serotonin and Endorphins).

All these reasons contribute enormously to the desire for businesses to understand how "engaged" employees are at work. You might have contributed to answering a regular (usually annual) survey called an Engagement Survey.

The science behind the surveys actually does more than just check who is happy at work, it also explores the extent to which employees **say** good things about their employer (always a good sign if people who work with you recommend you to others), have an intention to **stay** (again, usually a sign that you're doing something right as an employer – unless somebody feels totally trapped with no option but to stay) and **strive** (quite simply, somebody who is more engaged at work is likely to want to go the extra mile because they clearly understand how their efforts result in a better outcome for their employer).

Even though some employees sigh and roll their eyes about completing engagement surveys, the truth is that unless you're having super Emotionally Honest conversations with your manager the survey might be the only chance your employer has to understand what's stressing you out and how you're handling that stress.

Only then can employers start to work out what they might be able to do to support you.

Every organisation causes stress.

Most businesses exist primarily to make money. If they stop making money, they are likely to cease to function, therefore it makes sense that they will always be looking for ways to either keep making money or make more money.

Almost all businesses will do fundamental things to create stress like: streamline processes, bring in new products, ask employees to deliver more outputs, redesign the company.

Some businesses will do more complicated things to create stress like: promote people to roles without checking they have the right skills, communicating in ways that don't always result in the right message being heard by everybody, forgetting that new people take time to settle into their jobs, neglecting to create clear career pathways for all employees.

A few companies will also do pretty terrible things to create stress like: allow bullying, harassment or discrimination to occur, permit a blame culture, expect employees to work in poor physical work environments or for unreasonable hours, pay under the valued rate for a role.

For the ever-growing number of self-employed people (given the growth of freelancers, Giggers, casual workers etc.) these workplace stressors are likely to be on top of the everyday stress of wondering where the next pay cheque is coming from.

For them, there is the additional need to connect to find work, building a pipeline of work and then delivering the work at a place where any of the above stressors might also come into play.

As a result, recognising both the physical and mental signs of your own stress levels, and then implementing support strategies to take care of yourself (as far as possible) is paramount.

Coaching moment: your goals for Self-Care

Create an overview of what you need to have in place to know that you have created the conditions for optimum wellbeing. Look at the definitions of physical and spiritual wellbeing at the start of this chapter:

1   What are you going to do to look after your physical wellbeing? How often?
2   What are you going to do to look after your spiritual wellbeing? How often?
3   When are you going to start doing these things? How are you going to ensure that they get done, or get back on track if they don't get done?

Reality: what is your Self-Care currently like?

When you are asked about how your job or your week is going, what do you normally say? What do your colleagues normally say?

If you can get beyond a non-committal response (like "good" or "fine"), you are likely to find a response that is at some level influenced by perceived stress: "I'm swamped right now", "I'm running behind on my deadlines", "I'm totally overworked".

Stress has for some of us, become a badge to wear with honour. If something at work isn't stressing us out then perhaps we're not trying hard enough, or pushing ourselves far enough, or maybe we're not important enough to have a stressful job.

However, not all stress is bad.

Stress at its simplest is just our body's response to stimuli that creates demands on us (the VUCA world changes we identified earlier in the book – it's likely that some elements of VUCA create energy for you, not just negative pressure). It's the chemical response we have, our heart rate, our blood pressure.

It's our way of either responding to something external (the thing that happens in our environment which creates a demand) or the emotional response within us that the thing creates.

Eustress is the scientific name for good stress. Good stress can drive us into action and have a positive impact on both our wellbeing and productivity. It can provide us with the push we need to put aside our procrastination and focus on actually doing something, it can give us an injection of energy when we need to deliver an amazing presentation, it can help to focus our thinking and decision making.

Eustress is typically short term, and it feels a little bit exciting.

On the flipside, Distress is the scientific name for bad stress.

Bad stress can be short term or long term, but unlike Eustress it doesn't feel exciting, it feels unpleasant. It causes anxiety or concern within us and tends to lead to a decrease in our performance. Often the things that cause us Distress are things we believe we are not capable of being able to do and as a result, it can lead to physical and mental issues.

Because of the very personal nature of stress, it's critical that you find ways to take more notice of your own experiences of Eustress and Distress . . . and maybe next time somebody asks you how you're doing at work, you could even share it: "I'm really swamped right now, it's causing Eustress, so I'm finally getting the important things done" or "I'm really swamped right now, it's causing Distress, so I'm going to dial up my Self-Care and have some time out this evening" – what an interesting way to challenge our perception of the badness of stress.

Signs of overload

Remembering that all our lives have an element of stress in them, we all have a tipping point at which the stressors take their toll and fail to inject us with the optimal ingredients for energy and achievement.

According to the NHS (UK, 2017), the Top Ten signs of stress include:

1 Sleep issues
2 Pain of any kind; headache, neck/back pain
3 Neck/back pain
4 Finding it hard to focus

5   Shallow or rapid breathing
6   Digestive problems
7   Irritability and pessimism
8   Fatigue
9   Weight issues
10   Tearfulness

One of the tricky things about these symptoms is that there are lots of other factors that may contribute to experiencing them, for example: food intolerances, significant trauma or serious medical conditions.

The tools and resources in this book are only intended to address the stress issues experienced by those of us who are overall mentally and physically well, but things aren't going to plan at work.

They are not intended to replace the considerable support which may be required in extreme cases, under which circumstances you should seek medical intervention.

Coaching moment: noticing stressors

Think back to the time that you just recalled, as you considered your physical and spiritual Self-Care strategies in the past.

1   What are the main signs or symptoms that you notice about times when your wellbeing is strong at work? What are your clues from the list above?

Now reflect on a time when your wellbeing at work was not so great.

2   What are the main signs or symptoms that you notice when your wellbeing is starting to falter at work, and your stress coping strategies are no longer working?
3   What are the main signs or symptoms that you notice when you are under extreme stress at work; when you are well and truly over the tipping point of your coping strategies?

Starting to notice the point at which you transition from having a high state of wellbeing at work into a place where it is not so strong is fundamental to building resilience. We all travel this path every day, every week, every year – handling stress is part of the cycle of work and life.

The critical skill for a resilient person is recognising they have entered a less helpful state of wellbeing, and then take action to get back on track before they enter the dangerous zone of extreme stress.

The more emotionally arousing the event (whether positive or negative) the better it will be remembered, therefore if something happens to us at work which causes an extreme stress response we are more likely to store this as our default emotional reaction, and our body will react accordingly.

When you're in this extreme stress zone, it's likely that your body's chemical responses will be very unhelpful indeed.

The amygdala within your brain will send a message to the prefrontal cortex, telling it that there is a "fight, flight or freeze" situation and therefore a requirement to flood your body with adrenalin and cortisol, and your dopamine levels will be reduced.

There's some evidence that it's this increase in cortisol that causes your brain to "fix" this as a response to any perceived danger . . . which is helpful in some situations (I can smell smoke, so my amygdala sends a danger signal, the increased adrenalin and cortisol causes me to get out and then every time I smell smoke after this time I react the same.)

However, it is unhelpful if it becomes the default position every time there is a perception of danger (in fact, it can lay down the foundations for avoidance coping which we explore later in this chapter).

When your body is in this state, it is very unlikely that you will be able to create ideas and your brain will not be able to clearly define what is real versus what is imagined, so expecting yourself to come up with helpful solutions to resolve extreme stress is unrealistic.

Realising when you have entered your own zone of extreme stress is fundamental to asking somebody else for help, whether your manager, a career professional, a counsellor or a friend who will help you create solutions for getting through.

Finding somebody you trust who can help you to see this can be one way to grow your consciousness of when it's happening, since your adrenalin and cortisol response might prevent you from being able to tell that your extreme stress zone has been activated (perhaps you can return the favour and be the "stress spotter" for another person too).

By growing your ability to recognise when you're leaving the zone of being a bit stressed and entering an extreme state, you are likely to avoid burnout at work; the slow wearing down of energy and enthusiasm that can accompany long term work related stress.

Signs that you might be entering your zone of extreme stress:

- You generalise more often than normal (managers always treat me this way, I never manage to meet my deadlines).
- Your thinking goes around and around in circles focussing on trying to solve something that you have no influence over.
- You find it harder to distinguish between real and imagined threats (my manager is in a meeting which must be about my performance).

Booking a Stress Check into your diary every three to four months can help to prevent this from happening; use the Emotions Word List to reflect what your primary emotions are, and then explore the ideas presented in this chapter to create your plan of action if you think Self-Care needs to be dialled up.

Coaching moment: controlling pressure

Think about the issues at work that are causing an obstacle to achieve your career ambitions.

1   What are the aspects to these things that you could you control or influence?
2   What are the aspects to these things that you cannot control or influence, so you must accept?
3   How are you going to use this observation to decide where to dial up or dial down your Self-Care strategies? What action can you take?

Coaching tales: Brenda

Brenda worked for a consulting company. The focus on wellbeing at her workplace was enormous, from free Fitbit devices included in welcome packs, through to fitness assessments and of course an annual health check.

When Brenda came for coaching however, the focus of her coaching sessions was extreme stress.

This was somebody who worked for an employer that was absolutely beyond a doubt committed to providing a best in class environment for the wellbeing of their staff, and yet Brenda confided that she was not alone in the workplace pressure she was experiencing.

Through her coaching programme, Brenda concluded that because of combined influences (her own commitment to delivering her job, the pressure she believed there was on her to do so and her love of working in a fast-paced environment) she had avoided being honest with her team leader about the amount of focus she was able to give to accessing the wellbeing tools that the company provided . . . and it was taking its toll.

She decided that the buzz she got came from the enormous challenge of what she was responsible for; she loved the learning which she experienced every moment of the day, and the sense of achievement she got from connecting with clients and seeing the impact of what she did on their success. Except this had got out of control, and now she felt like she was reeling from contract to contract without any control or time to eat and sleep.

For Brenda, one of the biggest outcomes from her coaching pro-gramme was the recognition that she believed herself to be energised by the high pace of her workplace, but that in enjoying the "buzz" that this gave her, she had failed to notice that her work passion had crept ever so steadily into every area of her life.

All her time was spent in Learning and Connecting – with absolutely no time left for Emotional Honesty or Self-Care, despite the amazing opportunities available to her.

Working with her coach was all that she needed to design an approach which was more honest about the impact this was having on her. Over a period of weeks, she worked out ways to dial down her own focus on Learning and Connecting, which gave her the space to dial up her Self-Care.

Reflection: employers can provide state of the art wellbeing tools and resources for their employees, but unless they are being used, and their use is leading to positive change in employee wellbeing, there is little point in having them.

Brenda's experience highlights some important features of Self-Care:

1   Our workplace can be the cause of our need for Self-Care, but we can also self-sabotage our own wellbeing because of failing to notice (or ignoring) the part we are also playing.
2   Work can provide us with all the tools in the world to support our Self-Care, but if we do not use them, then we are also culpable in our own downfall; we cannot solely blame our employer for our Eustress experience at work.
3   The stress related trigger was a gift for Brenda, a warning sign that some-thing needed to change. For some of us, the warning sign might be sudden – while for others there may be a slow build before we realise that we are noticing there is a problem. Brenda chose to notice the trigger – and do something about it. Feelings and emotions are always part of a story, our opportunity is to listen to what they are telling us without judging them to be good or bad.

Coaching moment: Self-Care strategies

Physical Self-Care

When we are physically well, we can get through our day without excessive tiredness or stress and we consciously choose actions or behav-iours that we know will be helpful to our health (e.g. the food we choose, the activities we do) instead of actions or behaviours that we know will undermine it.

(continued)

(continued)

How does this definition compare with your own thoughts about physical Self-Care?

Think about a time when you were at a physical high. A time when you felt at your peak physically, whether you were at work or not.

1   What were the main actions or behaviours that contributed to this?
2   What effect did this have on your effectiveness or enjoyment at work or in life?
3   Write down the things that have changed since this time.

Now reflect on your last four weeks at work. Consider how much time you currently spend supporting your physical wellness.

1   What have you done to contribute to your physical Self-Care?
2   What impact did these activities have on how well you felt physically?
3   How does your approach compare to when you were at an all-time physical peak?

Coaching moment

Spiritual Self-Care

When we experience a sense of harmony between the life that we live and the values we believe in, then we are likely to experience a form of spiritual wellness.

If we have spiritual wellness, we have a sense of meaning – not just from the work that we do, but in the purpose of our life overall. This is likely defined by different aspects including: beliefs, values, morals and religious faith. If we take care of our spiritual wellness, then we are more likely to experience peace and inner calm, no matter what happens in the workplace.

Think about a time when you experienced a sense of calm, peace or relaxation regardless of what was happening around you.

1   What were the things that you did to create a sense of calm, peace or relaxation?
2   What effect did this have on you?
3   Write down the things that have changed since this time.

> **Now reflect on your last four weeks at work. Consider your sense of calm, peace or relaxation there.**
>
> 1 How does your current sense of calm, peace or relaxation compare with the time you identified above?
> 2 What do you currently do to cultivate a sense of calm, peace or relaxation at work?
> 3 What would need to change for you to experience a greater sense of calm, peace or relaxation at work?

Ideas: what could you consider?

You have identified what it's like for you to be at your optimum wellbeing at work, by recording or reflecting on a time when you had great physical and spiritual Self-Care.

You've explored your current commitment to this, by considering how well you are attending to both these areas, and you might decide simply to increase your focus on something that's worked for you before . . . or you might want to look at other ideas for dialling this up, should you wish.

Personal Stress Plan

Dr Lucy Hone is a founder of the New Zealand Institute of Wellbeing & Resilience. While her work currently primarily focuses on promoting wellbeing literacy and building resilience in school communities, her academic research informs some of the latest thinking to address the escalating levels of wellbeing issues at work.

Her work aligns very nicely with our exploration of Emotional Honesty, where we learned more about the impact of neuroscience, positive psychology and emotional intelligence on our approach to how we perceive and handle workplace stressors.

Lucy has designed a Personal Stress Plan template which helps us navigate the process when experiencing workplace stressors.

Avoidance coping

One way of coping with stressors at work is known as avoidance coping.

This is a way of trying to prevent ourselves from what we believe to be the realities of a perceived stressor. For example, if we have had a brutal put-down in front of the team after sharing an idea we might find that we stop sharing our ideas (in case it happens again). If you are in a role which you don't fully believe you can deliver you might try to keep a super low profile. If you think

Table 7.1 Personal Stress Plan

STOP	**Explore what makes you notice you are stressed:**
	• What are your emotional signals? • What are your physical signals? • What other signals do you get that you are leaving your zone of optimal wellbeing?
PAUSE	**Explore what you believe are the causes:**
	• Is what I am feeling the truth? • Is this good stress that will motivate me? • Will the stress get better over time? • Is worrying about it helping or harming me? • What can I change? • What do I have to accept? • What action could I take?
GO	**Explore what you will you do to diffuse the impact:**
	• Burn it off (physical activity) • Tune it out (distractions) • Tune it out (mindfulness) • Tune it out (other techniques) • Connect with others • Recover (unplug from technology) • Recover (sleep) • Reappraise the situation

there might be a problem with the quality of work that you do but use an avoidance coping technique you would avoid all possibility of feedback.

This is all well and good for a short period of time, in fact avoidance coping is fundamental to some roles; for example leading a team through large scale change and redundancy or telling somebody at your surgery that they have just a few months to live may mean you need to conceal your emotional response . . . but if you're still concealing them months later, particularly if you are experiencing any of the symptoms associated with less than optimum wellbeing then your strategy needs to be adjusted.

Dr Lehan Stemmet is one academic who has researched this topic deeply, with a project that involved almost 1,500 research participants from around the world.

He found that where we avoid dealing with issues from the past because we don't want to stir up memories or emotions we can accidentally prevent ourselves from learning from them, and this can prevent us seeking help and developing our resilience for the future.

Dr Stemmet suggests:

> People who avoid challenge at all costs may anticipate the challenge to be worse than it actually is and, therefore, avoid it rather than deal with it in a constructive manner. This could lead to unresolved personal or work issues, which could then lead to other consequences.

(Examples of other consequences would be health issues, performance issues or relationship issues.)

Signature Strengths and the PERMA + Model

The exploration into the psychological profiles of positive, successful, thriving people contributed to the disruption to the psychological world that we explored during Chapter 7.

Knowing the qualities that come most naturally to you, and then dialling them up to support our Self-Care can potentially have enormously positive effects on our resilience at work. We can all keep building and enhancing our Signature Strengths throughout our working lives.

The Signature Strengths

There are twenty-four character strengths, which we all possess – though to differing degrees. Understanding your profile, and then exploring ways to lean into your strengths can influence the way we handle obstacles, improve our relationships and contribute to our sense of wellbeing at work.

Table 7.2 Signature Strengths

Wisdom	• Creativity • Curiosity • Judgement • Love of learning • Perspective
Courage	• Bravery • Honesty • Perseverance • Zest
Humanity	• Kindness • Love • Social intelligence
Justice	• Fairness • Leadership • Teamwork
Temperance	• Forgiveness • Humility • Prudence • Self-regulation
Transcendence	• Appreciation of beauty • Gratitude • Hope • Humour • Spirituality

Imagine that you have been working for a company for five years and you've just heard that there is a large restructure planned. To dial up your Self-Care and align it with your Signature Strengths you might consider:

- **Gratitude**: create a gratitude journal to reflect on all the gifts your company has given you as a result of working there.
- **Spirituality**: pray for an outcome that results in positive change for the business and the people employed there.
- **Love of Learning**: research the latest industry trends, find out more about what's going on in the world your company works in.
- **Forgiveness**: put yourself in the shoes of the people running your company, consider what they will be having to handle and try to understand things from their perspective.

Martin Seligman also contributes to our ideas to dial up Self-Care at work with his PERMA+ ("PERMA Plus") framework. His research found that in order to experience wellbeing, there are five essential elements to consider. The model was introduced in his 2011 book, "Flourish".

The PERMA acronym stands for the five elements that must be in place for us to experience optimal wellbeing. They are:

1 **Positive Emotion:** in other words, to be experiencing wellbeing we must be experiencing the helpful and positive emotional states on the left side of our Emotions Word List. If not, we should ask ourselves what we can do to support ourselves into a positive emotional state.

2 **Engagement:** this happens when we are doing something that causes us to look at the clock and think, "holy moly, is that the time?" We are likely to be doing something that causes us to "lose time", and psychologists refer to this as finding our flow. Sometimes we need to minimise distractions to help us do this; luckily, you're learning about managing boundaries in this book.

3 **Relationships:** not just any old relationships but positive and meaningful relationships with people who contribute to our sense of wellbeing . . . if the relationships in your life are not positive, how much attention do you want to give them?

4 **Meaning:** in this sense, this refers to our belief that we are somehow serving a cause that is bigger than ourselves. It can be spiritual or religious in nature (e.g. a God or Deity) or it can be a cause that helps humanity in some way. It can be useful to explore your motivators, values and drivers at work to help you work this out.

5 **Achievements:** this doesn't refer to how busy you are but how proud you are of where you have spent your time, and what you are striving to accomplish – where you have clear goals and are deliberately taking steps towards them you will experience a greater sense of wellbeing.

The "Plus" part of the PERMA+ Model is included by the Wellbeing and Resilience Centre (South Australian Health and Medical Research Institute) and includes:

- Physical activity
- Nutrition
- Sleep
- Optimism

Five ways to wellbeing

In 2008, the New Economics Foundation was commissioned to review the work of over 400 scientists from around the world who specialised in wellbeing. The report aimed to find some evidence-based ideas for people to build into their lives, with a view to increasing wellbeing.

Their findings laid the foundations for the work of the Mental Help Foundation in Christchurch from 2009 and was especially widely promoted in the aftermath of the city's earthquakes.

1   **Connect** (talk and listen, be there – feel connected with other people around you)
2   **Give** (your time, your words, your presence – do something nice for somebody)
3   **Notice** (appreciate the little things, savour the moment – be aware of the world around you)
4   **Learn** (embrace new experiences, see opportunities, surprise yourself)
5   **Move** (do what you can, enjoy what you do, move your mood by finding what works for you)

Give, Notice and Move are all part of our Self-Care Foundation in the form of spiritual and physical wellbeing, while Connect and Learn (and Emotional Honesty) are separated given the findings of the Adaptive Resilience research team.

Finding ways to honour your Self-Care and do at least one of these five factors every day will directly contribute to your wellbeing.

Lucy Hone is one researcher who can prove this. Using information from 5,000 New Zealanders, she correlated every single one of these factors, and even adjusting for gender, age, ethnicity, marital status, household income and academic qualifications she found something interesting.

While every single one of the Five Ways to Wellbeing directly contributed to an increased sense of wellbeing; respondents felt good and functioned well as a result of committing to the Five Ways to Wellbeing . . . it was taking Notice that resulted in the biggest increase.

Frequently being aware of the world around you, and of how you are feeling . . . and by reflecting on the experiences that you have, you can increase your wellbeing by up to four times, compared with others who did less so.

1   Notice there's a problem or opportunity.
2   Notice that somebody needs to do something about it.
3   Notice that the somebody who needs to do something about it might be you.
4   Notice what might be different if the problem or opportunity was explored, unpacked, investigated.
5   Notice how you would feel if the problem or opportunity was resolved.
6   Notice that you have a choice.
7   Choose what to do.

What an incredible result to support our suggestion that Emotional Honesty is a critical and foundational part of influencing resilience.

Building evidence

During 2017, a team at the University of Canterbury are conducting research to explore the direct impact that Signature Strengths and the Five Ways to Wellbeing could have on our psychological wellbeing, as well as the effect of using Signature Strengths at work on our overall performance at work.

Using a control group, they are tracking and analysing the impact of using the Five Ways to Wellbeing on positive emotions and intrinsic motivation at work over a period of up to a year. In other words, they want to explore the link between playing the wellbeing game, and our levels of reported wellbeing and performance (supporting this with real indicators like cortisol sampling and physical health checks).

Their findings could have an enormous impact on building an even stronger case for using what we are learning in this book to build resilience at work.

Rewrite your story

All of us has a story.

Everybody has a whole life of experiences which helps to shape the person we are at work. Whether we are in our first job from school or our last job before retirement. During our journey, we have all had positive and not so positive experiences.

Focussing on what we have gained or learned from our journey and how it's helped us to become stronger can be hugely powerful for our sense of self, and our belief in our capability to become more resilient.

Coaching tales: Hakopa

Hakopa was born in Polynesia and moved to New Zealand with his family when he was a teenager. The move was the first time Hakopa had experienced such a significant life change, and despite his family's best intentions he began to struggle at school.

Because he was finding it hard to make friends, his parents enrolled him in the local football team in the hope that his love of sports would help him to meet new kids in the area.

Instead, Hakopa felt as though his parents were pushing him away and forcing him to cope with the changes all by himself.

Hakopa shared this story when he embarked on a coaching programme to support him through a significant change at work. His manager had noticed that he was taking on more and more responsibilities during the restructure of his team and was starting to come into work seeming ill and stressed.

In considering his story, Hakopa realised that he had created a belief that changes needed to be handled alone, and change was likely to be stressful and tiring.

With the support of his coach, he began to write his story. He realised the bravery it took for his family to make the move, he remembered that his sports had indeed helped him to regain confidence and make friends and he recalled that the initiative he had needed to resolve problems alone had been immense.

Armed with his new Story Strengths of bravery, confidence and initiative he totally changed the way he approached the restructure of his team.

Reflection: finding our Story Strengths can be empowering and can help us to rewrite the tales we tell ourselves about work, about our capabilities and about our future.

Coaching moment: your life story

Consider your life story so far. What are you telling yourself about who you are, where you've come from and where you can go from here?

1   What are the Story Strengths that your story has given you? ("if I hadn't experienced ABC, then I wouldn't be able to XYZ")
2   What are the not so positive parts to your story? The plot? The characters?
3   How might these things be influencing your experiences at work?

If you were to write a book or make a movie about the rest of your life, how would it evolve?

How would you like it to evolve? It doesn't have to be all "happy ever after", but if the story looks to be unfolding in a way you don't like, what could you do to change things?

How might you use the Story Strengths you've just identified to help you?

Turning your past or your perceived negative experiences into something that catalyses and ignites you can be an incredibly powerful thing to do. Brené Brown talks about reaching out to our most trusted connections to help us rewrite our story so that they can help us to reality-check it and keep things objective. Other ways you could do this include working backwards from the outcome you want instead (e.g. what's your "happy ever after" and how would you need to be different, think different, do different, in order to achieve this?).

Taking notice and mindfulness

We have explored the Five Ways to Wellbeing as one way to influence our Self-Care, and because taking Notice has been identified as having the biggest impact, we'll look at it in a bit more detail.

Noticing how we feel has been discussed during our chapter on Emotional Honesty so this is a more general discussion about the power of noticing.

Research has discovered that being mindful predicts judgement, accuracy and insight related problem solving (source: Kiken and Shook, 2009), that mindfulness improves job performance by improving vigour, dedication and absorption (source: Dane and Brummel, 2014) and that using mindfulness programmes can decrease stress at work (source: Aitken et al., 2016)

But just what does it mean to be mindful?

At work, it's likely to be our ability to be fully present and aware of where we are, what we're doing and the decisions we are taking . . . without being overly reactive or overwhelmed by what's going on around us.

What's the opposite of mindfulness at work?

- Perhaps we're in a meeting where our manager shares some news which causes us to be afraid, so we stop listening to the discussion and start imagining the horrors that might lie ahead.
- Perhaps we're working to a very tight deadline and finding it hard to stay focussed on what we're doing – so we do lots of other things instead, and perhaps we get cross with somebody in our team over something small.
- Perhaps we're receiving emails and texts at a rate of knots and it's influencing how panicked we are about what to do, so we run around being really busy without achieving much.

Developing mindfulness is like developing physical fitness; it takes time and regular practice (and then to stay fit, you must keep going).

Being more mindful at work doesn't always mean finding somewhere to lie down and be still. A more formal mindfulness like this is fundamental to developing the practice (indeed a minimum of twelve minutes daily is recommended), however it is not always possible at work.

A more informal mindfulness approach can be as simple as making sure you are listening completely to the person speaking to you (check what you've heard by repeating the main points back at the end of the conversation).

It can be as easy as switching off your phone while you are in a meeting.

It can be as effortless as taking three very deep breaths before you begin your work in the morning.

It can even be noticing how your breathing changes when your manager talks to you about the project you just handed in.

If you are looking for a slightly more robust way to be mindful at work, consider building it into a lunchtime walk. As you are walking, notice what is going on around you. Listen for three different noises, notice three different smells, look for three different shades of the same colour.

For more comprehensive ideas about building mindfulness, explore the tools and apps in the Tell me more! section.

Maximise your boundaries

Many of us have a major problem with lack of time. Despite the regularity of a 24-hour cycle to every day, we constantly pack our day and our to do list, fail to achieve everything and then experience stress.

There are heaps of awesome tools out there to help us with this, many of which are noted in the Tell me more! section.

Some quick ideas include:

- Consider your best time or place for doing these three things and then plan your day around them:

  o Creating ideas
  o Reflecting or thinking
  o Powering through your action list

- Use this knowledge about when your energy is typically high (or low); try playing with what you find – for example, what impact does it have to do high energy activities when your energy is naturally low?
- Consider a worry clock, or rumination clock. The science of resilience suggests that if we worry about something too much beforehand (or too much after it happened) then our optimum resilience is compromised.

  o Set an alarm, for say two minutes, and allow yourself to worry during that time. Write down all the things you have concerns about; what will get in the way; what could go wrong (or if it's after the event, all the things that went wrong, what you should have done differently, what you regret omitting). When the alarm goes off stop writing and focus on your job again.

The Self-Care elephants

It's all very well suggesting that we need to dial up our Self-Care but what if we are faced with any of these situations?

Self-worth concerns

Suggesting that somebody should consider the importance of re-energising by spending time on themselves, when they don't believe they are worthy of this, is problematic. Just because they are advised that it's important to spend time on this won't actually make it happen – some people need to create an urgency, which is often why a radical situation is the final straw that spurs us into actually doing something that we knew we should have been doing all along.

- Staying in a job you don't enjoy because you don't believe you deserve anything better and getting more stressed as a result
- Constantly putting yourself down and dismissing your own achievements
- Neglecting to take a break during the day because you are worried colleagues might think you are a slacker
- Asking for permission to have a lunch break to go to a fitness class (despite have a lunchbreak in your contract)

Coaching tales: Jennifer

Jennifer had taken three years out of her job to have a family. With two children under the age of two, she now faced the real challenge of returning to work in a role for four days a week, while also supporting the needs of her children, given that her husband had a full time role and travelled frequently with his job.

Because she wanted to give her employer no cause to doubt her commitment to work, and because she loved her job Jennifer quite literally worked every hour that she could, often doing as many hours as a full time employee. The remainder of her time was spent caring for children or running the household. She became more and more exhausted, and her employer encouraged her to meet with a coach to work out a plan to make changes to her work or her lifestyle.

During her coaching meetings, Jennifer realised that she had completely given up all focus on Self-Care. She quite literally existed for her work and her family, with no time for anything else. This realisation caused a very powerful emotional response, which was exacerbated by the perception that she did not have any support to help her.

Despite exploring ideas to build small amounts of Self-Care into her working day, to try out sharing some of the load with her husband or explore opportunities to swap childcare times with other mums in her village, she resisted.

Jennifer recognised that her actions would not result in supporting her resilience but did not feel that she could ask for help from either her husband, her employer or members of her social circles. She knew that she was emotionally and physically exhausted but felt it was her decision and therefore her responsibility to make the situation work. A few months later, Jennifer quit her job.

Reflection: returning to work after raising a family is an enormous and very personal decision. Designing the Foundations for resilience into your return can potentially make the transition smoother but relies on you dialling up all four Foundations.

You're addicted to technology

There is little to compare with the panicked feeling when we think we may have lost our phone . . . according to a Deloitte study (There's no Place Like Phone, 2016), almost a third of us check our phone within five minutes of waking and we look at our phones up to 150 times a day. How will we cope if we can't find it?!

Research shows us that another thing we can do to support our Self-Care is a digital detox (a sort of extreme version of managing boundaries).

But our inner voice screams if we contemplate turning off our screens: "what if we miss a critical email? What about the response I'm waiting for from accounts? I need to check the news every day! Without Facebook/Twitter/ Instagram how will I stay connected?"

We all know in our hearts that technology is not only an enabler of productivity, but also a disruptor. Constantly checking the various information sources takes us away from what we are "supposed" to be doing in our work, but we just can't help ourselves.

The constant pinging of text messages, messaging, emails, alerts . . . they all contribute to the additional noise of our life, but they can be incredibly draining.

Studies are relatively new in this area, but are suggesting some of these benefits as a result of turning off the screen:

1 **Deeper friendships:** having 500+ friends who share status updates instead of feelings can falsely lead us to feel connected. Catching up in person instead of via technology drives totally different conversations – we've already explored the very powerful impact that oxytocin can have on our feelings of connection.
2 **More confident body language:** we are more likely to make eye contact and stand up straighter without a smartphone.
3 **Improved memory:** likely to be because of being more present, and truly listening to the conversation content.

4 **Better sleep:** the blue light from phone screens suppresses melatonin, which influences our quality of sleep. When we don't check our phone or our computer just before bedtime, this is less of an influence.

5 **More time:** creating space for ideas to find you, instead of zipping between screens and suddenly realising that four hours of your life have passed you by. Realising that you do have time after all to read a story or go for a run.

There's no need to switch off forever, just finding the opportunity to have a break can be enough and can remind us that we are able to control it. Realistically this may not work easily in some roles (for example on call medics) but there will always be a time, however short, when we can manage this. If you really do find it an issue, try detoxing over time . . . start by switching off your notifications, or turning on the flight mode for a few hours. If the thought of this creates extreme anxiousness, you may want to seek the support of a professional to help you out.

You've forgotten what you enjoy

Some people have neglected their Self-Care for so long that they find it impossible to contemplate what they might do. The constant working late, or travelling on the job or other demands of life have led to a Self-Care void.

Tackling this might include remembering back to childhood, or a time when work wasn't all encompassing. Reflect on what you used to love doing in your spare time, and then try it out again. You might find that you've grown out of it, and it no longer fulfils your needs, or you might find that you're just as passionate about it as before, and it helps to re-energise you once more.

If you really can't think of anything, then play with the Self-Care strategies of others in your tribe. Join a colleague at their weekly rugby game, ask a friend what they do and then try it out for yourself, organise a group to attend an art show.

Coaching tales: Lewis

Lewis was the senior manager at a finance firm. He had worked his way to the top and was proud of his direct reporting line to the CEO. His team was responsible for a portfolio of projects worth millions and it was his passion to make sure that targets were exceeded every week.

Lewis also really cared about his team and made sure he was constantly available to support them, taking their calls at every hour and answering any questions that would mean they could deliver their work.

At home, Lewis' wife called the shots. A very confident and capable woman, she managed seamlessly to run their home, take care of their three children and on top of this had built a very successful photography business.

When Lewis was home, it was his wife who answered the questions, gave the orders and took control.

Over the years, Lewis spent more and more time at work and less time at home so when he began a resilience coaching programme and was asked about his commitment to Self-Care his answer was simple, none.

Lewis realised he had thrown himself into work where he had a feeling of worth, had accidentally removed himself from his own home life, and was neglecting every aspect of his physical and spiritual wellbeing as a result. He literally couldn't remember what he did outside work, and it took several months before he was regularly taking time out to re-energise.

Reflection: if your Self-Care has been neglected for a long time, it may take extra patience and commitment to find its way back into your life. Creating the time to make it happen regularly might be the hardest part.

Your company culture is the pits

Luckily the number of companies which fall into this category is minimal, but they still exist. These might be the organisations that expect you to give up your wellbeing in return for the privilege of a pay cheque from them each month.

If you are desperate to dial up your Self-Care strategies but find that your employer's expectations are undermining all your efforts, then it's worth considering whether this is a deal breaker for you.

Short term issues are expected in some industries (e.g. busy periods over Christmas, or stocktaking), extra challenging circumstances are to be expected in other industries (e.g. shift working or nursing roles), but if you are totally unable to find time for Self-Care, then you may need to explore some of the recommended resources for career transitions.

You can still choose an alternative outcome, even if the situation is so dire that you really can't see a way through it; there is always an option for you to leave. Find a champion to support you and help you to stay strong as you use the tools and resources in this book to help your coping strategies in the short term, while building your exit strategy.

Make sure you maintain your high standards of work until your plans are in place for the move.

Your own worst enemy

We know that making good choices about our physical health does not include reaching for alcohol, drugs, smoking or choosing poor nutritional food groups and yet we continue to do so.

We know that sitting at our desk from 7am until 7pm with limited breaks is not a good example of resilient behaviours and yet we continue to do so.

We know that attending meetings back to back all day, every day, will result in no time for us to complete the work that we agree to while attending those meetings, and yet we continue to do so.

We know that if we have an important deadline requiring large efforts of work, then we are best placed to pace ourselves to achieve it.

In an interesting and challenging article, Jason Eder encourages us to consider the role that Organisational Currency plays for us at work. He identifies the "Big Three" as:

1　**Email volume**: the team member who always has soooo many more emails than us – what does that tell us about how important they must be?
2　**Meetings**: the most essential people at work spend more time in meetings than others, don't they?
3　**Hours worked**: the more hours you are seen to be working the harder you are doing your job, right? Sending an email at 11pm shows everybody how overworked but dedicated you are doesn't it? This might be acceptable for a specific reason (e.g. meeting a ridiculously tight one-off deadline) but is not going to help your Self-Care over time.

Jason suggests that where these behaviours are rewarded (not with bonuses or currency but with status that's attached) then they begin to become the cultural norm and drive behaviours accordingly . . . for example, you feel a pressure to reply to the email sent at 11pm.

Of course, the company might play a part in this elephant too; for example, policies that insist on entire teams attending training events instead of tailoring the learning for those that need or want it, but the truth remains that some of this behaviour is ours to examine and to own.

Coaching moment: Organisational Currency

Consider the Organisational Currency in your workplace, or in your role.

1　What behaviours are being rewarded or sustained in your workplace?
2　What impact is this having on your sense of being resilient?
3　What could you do to break the cycle of Organisational Currency in your work?

Lack of role models

What if you want to look after your wellbeing, and have a clear idea of what you need to do to function at your best, but your manager sends you emails or calls you 24 hours a day (and expects an immediate response), your colleagues are at their desk no matter how early you arrive (or how late you stay) and everybody in your workplace seems to thrive on workaholism, what are you to do?

You could explore some of the Boundary management tactics that are discussed in this chapter, you could look outside the organisation and use the Mentor strategy of our Connections chapter to find somebody who's working style is more aligned to what you want to achieve.

You could also dial up your Emotional Honesty and consider how this working life compares with previous employers . . . if all of your career has started with good intentions, but then gravitated towards a hectic work pattern that doesn't allow for Self-Care, then this may be a pattern you want to explore with a career professional.

Alternatively, if this is something new, you could consider an honest discussion with your manager about the impact it is having on your wellbeing at work. There may be things that you can do differently to rebalance things, and if not, then perhaps it's an opportunity to reconsider your employer.

We are our stressor at work

One of the interesting things to remember about stress is that it can be a good thing – up to a point. We all have an optimum stress response, where the adrenalin and cortisol response created can catalyse us into action and boost our goal achieving capabilities.

Recognising this and understanding our own personal drivers and motivators at work can be hugely powerful . . . particularly when we acknowledge that having some stressors at work can be a positive thing.

However, another useful perspective to consider is the role that we sometimes play in creating our own stress:

- Sometimes, we push ourselves harder and harder because we actually enjoy the challenge.
- Sometimes, we forget to enjoy ourselves along the way and just push harder and harder and harder instead of relishing what we learn on our journey.
- Sometimes, we love what we're doing so much that we work longer and longer hours to do it, even though it prevents us from doing other things that we also want to do.
- Sometimes, we know that we should focus on Self-Care, but we make it a low priority in our life.
- Sometimes, our definition of what we want to achieve isn't clear enough – so we get stressed about the journey to reach it.
- Sometimes, we blame other people or circumstances for our stress when we could do something to address it ourselves.

Boundary management is something that can influence the extent that we experience some of these issues. That is, the ability to respect the lines that we want to draw to protect our wellbeing, while still respecting the needs of our team and our organisation to achieve their goals.

Of course, the reality is we will continually need to adapt or tweak our boundaries as we go through our working life – but a few weeks of long hours because we know it's the "busy season" at work is typically more bearable than a seemingly endless road of early starts and late finishes.

Coaching tales: Dave

Dave is the most senior person in his company. He is doing what he loves, in a company that he is passionate about.

As a result, he found it almost impossible to identify where the lines for his boundaries could be drawn, despite a 360-degree feedback report identifying concerns from his team about the amount of time he was perceived to be working.

Although he was always very careful to specify that it was his choice to work outside his normal contracted time, and he didn't expect the same from them, this was not always how it was perceived.

On considering where his energy and focus was being directed, Dave realised that he was totally devoted to Connecting and Learning, but that he had completely left out Self-Care.

An avid diary user, he began scheduling Self-Care into his diary; with daily half hour slots for a walk around the block and at least two nights each week where he left at 5pm on the dot (and didn't do any work in the evening).

He also started booking tasks as well as meetings into his diary, and turned off his email notifications, instead checking his in-box a couple of times a day.

A keen cyclist, Dave started attending a local cycle group once a week (which also helped him get out the office at 5pm). He noticed a side effect from this decision of further increasing his Connections.

At first, Dave was pretty stressed out by his plans. He worried that his team would think he cared less about them, and he was apprehensive about the impact it might have on his workload . . . so he made the changes gradually over a few months.

After a year, Dave was blown away by the impact his changes had. He didn't need to do another 360-feedback check to notice that his team were much more relaxed than before, and yet their energy and productivity had increased. His personal fitness levels had soared and he even shared that his family were stoked with getting him back in the evenings and at weekends.

Reflection: investing in Self-Care not only creates the optimal conditions for our own wellbeing, but also gives permission for other people around us to do the same.

Coaching tales: Harvey

Harvey worked on a project that operated in a highly pressurised environment. His role involved working from multiple sites and he regularly flew to offices around the country a couple of times a week.

However, Harvey found his job getting more and more stressful and he realised he was at breaking point. His health was suffering, he wasn't sleeping well and his relationships at home were starting to crumble. He approached a coach to help him get back on track, or to help him find a new job.

The coach noticed immediately that during meetings, Harvey was constantly checking his telephone for messages, and sending texts. One two occasions during a coaching session somebody from his team came in to speak to him about a client issue, and Harvey discussed what to do.

In organising coaching sessions, Harvey booked his meetings straight after meetings which were already in his diary, and which were in another building – so he knew that he would be late from the start.

Harvey began to realise that his actions were totally out of alignment with his Goal. He wanted to more effectively manage the stressors that were contributing to his wellbeing at work, but the pressure that he was feeling about his workload was causing him to react instead of pausing for a moment to make a better decision about his time management.

Despite realising this, Harvey decided not to change how he managed his diary, nor how he responded to demands on his time. He concluded that because the project was short term, his priority was to continue delivering and that he would use his observation about his working style to become more organised in his next project.

Reflection: assuming Harvey does indeed make changes to his working style on his next project then this is a good example of how awareness is sometimes all we need to make a change to our wellbeing at work – therefore building resilience by becoming stronger when we face the situation again. If, however, this is a pattern which he recreates in his next role then he will need to dial up his Emotional Honesty about the impact his own working style is having on his wellbeing and take some real action.

Extended Signature Strengths

Knowing our Signature Strengths puts us in a very powerful place, but while repressing them at work can have a negative impact on our wellbeing, equally over extending them can bring issues for consideration.

For example, if your workplace pressure is because of the company being too slow to innovate and one Signature Strength is **Bravery** – you might find yourself "going to battle" over your beliefs, rather than finding helpful ways to influence change. If your company is restructuring and one Signature Strength is **Fairness** – you might find yourself "siding" with people who are impacted, who may only have access to one side of the story. If one Signature Strength is **Perspective** and it's over extended, you may find yourself under considerable pressure as people become overly reliant on your wisdom to support them.

Overstretched resilience

As we have learned through the book, resilience isn't about staying strong at all costs. Neither is it about dialling up our Resilience Foundations to extreme levels which create additional pressure.

Identifying your "deal breakers" can be useful for deciding when it's time to call time on a role or an employer and look for something new.

Perhaps the role has become too physically demanding and despite every effort you are no longer able to complete the tasks required (although a resilient outcome here might be that you focus on developing new skills that allow you to move into a new, less physical role).

Perhaps you are holding out for a transition into a new role, which keeps being promised but has yet to come to fruition. If you are certain that you have dialled up your Resilience Foundations (particularly Learning, including feedback) then you might consider a deadline on your waiting. A regular review of your progress can prevent you from suddenly realising a couple of frustrating years have passed by and you are no further on in your career.

HR and Business reflect

- "Monthly reviews at our workplace include a 5-minute Wellness Check at the start, where managers not only discuss the attendance data for that month with employees, but also ask about overall wellbeing."
- "When you are promoted to a leadership role, there is a 2-hour Wellness Workshop which demonstrates how to discuss attendance data, how to discuss wellness and the warning signs to notice if somebody might not be as well as we would like."
- "We believe that starting out with this topic reinforces our commitment to supporting team members, the focus on data keeps things objective and the discussion keeps it conscious in everybody's mind so we can both notice any change."
- "Don't expect that changing your role will equate to instant happiness. Too many people don't check out their next career move in enough detail, then when they are promoted or moved into a role they have requested, they are surprised by the extra (and often new) stressors that they experience."
- "If you are having a really bad time at work, and you're totally in the zone of extreme stress don't use it as an excuse to become the office martyr. Stay solution focussed, ask for support and find other people who will help you (not sympathise with you)."

- "Time with friends and family and self is absolutely critical to Self-Care. Stop for a while and imagine the waiting process (for your career ambitions) is like a living organism, it needs to rest and replenish."
- "Stay away from negative people who drag you down."
- "Ask if your organisation will support you in talking with an external career professional to assist your career strategy planning and interview techniques."
- "Clients I work with want support in finding a new job when they get frustrated in their current one, but when they change jobs they often meet the same issues that they had before. They just swap companies and keep their issues. I wish more people were active about improving their current job instead of just moving on."
- "If needed, request a job review – HR can contribute to assessing stress levels in role, demands of the job etc."

Management corner

As a manager, there may be opportunities for you to notice when a member of your team needs to dial up their Self-Care strategies.

You might see a sudden spike in sickness or absence, or a change to behaviour (suddenly working late or suddenly leaving early), you might notice patterns in when somebody takes time off. Of course, we rely on our team talking to us about these things but if they don't we could consider asking them.

If you're at all worried about having this conversation, talk to your HR team (or advisor) first. "Go with flowers" by sharing that you want to have a conversation about their wellbeing because it's so important to you. The wellbeing of everybody in the organisation is paramount, and you've noticed that some things don't seem right for them.

They might of course, choose not to tell you (in fact, you might even be part of the problem) so have a backup strategy ready if this happens (potentially another person in the business they can talk to). If they choose not to talk, perhaps you could share this chapter with them so they can consider the impact they may be having on their own wellbeing by choosing not to handle things.

Here are some conversation starters to try out with your team. Please amend the questions if you prefer.

- When have you felt great at work in the past? A time when you didn't feel stressed or pressured (explore)?
- What are the strategies you've used in other jobs to manage your workplace stressors?
- What would you need to do differently to handle your stress better at work? What could I do to support you with that?

Five vital facts: Self-Care

1   **It's critical**: if you are exhausted by your resilience journey then it might be useful to check how much energy you are giving to your Self-Care Foundation. For many people, this is the "nice to do" when you have the time, but it's absolutely critical for optimal wellbeing, and resilience.

2   **We are accountable:** whether or not we are provided with tools and resources for our wellbeing at work it is up to us to choose to act in the interests of our Self-Care. Notice before you make a choice about what to eat, how to spend your time, what to talk about. You can still choose to eat the chocolate, do the procrastinating or have a gossip – but do it consciously, knowing it is not contributing to your resilience.

3   **Stress can be helpful:** remember that Eustress is a form of stress which creates the pressure that many of us need to energise us and create action. It's only when the pressure becomes negative, triggering adrenalin and cortisol responses that we have a distressful experience. Notice what happens to your own body when you move out of a positive stressful response and into a negative one.

4   **Signature Strengths:** these can play a critical role in helping us to experience optimal wellbeing at work. They can help us to tailor our dial up response for Self-Care even further.

5   **Find ways to be present:** mindfulness, presence, noticing – these are all ways that can most influence our optimal wellbeing at work.

What resilient people say about Self-Care:

Figure 7.1 Self-Care "flower": what people say

Tell me more!

Read

- Adrenalin Junkie. Matt Church. www.mattchurch.com/chemistryofsuccess/
- Why Zebras Don't Get Ulcers. Robert M. Sapolsky, 2004
- The Human Potential Centre. University of Auckland New Zealand. https://humanpotentialcentre.aut.ac.nz/
- How to Stop Worrying and Start Living. Dale Carnegie, 1948
- GRIT. Angela Duckworth, 2016
- https://allright.org.nz/ (A collaboration of Healthy Christchurch, Canterbury District Health Board and the Mental Health Foundation of New Zealand.)
- www.mentalhealth.org.nz/home/ways-to-wellbeing/ (Includes ideas for the Five Ways to Wellbeing; Connect, Notice, Give, Learn, Move.)
- www.theworrybug.co.nz/ (The Worry Bug and Rising Tide, two resources designed for growing resilience in children facing mild to moderate anxiety as a result of the Christchurch earthquakes – Sarina Dickson and Julie Burgess-Manning.)
- www.greatergood.berkeley.edu (The Greater Good Centre at University of California, Berkeley.)
- The Hands-Free Mama; Only Love Today – Rachel Stafford (Reminders to breathe more, stress less and choose love.) www.handsfreemama.com/onlylovetoday/
- www.wellbeing.bitc.org.uk (This, the UK framework, is very closely aligned to the Five Ways to Wellbeing.)
- www.mentalhelp.net
- The Third Space. Adam Fraser (The moment of transition between one task and the next.)
- Mindful Coaching. Liz Hall, 2013

Play

An assortment of the latest apps to support your Self-Care Strategies . . . ask around for other recommendations, there are even breathing apps to help support this very fundamental approach.

- Catch It
- Headspace
- Spire
- Mental Workout
- Calm
- Whil
- Simple Habit
- Smiling Mind
- Mindfulness Coach.

Watch

- www.youtube.com/watch?v=jqqHUxzpfBI (Professor Seligman on the PERMA model.)
- greatergood.berkeley.edu/video/item/how_to_be_an_emotional_jedi (How to be a mindful Jedi.)
- greatergood.berkeley.edu/video/item/overcoming_skepticism_mindfulness_at_work (Overcoming the scepticism to mindfulness at work.)

Do: it's time to write your story (Action Plan)

This chapter about Self-Care has underlined the importance of . . .
It has given me a better understanding of . . .
What I've learned about myself is . . .
What I'm particularly thankful for is . . .
What I'm going to do immediately as a result is . . .
What I'm going to do over the next twelve months is . . .
The impact this will have is . . .
What could get in the way is . . .
   (If this happens I'm going to . . .)
I will know I have succeeded because . . .
I am going to check what I've achieved on . . . (date)
The person who will help me to stay accountable to this plan is:

SELF-CARE

GRID	Here are some questions for you to consider as you reflect on what you have learned in this chapter. They have been designed to help you decide how to use what you have read. **You may wish to consider the questions alone, with a friend or with your manager at work.**
GOAL	• Self-Care strategies refer to your spiritual and physical wellbeing. How would you like your strategies for these to be different?
	• When was the last time you felt great about the Self-Care strategies you were using?
	• What do you wish you could do more of regarding your Self-Care strategies?
	• Consider the amount of time you give to your physical wellbeing and spiritual wellbeing right now; how does it compare to what you need to feel at your most resilient?
	• What causes you to believe that you need to invest more in your Self-Care strategies to be more resilient at work? What are the signs in your own body?
	• What are the conditions required for you to be at your most energised at work?

REALITY	• How much focus are you giving to your spiritual and physical Self-Care right now?
	• How much time are you giving to your Self-Care strategies at work?
	• What are you noticing about your stress levels at work which cause you to think you need to adjust your Self-Care focus?
	• What is stopping you from adjusting your focus towards a more helpful Self-Care approach?
	• How have your coping strategies to overcome stress in the past helped support your Self-Care?
	• What are the signs that you have recognised that you're moving out of your pressure zone and into your extreme stress zone at work?
	• How might your Signature Strengths be influencing your attention to Self-Care?
IDEAS	• What Self-Care strategies have you used in the past to manage your stress response at work?
	• What strategies have you noticed other people use?
	• What new Self-Care strategies have you considered trying?
	• How does your employer support Self-Care strategies at work?
	• What are the different choices you could take to support your spiritual and physical wellbeing in a more positive way?
	• How could you overcome some of the obstacles that are preventing your Self-Care focus?
	• Who could help you to explore new ways of more effectively managing bad stress at work?
	• How could your Signature Strengths help you to achieve better Self-Care?
DO	• What one change could you make immediately?
	• What will you have to plan to introduce over time?
	• How could other people in your workplace support you with achieving your goals?
	• What are you going to do as a result of learning about Self-Care in this chapter?
	• What signs are you going to see that your strategies are working?

8   Connecting

Building and maintaining sincere
connections with others whom you
want to help, and who want to support
you, is critical to strengthening resilience

Resources in this chapter:
  Coaching moments:

- Goals for connecting
- Your tribes
- Sharing "You"
- Connecting energy
- Your Top 20
- Quality connecting
- Your "Go To" skills
- DOSE: the science of connecting
- Questions to help you connect
- Identifying a mentor
- Mentor questions
- GRID for mentoring

What is this chapter about?

The N-Word has a habit of striking fear into many hearts. Talk to a colleague about their "Networks" and somehow there's an inference of flakiness and insincerity. A perceived need to change something about ourselves to sell the value that we bring.

And yet we connect every day on many levels. It is a fundamental human need to be and feel connected, so this chapter explores the impact it has on our resilience at work, and how we can dial it up should we need to do so.

Connections at work might lead to new opportunities in our current employer, or new opportunities in a different employer. They might support us through challenging times or encourage us to think about things in different ways.

Dialling up our connections can be one strategy for building our resilience, so let's explore how to do just that.

Goal: what do you want to achieve?

The truth is that when you ask most people how much they like networking, they'll tell you they would rather do anything other than make small talk with a room full of strangers or chat about themselves . . . and yet research indicates that up to 80% of jobs will never actually be advertised, particularly those that are within the organisation where you already work.

Of course, this percentage will shift depending on variables such as your industry, level of seniority and technical expertise, but typically sits around 45–50% on average.

Imagine knowing that, whether you're already in a job and considering how to be considered for a promotion or actively looking for a job outside your company, you are only really seeing about half of the jobs that might be available advertised on job sites or in the media.

One of the business outcomes from the SCIRT Strength to Strength resilience programme was this: "employees who are skilled to make better connections, both inside and outside our organisation and who continue to broaden their thinking about how we get the job done."

If we consider some of the many ways that having good connections at work might be helpful to us, they might look something like this:

- External job search
- Growing professional connections internally
- Connecting to information
- Staying in touch with an industry
- Maintaining previous friendships
- Finding a mentor
- Sharing opinions
- Enhancing professional reputation
- Finding a support group
- Introducing your network to other people
- Challenging and extending our thinking
- Being noticed
- Sourcing work opportunities
- Making a career change
- Finding out about a possible job

Coaching moment: goals for connecting

What are the main reasons that you have chosen to dial up your Connection Foundation?

1   How will achieving stronger connections help you to achieve your career ambitions?
2   What might happen if you don't dial up your connections to support your resilience?
3   Who could help you lean into stronger connections? Do you know anybody that has lots of connections, or is good at connecting? How could they support you?

Figure 8.1 Word cloud: blockers to connecting

So, if networks and connections at work help us to be more resilient and can support us in achieving our career ambitions, what stops us from focussing our time on doing more of it?

Coaching moment: what's stopping you?

Think about your own approach to connections. What are some of the things that are stopping you from dialling up your connections at work?

1   What impact is this having on you right now?
2   What is it stopping you from achieving?
3   How is it feeling as a result?

At work, social wellbeing can be created in many forms; it's the ability we have to relate and connect to other people, establishing and maintaining positive relationships with family, friends and colleagues.

Notice that we have to not only establish relationships with others to create social wellbeing, we must also maintain them. This is not just about talking to people once, exchanging business cards and never speaking to them again

There are many potential sources for social wellbeing and connectedness at work; the team we operate in daily, the teams we join temporarily, the employees who work in our company, the "tribe" we hang out with in the café or lunch room, the sports or social teams we belong to.

Coaching moment: your tribes

Who are the teams, tribes or groups that you connect with at work?

1   What impact does it have on you to hang out with them? (You may want to use the Emoji Island from Chapter 5 or the Emotional Word List from Chapter 6 to help you.)
2   How are they currently supporting your resilience at work?
3   What other ways could they support you that you're not tapping in to right now?

Building your Connection Foundation for better resilience at work can be achieved in different ways.

- Consider using your Signature Strengths to help you. (Brainstorm how to use your top three strengths at work every day with somebody who has similar strengths.)
- Share one personal thing about yourself to see how it influences your relationships (for example, something surprising about your life or a hobby that you're passionate about).

The science of connecting

When we have social wellness, we live a life where we use our communication skills to create meaningful relationships and a helpful support system.

On top of this, research shows us that not only is there a significant link between social wellness and psychological wellness, there is also a link between social wellness and the ability to manage stress, stay healthy and be resilient.

Matthew Lieberman, a neuroscientist from the University of California, suggests that there are three main networks which are responsible for driving our social connections.

He found one which enables us to feel social pleasure (and pain), one which helps us read the emotions of other people and one which helps us to absorb cultural beliefs and values – this is what helps us connect with social groupings.

He concludes that we are actively hard wired to search out connections; reaching out and interacting with others. As a result, by growing our connections at work we are far more likely to create conditions for happiness and health.

To understand this further, we can explore the chemical response that occurs when we make connections. We release oxytocin which subsequently triggers the release of serotonin. This chain reaction of chemical response creates a sense of calm, love and happiness – we quite literally feel good when we are connecting with other people.

Table 8.1 DOSE and the science of connecting

DOSE	Optimal DOSE may contribute to . . .	Ideas to grow it . . .	Low levels may result in . . .
Dopamine	• Motivating you towards goals • Can surge when you achieve goals	• Set smaller goals • Celebrate achievements • Create a string of goals	• Procrastination • Self-doubt • Low enthusiasm
Serotonin	• Feeling significant and important • Calming the mind	• Relive past successes • Practice gratitude • Go outside and get some sunshine	• Loneliness and depression • Attention seeking behaviours
Oxytocin	• Creating intimacy and trust • Strengthening relationships	• Be encouraging • Listen • Share gifts and hugs • Reach out	• Sense of rejection • Not feeling connected
Endorphins	• Alleviating anxiety • Diminishing perception of pain	• Exercise • Laughter • Aromatherapy	• Anxiousness • Low tolerance for pain

In very simple terms, Table 8.1 is a summary of the four major chemical (called neurotransmitters) responses of your body for creating the conditions for healthy connections at work.

Neurotransmitters are, of course, far more complex than a simple table like this and if you believe that you have a serious issue with the balance of your DOSE levels you should always consult a medical professional. It's possible to have your urine or saliva tested to find out more about the levels of neurotransmitters in your body; this is likely to be a more evidence-based approach than just "taking some because you feel a bit low vitamins".

Serious issues can be caused by having too high levels as well as too low levels in your body, hence the reference to "Optimal DOSE", which is your personal balance between the two.

A DOSE of connection?

Dopamine, oxytocin, serotonin and endorphins are the main chemicals in our body which cause us to feel good. As a result, finding ways to create more of them can only be a good thing, surely? Or can they?

The academic research and neuroscience is catching up on the impact of technologies like Facebook, LinkedIn and Twitter on our sense of connectedness and how this subsequently impacts our sense of wellbeing.

Technological connectedness can lure us into a sense that we are connected (after all, why else would we have over 1,000 Facebook friends if we weren't well connected?). Add to this the suggestion that sharing (by tweeting and updating) activates the Temporoparietal Junction which creates oxytocin, which in turn activates trust, bonding and connection and you have a recipe for wanting to share more and more and more . . .

So far, the evidence from neuroscience is suggesting that the similar addictive behaviours and patterns which cause us to seek our DOSE of happiness from less healthy sources (for example, drugs, alcohol, gambling) are potentially influencing how we use social media to feel good about our social connections.

It might be one of the reasons why, when you're waiting in a queue, you reach for your phone to see who has "liked" your most recent post.

As a scientifically-based theory, understanding our social media selves is relatively new just now . . . though the likelihood is that it's just a question of time before research catches up and gives us even more proof about our social media inclinations, so we can choose to use them more wisely if we prefer.

In the meantime, it's worth considering other ways of creating a DOSE of connection which don't just make you feel good but result in building real "feel good" responses in others too; like face to face connections.

With the knowledge that when we share, we create higher levels of oxytocin which in turn help us to feel good, bonded and connected we can consider ways to achieve this at work.

Coaching moment: sharing "You"

Think about the amount of sharing that you do at work already. How much do your colleagues know about the real you? There is no reason at all to feel pressure to share everything about yourself (in fact, this has the potential to backfire, particularly intimate stories, if you don't really have a relationship established with your colleagues), but by sharing some things you might just create a more trusting experience for yourself.

1   What would you feel comfortable sharing? Topics to consider might include: a place you'd love to go on holiday (or have been on holiday), your favourite restaurant, your favourite movie, a sport you love, a hobby you enjoy outside work.
2   Consider what you might share about your learning from reading this book so far? Perhaps what you've learned, or what you're planning to do?
3   What else would you feel safe sharing about yourself?

My story: Jason

Jason is a senior manager in a retail organisation and very committed to creating better connections with his team. After learning about the science behind connections on a leadership development programme he decided to find more ways to share.

(continued)

(continued)

He realised that he hadn't ever really connected with his team, other than conversations about store performance and business results.

He created an idea which he called, "Dates with Jase". He decided he wanted the experience to be light-hearted and knew this would appeal to the people he worked with. He also knew that they would find it very strange to be invited to share things with him out of the blue, so he began by sharing himself.

Once a week, he took a different member of his team out for a coffee and began by apologising for not having taken the time to get to know more about them.

He then shared some of his story; the hopes he had for his career, the reasons he enjoyed working at their employer, the things he loved about his job and the things that frustrated him.

By setting the scene and taking his time, he soon began to find that the team also leaned into this more sharing style of conversation – and began to share their stories too.

Reflection: with knowledge about what happens to us chemically and emotionally when we share, we can choose to create the conditions for better trust at work and in our team.

My story: SCIRT Peer Workshops

At SCIRT, the conscious focus on creating the opportunities for people to share (and therefore build the shared trust and connections as a result) lead to the introduction of Peer Workshops. These workshops were held for the project managers and engineers.

A topic was selected for a 30-minute presentation to start the workshops (typically given by either a local expert of an industry expert). Then the group of around 100 employees broke into smaller sub groups of around ten to discuss what they learned.

At first, these workshops were self-guided and the attendees were left to have their own discussions, but we quickly realised that this was an approach which was very unfamiliar to the attendees.

As a result, questions were designed to support each workshop to encourage open discussion and sharing. Examples include:

- When have you faced a situation like this at work?
- What did you find was the most successful strategy?
- If you faced the situation again, what would you do differently?

In total, these workshops ran five times to try to create the conditions for better sharing and trust from the early days of the project.

Reflection: sharing does not come naturally to everybody, nor should sharing very personal details about life, so finding a way to share about work experiences can be a good place to start.

Coaching moment: connections energy

Consider a time when you have felt at your best at work, for example, vibrant and energised or happy and grateful for your job.

1 How much time were you giving to connections at work?
2 What role did your connections play in creating this sense of positivity? What did you do with your connections? How did they support you?
3 What might you be able to take from this observation to help you dial up this Resilience Foundation?

Reality: how are you already connecting?

Before we design some ideas to grow your connections even more, let's explore how you are already connecting.

Many of us have a preferred way of meeting people, perhaps we say hello to the parents as we drop our kids off at school, sometimes we meet new people because of sports clubs; or other hobbies and interests – we don't just make connections at work.

Noticing this can help us to grow more authentic connections, at home and at work. We can use the modus operandi that is natural to us to grow more connections.

Coaching tales: Tane

Tane was considering his next job. He had worked with his employer, a building company, for six years and was feeling frustrated with not being offered a management role. He was regularly told he had the skills for the job, but because they were a small company he would not be able to step up until somebody resigned.

(continued)

(continued)

Tane recognised that he "wasn't much of a talker", an observation he shared with his coach. He felt that this was really holding him back, as despite wanting to grow connections with other building companies to find management opportunities, he couldn't find the courage to strike up conversation, or call companies out of the blue to discuss this.

Relying on advertised roles wasn't helping, as they were few and far between.

When Tane thought about connections in the rest of his life, he realised that they largely came from sports clubs. He also realised that over the last couple of years, he had stepped away from team sports, and spent more time doing solitary exercise at the gym. When asked to think about a time he felt like he had strong networks and connections he kept coming back to sports clubs . . . so he formed an idea.

Tane launched a Friday social for the local construction companies. At 5pm on a Friday, there was an open invitation to meet for a game of rugby or football at a central park. After an hour of playing, the people who showed up went for a quick drink before heading home.

Tane hasn't quite identified his next role in management, but his networks in the industry are considerably stronger, so he's in a much better place to hear about them when they come up.

He also shared that he feels alive again, his work energy has been revitalised by dialling up his Connecting (and sneaking in a bit of Self-Care at the same time).

Reflection: networking is not just attending an event and handing out your business card. Connections are everywhere, and building relationships is at the heart of successful connecting. How you do this is likely to be personal.

Ideally, you will have at least one person in your connections who is high quality (takes pride in doing an exceptional job), positive, solution focussed and supportive.

Coaching moment: your Top 20

Look at the top twenty people that you email or call in your life. Think back to when you first met them.

1   How do you know these people? (What's the story behind the way you met them?)
2   What are the reasons that you stay in touch with them?
3   How could you use this knowledge to help you grow more confident in developing connections for work?

It can be helpful to think about your connections as a tree – you have strong roots which are the connections in your life that have been with you the longest. These might be your closest friends, or your family.

The main tree itself is made up of all the people from your life and your work so far; make a note of who they are, what they do and where they work. Some of these branches will likely bear fruit – notably the ones that are most closely aligned to who you'd like to meet to achieve your career ambitions.

Looking for a mentor who has experience of setting up their own business? Perhaps you forgot about Bob from school who launched a design consultancy back in 2004. I wonder how talking to him might help you to find out the true experience of starting up and help you to plan your journey.

Like a tree, your Connections will need nurturing. Regular reminders to let people know you're thinking of them are a good idea; spend ten minutes calling a few of them to see how their day is going, meet for a coffee.

Without this nurturing, your Connections tree will dry up and may even die. Either way, you're going to have to do a lot of nursing (and it will take longer) to get your tree back into shape.

As a career coaching tool, this is sometimes presented as a Career Genogram. Like a family tree, this is a way to reflect on the different roles that people in our family have had over the generations, and can help us consider who we are today.

Making a note of what your family members did for a job, the core skills they had (and even how they felt about their job) can be a valuable way of exploring patterns and understanding where our thoughts about work might have come from.

By expanding this Genogram to include our existing Connections, we can start to see where we have nurtured our friendships and whether we are surrounding ourselves with people who are in jobs they love.

Coaching moment: quality Connecting

Think about the most important relationships that you have at work. The key people you interact with, your leadership team, the customers you connect with.

1   Assign a score of 1 (terrible) to 5 (awesome) to each of these relationships.
2   For each person, make a note of what has influenced your score (what is causing it to be a such a low score or high score).
3   For each person, make a note of what you could do differently to increase the score by at least one point, assuming it's not already a 5.

Now reflect on those same relationships and consider what score they would give you if they were invited to do the same exercise. Connecting is a two-way process.

Catch your conversations

So, you've just had a shocking day when your boss pulled you up in front of the team for a mistake you made, and then you were late to a super important meeting as a result.

Venting and ranting about this with your colleagues can seem like a really good idea, in fact it probably feels pretty good and can help you to let off steam. And you're likely to feel like you are connecting.

Continuing to rant or complain however, is a totally different story. Affective Events Theory (AET) suggests that when we have experienced a negative event and then complain or criticise, it then it becomes more likely to reduce our workplace engagement and can persist as a mood over time.

The psychological theory suggests that things in our work environment (like what we do, how we interact, the people we work with etc.) have a very real impact on whether we experience inconveniences or encouragements in our job.

Because of whether we perceive that we've experienced inconvenience or encouragement, we will have a positive or a negative emotional reaction, and this will then directly influence both our job satisfaction and our job performance (which will both be higher if we have experienced encouragements at work).

As a result, AET suggests the inconvenience of being pulled up for a mistake and late for a meeting leads to a negative emotional reaction and therefore a lower level of both job satisfaction and job performance . . . and I'm not sure lower job performance is something any of us have in mind if we want to achieve our career ambitions.

Luckily, we can intervene.

Just when we're on the verge of having an emotional response and deciding whether we feel positive or negative about what just happened, we can use the new superpowers we developed in Chapter 6 (Emotional Honesty) and dial up our optimism.

Instead of meeting our work colleagues for a gripe and a moan, we can choose to be very disappointed (we can even choose extreme emotional responses), and then we can choose to dial up another Resilience Foundation of our choice.

Perhaps we want to dial up Self-Care and go for a run, or a yoga class. Maybe we want to go and sit quietly in a church to reflect on what happened. Perhaps we want to dial up our Learning and explore what caused the mistake in the first place, so we don't have to go through that again.

Perhaps we want to dial up a DOSE of Connecting in a way that creates more of the good hormones; brainstorming ways to overcome the issue or avoid it happening again.

Ideas: what could you do to grow your Connections?

Inbound networking

What if you could turn networking on its head so that instead of you going to other people to talk about things, they came to you?

This approach has been used for years in the marketing departments, where interesting topics are shared to identify who is attracted to finding out more – then the people who are identified as the "targets" because they visit the website become easier to convert.

Coaching tales: Miles

Miles worked with the SCIRT project for four years, on a secondment from the consultancy that employed him. He gained experience that he would not otherwise have been able to, had he stayed with his original employer.

As the end of his secondment to the project approached, Miles started to worry about how he would find his next job. Would his employer just stick him back in the team that he had left four years ago? Who would he know at work? How would he reconnect with people he used to work with?

Miles decided to organise a couple of learning sessions at his original employer to share what he had been responsible for delivering, and how he thought his knowledge might be useful to his consulting firm.

He organised a lunchtime event, encouraging attendees to bring some food to share, and created a 15-minute presentation which included some examples of what his team at SCIRT had achieved, the skills he had gained, the fun stuff he had done and ideas for potentially using his new skills at work. He invited people from his old team and his old boss.

The feedback he received was overwhelmingly positive. Of course, people might not have shown up, or they could have been sceptical – but what happened was that he reconnected with his old friends, and his boss identified possible ways to enhance his role so his new skills could be used.

Miles was also invited to take on a "champion" role, becoming an expert for his company in some of the skills he had developed on his secondment. From now on, people would come to him to find out more.

Reflection: by being brave and doing something a bit unusual to demonstrate our capability, we can use our knowledge of creating connections to draw people to us. A presentation worked for Miles, or you could consider blogging about your skills, becoming a major contributor to conversations and debate.

My story: Glenn

Glenn was facing down one of the most stressful moments of his career. He had career ambitions to progress within his company to a more senior role, but he didn't believe he possessed the skills (or the passion) to take on a management role.

He had always enjoyed being a technical expert but had been placed in a project where his role demanded management capabilities, and he found himself becoming more and more pressured.

"I was on the verge of leaving a company I had worked in for a long time, and I wanted to make sure that I wasn't thinking too emotionally . . . I needed to ask myself; do I really want to be on this bus?"

He realised that first, he needed to be more Emotionally Honest with himself about the demands of the job. From this point, he saw that his own perception of his management skills was not based on real evidence, so he decided to ask for feedback.

He used a leadership 360-degree questionnaire to explore this more conclusively, and deliberately chose a mix of people he worked well with, and people whose relationships were not so positive, to seek responses.

"Asking for other people's thoughts about me as a person was a huge risk . . . I knew that what they shared might make me uncomfortable, but I realised that something needed to change, and it wasn't about to be the company or the job, so it needed to be my understanding of me".

Working with the feedback he received and then tailoring his Learning, Glenn began trusting in his leadership skills as well as his technical skills.

Glenn's focus became that of intentionally Connecting. He realised that this was his super power; generating trust across his peers, his team, his customers and his managers by being 100% honest and professional, and by quietly encouraging others to do the same.

Recognising this gave him energy and purpose again, and he realised that he did want to be a leader after all. He had challenged his perception of what leadership looks like and his perception of himself in a leadership role.

Since then, Glenn has regularly been head hunted internally by his employer and is a highly sought after leader on international projects. His strategy for creating authentic connections is paying dividends, with team members asking for him to lead their team – and suppliers demanding that he is responsible for handling their accounts. He has even been approached by people from other organisations who want to work for him now.

"I think becoming resilient demands bravery" he shared, "if you're going to get stronger, you need to look closely at who you need to be, and some people aren't comfortable with this. Walking away wasn't the answer for me, I needed to examine the question more closely – and yes, I want to be on this bus".

Reflection: walking away from something that is demanding is not what resilience looks like. A more powerful solution is to define the outcome you're looking for, find balanced evidence to explore this and then you can make an objective decision. You may still choose to walk away, but you will be more informed and confident in your choice.

Coaching moment: Your "Go To" Skills

1   What are the "Go To" skills that you could become known for, right now, at work?
2   How could you demonstrate your skills to the people who work with you, so they become more aware of what you're capable of or interested in doing?
3   What would you love your "Go To" skills to be in the future – in a year, what would you love to host a party for? How can you dial up your Learning Foundation to help you achieve this?

To Link or not to Link

According to LinkedIn statistics (therefore open to question because of the data source, but let's work with it) over 25 million LinkedIn profiles are viewed every day. Regardless of whether you believe the number, that's a heck of a lot of opportunity for you to find a tribe or grow your connections so it's an obvious discussion point in this chapter.

The conundrum about whether to sign up for and use LinkedIn is an interesting one. For some people, it's a natural extension of their connectedness and for others it's the worst thing you could possible suggest.

True LinkedIn connections are the people that you have worked with or been introduced to by the people you work with. They are likely to have met you, or at least know about your work and your interests. Wider connections can include the people you are interested in meeting who work in industries or roles that you want to find out more about. They are still "real" connections, but they are not as close to knowing the real you.

Connecting with people who simply send you an invitation out of the blue is not true connecting in any sense, this is likely to be the equivalent of spamming

So, what are the pros and cons of using LinkedIn? They are listed together, so you can decide whether they are an advantage or a disadvantage for you.

- **Quiet connecting**: it's great for quiet connectors. Not everybody likes to chat to somebody in a café, some people prefer building relationships quietly by sharing data, engaging in conversation and building ideas in writing.
- **It's a start:** sometimes it's easier to start with a connection, followed up by a longer email introduction which leads to a face to face meeting or phone call.
- **Global resources:** the research potential within LinkedIn is amazing. Instead of just searching for people, try looking for jobs, companies, posts or groups. It's an incredible way to connect to likeminded professionals who are also interested in growing their connections and their learning. Experiment by asking questions of your LinkedIn connections as well as your colleagues at work, explore what happens to the volume of ideas that you create.
- **Global learning:** the learning portal has plenty of free and accessible resources to support your development at work, wherever you are. Just make sure the sources are credible.
- **It's customable:** with the click of a button you can control the subjects and authors that reach your feed, allowing you to find content that matters from the people within your tribe.
- **Extend your CV**: if you're actively job searching and don't feel you are able to present the whole of your work history into your CV, you can use LinkedIn as an extension by completing all of the sectors. It enables you to flesh out what you might write on a resumé.
- **You are visible:** (although, this is a bit of a downside too). Recruiters can look you up and potential customers can look you up as well as current and future connections. Make sure your profile is professional or at least sets the example you'd like to make. Also remember that every time you check out the profile of somebody on LinkedIn, the system tells them you've had a peep. There's no invisible stalking function.
- **Information overload:** there are always going to be too many technological places for us to visit and check. Smarter use of technology includes compartmentalising what you do and when you do it. Book a diary meeting for your LinkedIn time, then treat it like a meeting – don't get tempted to spend all your time there. Use the filters to control what goes into your mail box, and always remember you can either disconnect from people who spam you or turn off your LinkedIn applications.
- **Setting up time:** setting up your LinkedIn profile can take time, so simply pace yourself. All you need to start with is a professional picture (if you want a picture) and your basic employment details. You can develop everything else over time.

- **It can be tailored:** there is an investment requirement to do some of this. By choosing a premium account, you will be able to tailor your LinkedIn experience. As of 2018 the premium accounts include; basic (free) job seeker, business plus, executive, sales navigator and recruiter lite. The LinkedIn Help Centre has pretty much everything you need to know to decide what's right for you.
- **Interaction is limited:** it isn't as quick and simple to interact on LinkedIn as it is on Facebook. Making comments and uploading materials are fairly cumbersome compared with other social media platforms.
- **Endorsements:** sometimes a connection endorses you for a skill that they have never encountered from you, which is another reason to be sure that your connections remain as true as possible. Make sure that your profile is truthful and presents evidence of the knowledge, skills and experience that you claim to have.

My story: Anthony

Anthony was self-employed and growing a new business. He knew that his target market was employers in the region who had between fifteen and thirty employees, so he accessed local business data to check out the companies that included.

Once he had done this, he used LinkedIn to find out more information – whether he knew anybody that worked there (or had links there), what the latest research showed in the industry, what the competitors looked like etc.

As a result, Anthony's details came up for the CEO when he visited his own LinkedIn page. The CEO could clearly see that Anthony had looked him up. As a result, the CEO returned the favour and checked out Anthony's LinkedIn page (hence the reason for having a professional looking profile!).

Within two days, the CEO connected with Anthony and asked to meet for a coffee. Anthony was on the road to making a new connection, in a target employer – even if the coffee was just a coffee, a new connection had been made which could lead to all sorts of adventures.

Reflection: connections can begin to happen simply by reaching out and looking for them.

Coaching tales: the real LinkedIn

During a Strength to Strength workshop at SCIRT, we were discussing the varied use of LinkedIn as a networking tool and debating how widely it might be used.

(continued)

(continued)

In the space of two minutes, one attendee confessed to being on a board that had rejected applicants because of their LinkedIn profile and one attendee shared that they had sourced a geotechnical recruitment opportunity after scanning LinkedIn for the people in Australasia with the required qualifications and then contacting people to invite applications.

Reflection: whether we like it or not, LinkedIn is a powerful tool to enable or undermine our connections at work.

If you're going to use LinkedIn or other online networking resources, consider how you can bring yourself to life. Don't just sit at home reading the streams and streams of data, blogs and information that will no doubt cascade into your data feed.

Take a few minutes to join the special interest groups or closed groups which are aligned to your career ambitions. They will be more specialised, and likely expose you to a more targeted audience. Make a point of "giving" to online networking groups; through sharing relevant thoughts, ideas or research that you have found.

Remember to ask open questions about what they are doing, then listen to their responses. This is a great way to gather information from a global connection of likeminded people.

My story: Sarah

Sarah was the general manager of a pharmaceutical company. She enjoyed the challenge of ensuring that her business thrived, the thrill of watching the positive impact it had on the lives of those who accessed treatments and developing a successful team.

After the earthquakes in Christchurch however, the company went out of business and she was faced with the challenge of finding new work in a city that now had limited opportunities for senior managers.

Working with a career coach, Sarah decided that she would become an independent consultant, supporting organisations in related industries to rebuild their practices, and quickly found work at several medical organisations.

For three years, Sarah was kept very busy and she enjoyed a successful (though unexpected) career. As the city began to stabilise, the consulting opportunities slowed down and Sarah decided that she wanted to return to a senior management role where she could get more deeply embedded in business success. She confessed that the consulting work wasn't fulfilling her love of developing a team, nor seeing the impact of the medical advancements on her clients.

For twelve months, Sarah applied for suitable roles that were advertised. She always made it to the final interviews and was always let down by the results. As a result, her confidence began to plummet and she found herself questioning capability in everything that she did.

Sarah talked to a coaching professional again, to reflect on what was happening to her. During the discussion, she realised just how deeply the constant rejections were having on her spirit and became very emotional.

She realised that as her confidence dipped, she was withdrawing further and further from her connections, which in turn was causing her to panic about where her next contract was going to come from, and how she was ever going to find a job. Her resilience levels were getting lower and lower.

Reflecting on when she had felt at her most resilient, and her most confident she realised it was when she spent time in social situations, not talking about herself but talking about others.

This insight helped Sarah to realise that there were subtle shifts she could make in her approach to connecting. She needed to be kind to herself and remind herself about how much she loved connecting, re-framing the process as something to be enjoyed, not endured.

She began meeting people that she had worked with previously in social situations (not situations where she was looking for work) where she focussed on talking to them about their own work and lives.

Finding that this gave her energy again, she began being a little braver – sharing her own story about the work she had been doing and asking the people she knew whether they knew other people who might be interested in talking to her.

By dialling up her Connecting Foundation gradually in this way, Sarah soon began to feel more like herself and her self-confidence grew remarkably. Sarah hasn't found that new general manager role just yet, but is now enjoying a much happier consulting practice, working with old friends and new.

Reflection: Emotional Honesty can sometimes be a catalyst for realising that you need to dial up one of your other Resilience Foundations. Connecting doesn't have to just be about finding a job, sometimes it can be more focussed on finding yourself again.

Great connectors

Great connectors typically do three things well:

1   They ask open questions.
2   Their questions are about the other person.
3   They do great listening.

One of the secrets of great connectors is that they often have an inner list of questions to help them to connect, so they don't have to stress about all the things we just identified that stop us from connecting confidently.

Questions to help you connect

To help you get started with your connections here are a few ideas for questions you might ask. Feel free to adapt them to words you would choose.

Notice how they are all questions that start with: what, where, who, when and how. Using open questions like this will give you a much better chance of having a conversation that flows.

Safe starts

1 Where do you recommend as a great place to eat around here?
2 How did you hear about this event? (If it's an event.)
3 What do you love the most about your job?
4 What are the most challenging things that you are responsible for?
5 How did you find your way to being a <insert job title>?
6 What advice would you have for somebody who wanted to work for your company?
7 What are you passionate about? In work? In life?
8 Where do you live now? Where have you lived previously?
9 What are the latest trends in your industry?
10 How have the changes in your industry impacted your job in the last few years?

When you're a little more confident you may want to consider playing with some of these questions:

Courageous curiosity

1 If you could do any job in the world, what would you do instead of the job you're doing now?
2 What separates your company from the companies you compete with?
3 What's the strangest thing you've ever had to do at work?
4 How can we make sure your time spent with me is valuable to you?
5 What gets in the way of being able to do an awesome job at work?
6 What is the latest thing you did to develop your professional skills? How did you learn?
7 If you had to pick three words to describe yourself, what would you choose?
8 What would make me the ideal person to work in your company?
9 What do you recommend as "must have" items on your CV to be successful at work?
10 What sort of person are you looking to meet so that I can introduce you to people from my own networks? (Or explore clients, customers etc.)

Once the conversation has been started, you can encourage the person you're talking with to keep sharing by nodding, using silence and asking follow-up questions like "go on . . .", "tell me more . . ." and "then what happened . . .".

And, of course, pretend you're on a very important date while you're talking to them; don't answer your phone/check your emails/look across at other people to see if they might be more interesting.

Be present and expect to learn something awesome. In fact, a great tip might be to come away with three bits of information about the person you just met.

Coaching moment: planning more connections

Make a list of the people you already know. Use your phone book, check who you've emailed in the last few months, look at your LinkedIn connections.

1   Note anybody who works in an industry you'd like to find out more about.
2   Note anybody who works in a job you'd love to find out more about.
3   Notice whether there is anybody that you admire for their career achievements or their connections; what could you do to learn from them?

Own the follow-up

How many times have you genuinely said to somebody, "we should meet up soon" and they say, "we sure should", and then you both leave with good intentions and it never happens?

Make a date for a follow-up meeting at the time you are with them, even if it's a few months away. Having sometime in the diary will mean it's more likely that you follow up and meet, and if you can't make the agreed date and time, you can always rearrange.

If you don't book a time specifically, don't just wait for several months, then send an email or a text to say "Hi". Call, leave a message and follow up until you have a meeting booked.

Don't become a weird stalker – perhaps a four or five messages unreturned is a sign they may not want to meet up after all.

Share learning

A really great way to network is to find ways of sharing something that will help the other person. Perhaps you've read an article that's about an issue you discussed when you met them, or you meet somebody that you know will make a difference to their workplace.

Make a point of sharing it with them, even if they choose not to read the article, watch the video or meet the new connection, you are demonstrating your support for growing them. This creates the right environment for them to want to do the same for you.

Note: don't just do this when you want people to help you out. It has to become your way of "being" or you're going to seem a bit odd.

Make recommendations

Once you've asked questions and done great listening to find out more about your connections, find a way to support them; review their products online or recommend them to other people (assuming you have experienced their products – don't make something up).

Talk positively about the connections that you have made; sharing information about what they are doing with the people who might be interested.

And say "thank you", a lot.

If you take a few minutes to thank the people who pass through your day with you, and even better you specify why you're thanking them, then the world of connections will open up to you.

My story: Joy

Joy loved her job as the front of house for a very successful café in the city. She thrived on building relationships and helping customers to have an amazing experience every time they came for a coffee or for lunch.

She was very well known for her customer service skills, and exceptional standards of service so, when she announced she was leaving for a new career her regulars were devastated.

However, when she shared that her new career was in recruitment, there was widespread agreement that she would do an amazing job.

Her ability to build relationships and work out just what somebody else was looking for were second to none.

Several of Joy's regular customers worked in industries that either recruited heavily or were restructuring and shared that they would be staying in touch.

As a result, although they had originally met over a coffee, Joy's initial flow of work from employers looking to hire and employees looking for work was very high.

Reflection: look for ways to build connections all the time. Ask questions, find out . . . you never know where the connection is going to lead.

What we can learn from expats in Sweden

According to the HSBC Expat Explorer Survey, Sweden is one of the worst places in the world for foreigners seeking to strike new friendships and make connections.

There must be few roles that compare with the amount of networking required for an occupation like working as an expat, which require the same extent of connecting and relationship building.

Can you imagine regularly uprooting your life (and perhaps your family), starting a new job in a new country, your children beginning at new schools and you may even be immersed in a culture where you don't speak the language fully?

Exciting? Absolutely, but my goodness you must likely develop incredible capabilities for making connections. So how about learning from the people that do connections for a living?

- **Ask to be recommended:** making the initial connection can be the hardest, so asking to be introduced can be a way of achieving this. If you're going to an event, take a more confident friend who can break the ice with new people and then introduce you. Or perhaps you know somebody on LinkedIn that has a connection? Or you have a "friend of a friend" who works in the industry? **Moral: you don't have to build connections alone.**

- **Develop a networking mindset:** seeing the people that you meet as "nodes" who you want to approach for help can be excruciating. Finding a way to shift this thinking more to a place where you see yourself as the node, and other people you meet as possible people for YOU to put in touch with others can help to turn this around. **Moral: consider inbound networking strategies.**

- **Many connections are from childhood**: in Sweden, many of the connections at work can be traced all the way back to school days. **Moral: consider whether you have people in your connections already from way back who could play a role in helping you dial up your resilience.**

- **Food focussed:** organise something that involves food and invite people along who you'd like to meet. Keep things casual, don't focus on work – for example, celebrate the seasons, honour a sporting event or do something for charity. Socialising in Sweden is mostly done over a "fika" (from the outside it looks a regular coffee break, but it's where the most important connections are made and has become a social phenomenon). **Moral: accept every invitation you can for a coffee catch-up, you never know where it will lead.**

- **Have a goal:** you might decide to meet three new people at an event or talk to somebody new at lunch for at least ten minutes; this will help you to believe you are achieving something with your connecting, not just turning up, feeling shy and going home (only to berate yourself). **Moral: choose one thing that you want to take away from each conversation with a connection.**

My story: Gareth

Like many great career decisions, Gareth's choice to leave his UK job and move to Sweden was made over a bottle of wine.

Gareth and his wife had enjoyed several holidays there over the years with their Swedish family, and with a new baby (combined with Sweden's envious reputation as a family-friendly lifestyle destination) the decision was made.

Giving themselves a deadline of a year to make the move work out, they arrived into the country filled with hope, since they both had enviable skills, qualifications and experience.

Language was never a problem, due to the exceptional language skills of Swedish nationals however one area that both Gareth and his wife both overlooked was that almost all jobs in Sweden are secured through networks, including that of school friends.

On top of this, Gareth found that the other overseas workers stuck together – preferring to stay in their "national tribes", and as a result Gareth struggled to build his connections, since he found himself spending most of his time with other Brits, few of whom had established networks in the country.

Gareth needed to think laterally, and think fast.

His first job was as a labourer, a far cry from the City job he enjoyed in the UK. But it got him known and it got him talking to Swedish nationals. He has a friend from his City days who has lived in Sweden for six years and still doesn't have a job. "He just doesn't have the fight" says Gareth.

"I must have sent over 100 job applications without getting a reply of any kind, never mind an interview. Most people give up". Gareth knew he needed to just find a job, any job to begin with and his connections would start to grow.

"I've lived outside of the UK for most of my life and I've never found a place that's so hard to crack" he shared.

It's now twelve years since their move from the UK.

Gareth finally scored a job at an investment bank after chatting to somebody at a company barbecue. It's much better suited to his skills, and his connections have grown, but not because of his conscious networking efforts; "working in an industry where there is high turnover, I regularly find that colleagues leave to go and work for rival companies. We stay in touch, and so my networks expand".

Reflection: Gareth's determination to get a job at all costs was a gamble. Luckily, his decision to take on a significantly underpaid and under skilled role paid off, and he quickly used it and his confidence in connecting with others to find other, better suited opportunities.

Gareth could have followed up on those 100 applications more persistently, searching for feedback to strengthen his application, but thankfully, he found a role that suits him despite this.

By staying in touch with his connections when they leave his current workplace, he has reduced the need to "dial up" his networking skills in the future. A great example of how important it is to continue cultivating connections once they have been established.

One of the biggest reality checks for our connecting intentions is often time, so how on earth can we make maximise our investment?

At SCIRT, the Strength to Strength programme attendees came up with an idea of having Gold, Silver and Bronze connections to support your career resilience.

Here are their recommendations:

- **Gold:** these connections are people in roles or organisations that are well and truly on your Wishlist of career ambitions. You prioritise personal catch ups (face to face or Skype) and make sure you catch up with at least one gold connection every month.
- **Silver:** these connections are people in roles or organisations that are not aligned with your future career aspirations but can help to stretch and grow you in your current role. Consider group catch ups with people from your silver connections every two or three months.
- **Bronze:** these connections are people who have no connection at all with your career ambitions, but who you couldn't bear to lose touch with. Catch up with somebody from your bronze connections whenever you like, particularly if you want to re-inspire and energise yourself at work.

The impact of mentors

Mentors can be the ultimate in connections. In surveying methods to grow resilience at work, an overwhelming number of HR and Business professionals suggested a mentor.

When we find a good one, they can help to challenge our thinking, inspire us to aim high and potentially put us in touch with people from their own networks to support our career ambitions.

Finding a mentor can be a simple process. Think about the people that you've come across in your career, and highlight anybody who really impressed you, or who is doing a role that you'd love to do one day.

They don't have to be in the same company as you, in fact it can be helpful if they are in a different company to give you a new view point (and new connections).

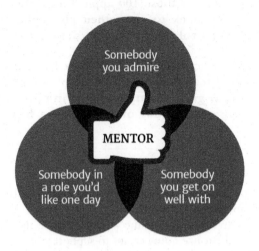

Figure 8.2 Identifying a mentor

A mentor doesn't have to be for life . . . a good way to start the mentoring process can be to agree on three meetings to begin with (to check it's working for both of you) and then consider an annual review. Mentoring can be as casual as a one-off catch-up to ignite and inspire your ambitions, or can be an ongoing arrangement, it depends on what you (and of course your mentor) would like from the relationship.

Identifying a possible mentor

Mentors can come from formal mentoring organisations, or they could literally be somebody you met or worked with previously.

"Unofficial mentors" that are more informal are also entirely plausible. These are people who you admire, connect with and are in a role you'd love to do one day . . . and you catch up to talk about their career in the same way as a more formal mentor but there is no official mentoring relationship; the question doesn't come up. As long as you are both happy with this, there is no reason to create paperwork, and you might find that you both become friends.

Starting the discussion about whether somebody might mentor you could be as simple as sharing that you have met them previously (assuming, of course, you have) and you were really impressed by what they have achieved in their career.

As a result, you'd love to find out a bit more about how they did that, and talk about the advice they would have for somebody in your position.

You might meet up once and be inspired enough to continue your journey, armed with more tools and resources and ideas than you were before you met your mentor, and therefore more resilient to achieve your career ambitions.

You might meet up a few times, or monthly . . . or have an annual mentoring discussion – the way you structure your time is entirely down to you and your mentor.

You may choose different mentors at different points in your career, or even have multiple mentors at one point in time, each supporting you in achieving something.

Hopefully your experience will inspire you to mentor others, on their road to career resilience.

GRID

We could use the GRID framework to consider our mentoring discussion.

What is your Goal for mentoring? Reasons for mentoring sometimes include:

- To challenge my thinking
- To give me advice
- To help me achieve something in my career
- To grow my understanding
- To encourage me to excel
- To tell me how to improve
- To share their journey
- To help me bounce ideas
- To connect me with others.

What is your mentoring Reality? Do you already have a mentor? Have you ever had a mentor? What has been your experience of mentoring in the past? How did you structure the relationship? Who have you met, that you could consider a mentor? If you haven't met anybody yet, how can you dial up your connections in the area you would like to work so that you might identify one?

What Ideas do you have for finding and working with a mentor? How are you going to choose a mentor? What are the most important qualities for you in a mentor? How often would you like to meet them? Where would you like to meet them? What would you like to talk about? How are you going to make the initial connection with them? What are you going to say?

What are you going to Do, about mentoring? Reflecting on all that you've learned about mentoring, what are you going to do now? Who could support you in doing this?

Mentoring moments: here are some ideas for questions you might ask your mentor during your journey together. You could use the questions from earlier in our chapter to build the relationship from the start.

1 How did you get the job you're in now?
2 What advice would you give to somebody like me?
3 When you were faced with XYZ <insert challenge>, what did you do? How did that turn out?
4 What have been the best decisions you've taken in your career?
5 What are you proudest of having achieved so far?
6 What have been the worst decisions, and what did you learn from them?
7 What has been the biggest lesson you've learned in your career?
8 What have been your biggest challenges in your career, and how did you overcome them?
9 What's the best piece of advice you were ever given by somebody about work?
10 How have you built connections for your own career?
11 Where do you go for advice?
12 Who do you know who might be able to help me achieve my goals?
13 If I follow a similar path to you, what do you think are the advantages and disadvantages?
14 What legacy do you want to leave to our industry?
15 How can I help you with that?

You will often find that mentors offer their time for free, so it is a great idea to find out a bit about what they are passionate about and get them (or make them) something to say "thank you" from time to time.

Also, reverse mentoring is an interesting and growing phenomenon. It's a term that's been used since 2000, but it has grown in popularity over the last ten years. A more experienced employee is paired with a newer employee, to grow connections in different ways; like creating shared empathy (to get rid of some of the clichés about generational differences), growing ideas from a fresh pair of eyes and providing support with technical challenges.

The Connections elephants

Too much like me?

It can be amazing to meet people who are just like us . . . when we have a catch up, and it's like we already know them. They think like us, react like us and sometimes they even look like us. This can help us feel safe, but it doesn't help us to consider work from different angles. We may even miss opportunities and ideas because we are approaching things from the same viewpoint.

From a scientific perspective, the part of our brain known as the Rostromedial Prefrontal Cortex lights up when we connect easily because of this and it helps us to feel comfortable with who we're talking to. It's a nice place to be.

However, in growing our consideration of and connection with others, it can be useful to consciously look for people who aren't just like us – to challenge our thinking, grow our view points and create new neural pathways for our thinking.

Here are some ideas for you to consider. Build your connections with somebody from:

- A different culture, or religion
- Another department
- Somebody who works differently to you – they like more detail, or they make fast decisions
- A new joiner
- A customer
- An extravert (if you're an introvert, and vice versa)
- Somebody who loves doing what we hate doing at work
- Somebody who doesn't seem very happy at work.

Computer free zone?

You are far more likely to make helpful connections if you can find a way to meet people in person. You might start by using emails or LinkedIn messages as an introduction or to pave the way, but there's just no substitute for a face to face conversation, whether it's in person or via Skype.

Coaching tales: Mark

Mark worked for an event management organisation and it was his responsibility to identify and confirm speakers for significant events in the City.

Mark was sent for coaching by a manager who had grown frustrated with the length of time it was taking him to organise speakers, sometimes resulting in events being postponed and he was on the verge of being managed out of the company.

Working with a coach, Mark realised that he was frightened of calling people out of the blue. He relied on texts and emails to find potential speakers, and then spent a lot of time waiting for them to respond.

The more his manager told him to have face to face conversations, the more panic-stricken Mark became about his role.

Some serious questions needed to be considered: firstly, whether Mark was in the right job given that the heart of his role involved doing something that he was very frightened of doing.

Mark confided that the buzz he got from being there when the event happened, and knowing he played a part, was incredible, and that was the main reason he wanted to stay in his job. He confirmed that he wanted to do anything it took to keep his role.

Exploring what was causing this fear, Mark realised it was the uncertainty of the way conversations could go when he was lining

(continued)

(continued)

up speakers. He didn't like thinking on the spot, and therefore resorted to emails and texts.

To overcome this, he created a flowchart for supporting his conversations on the phone. Instead of calling out of the blue, he had a series of questions and possible directions to take the conversation. The potential speaker didn't know he was following a script, but it gave Mark more confidence with what he was saying.

Mark created a strategy for himself: identify the potential speaker, send them a text to let them know he was keen to talk to them, follow up with an email which contained information about the event and some FAQs, follow up with a phone call and, if they were keen, organise a face to face meeting.

By the time the meeting took place, Mark was more confident of his connecting skills because he had been in touch and had been supported in his conversations.

Reflection: calling out of the blue isn't the only way to build connections. Reflect on what works for you, and how to set yourself up for success.

Coaching tales: Michelle

Michelle had been made redundant from a large agricultural employer and was actively looking for a job. She had a very clear idea of what she wanted to do, and the sort of company she wanted to do it in – which is a great job search strategy, except – she was sitting at home in front of her computer waiting for the job to be advertised on job boards.

For over a month, she worked with a coach who explored different ways to create opportunities to connect with others. Together they explored real companies Michelle wanted to work in, identified friends and ex-colleagues who could put her in touch with those companies and they planned what she would say when she met them. They even discussed friends who could help Michelle find the courage she needed to get the ball rolling, and looked online together to identify the LinkedIn connections that might help her.

Together they put together a plan of who to contact, what to say and how to stay in touch. At the end of every coaching session, Michelle was full of positive intentions and high hopes of dialling up her Connecting Foundation.

Yet still Michelle sat at home in front of her computer waiting for jobs to be advertised.

Over a period of weeks, Michelle became more and more frustrated, and soon her frustration became anger. Now her coaching sessions also had to focus on how she might come across during an interview with any potential employer, since she was so panicked about finding a job and disappointed that they weren't appearing for her.

Michelle was convinced that the best way to find her job was to wait and be patient, despite all the evidence presented to the contrary.

Soon she gradually began to withdraw from her friends too, as she became more and more despondent.

Reflection: finding a positive, supportive champion to keep you energised during your resilience journey is vital but does not guarantee that you will succeed. Learning about how to be more resilient is only part of the story, you have to DO resilience to really build it.

Be genuine, or don't be

If you find that you are putting on a front and pretending to be something you are not during a meeting with a connection, then you might want to check out of the connection.

There is little point in continuing to meet somebody that you don't have a genuine interest in, because they are very likely to see through you and that might not end well. Dial up your Emotional Honesty and consider how meeting with the other person makes you feel.

You may end up in a job that you're not well suited for (and then you're stuck pretending to be the person who got the job) or you risk damaging your reputation if the other person catches on.

The structure sucks

For some of us, working in very traditional organisations can get in the way of how we build our connections, especially if we must overcome the perceptions of others to do so.

- "You've not been a junior for five years yet, so no, you can't talk to a partner to find out what it's like in a senior role".
- "You're female and you're not from an industry background, so no, you cannot be considered for a management role".
- "Nobody is allowed to meet the CEO, he doesn't have time to talk about his vision with the team; that's what your manager is for".

Worryingly, these are all stories that have been shared by clients I have worked with. All these people managed to create connections and progress their careers, but they had to work a little harder (and be a bit more creative) to achieve this.

Some more modern companies recognise the importance of encouraging connections that are broad as well as deep, and that span the whole organisation. Many deliberately design projects or events that enable this to happen.

Even more future focussed organisations are using Organisational Network Analysis to create sociograms and understand how their teams are networked, and how information is shared.

Software like Orgmapper and Orgnet can help to visually understand who talks to whom across the business and can be a great place to get ideas for how you might build your connections.

For traditionally structured organisations, this can help them to understand who the main communicators are, for example, is the best person to talk about IT strategy always the IT manager? Sometimes it's the quiet coder that is passionate about understanding the industry trends instead.

Coaching tales: Helena

Helena worked with a government agency that was relocating to the Christchurch CBD after spending four years in temporary office space.

Passionate about connections, she realised that the temporary office space had resulted in losing some of the friends and colleagues she had previously worked with. She acknowledged that for her, "out of sight was out of mind" and she had not nurtured those relationships.

Her career ambitions had been sidelined while she took care of earthquake related support for the people of the city, but she decided it was now time to lean back into her goals.

Working as a project manager in her temporary role, she realised that she now had made many connections across the business, and that this could be very valuable to supporting her ambitions of finding a senior role in the policy team. She recognised that the different viewpoints and perspectives would help her design stronger policies.

Despite the new offices the government agency was very formally structured, with teams working in separate buildings and even issues accessing phone numbers for team members in a different building.

Realising that she wanted to stay connected to these people, and not lose sight of them as she had before she decided to organise a Business Breakfast Club, where once every couple of months they would get together early in the morning.

The topic for discussion was agreed by the group each time, based on what was current for the organisation, and was organised through the Social Club, which had a website which was available across the entire agency.

Reflection: look for the lessons learned about how you best make (and keep) connections and then lean into them. Taking responsibility for keeping connections alive can make you a very valuable person. Helena is often sought out by leaders in her agency to find out what the latest thinking is across the business.

Coaching tales: Debbie

Debbie was being made redundant by her employer after twenty years of working as a social worker. Instead of reacting negatively to the situation, Debbie saw this as an opportunity to do something completely different and came for career coaching to decide what to do.

For Debbie, after twenty years of a significant commute (involving different bus routes joined together for an hour) she decided that the main priority would be walking to work and getting there within twenty minutes.

As a result, instead of psychometric reports looking at transferable skills or reflections on what she would like to be doing as a second career (and then building connections accordingly) the only thing she did was walk around her neighbourhood.

Carrying a pen and paper, she walked a concentric circle of 20 minutes and made a note of all the employers that she saw which looked appealing. When she got home, she researched each of the companies that she had noted and created a short list of employers that were within a twenty minute walk, that had great street appeal and which had jobs that sounded interesting.

She narrowed it down to a PR company and a learning centre.

Debbie's next task was to check her CV and look at how she had pitched her knowledge, skills and capabilities. She updated it from a social worker CV to a much more generic one, which focussed on the skills likely to be required by the PR company and learning centre.

Armed with her new CV and a lot of bravery she then walked into the companies she liked the look of and introduced herself. There weren't any immediate roles at either of the places she visited, but the learning centre took her on as a casual facilitator and introduced her to another learning centre across town.

Several months later, Debbie reconnected with her career coach to share that she had spent the time delivering communication and conflict training for the two learning centres and had just been contacted by the

(continued)

(continued)

PR company to work with them on a project. It wasn't full time work, but it was mostly closer to home, and using new skills that energised her once more.

Reflection: building connections doesn't have to be obvious. It can be very powerful to think laterally and create connections in potential new fields for the future. Also, sometimes it's not the job that drives the connection but the wider motivation behind work.

Your connections are the problem!

What if your connections are causing your resilience issues in the first place?

If you search for research about the biggest causes of stress at work, the reasons at the top typically include, "working with difficult people", "office politics" and "feeling criticised by colleagues".

When the people that you work with every day are the biggest source of your stress, you may want to ask yourself a few tough questions. If you've always found that your work colleagues stress you out, and you've never worked anywhere that you felt supported or encouraged then you might consider working with a career professional to explore the causes of this more fully.

You don't have to be best friends with everybody at work, but you should be able to work in a team where there are at least a couple of people who support you, work through problems with you and celebrate your successes.

If you genuinely can't think of one person, or if this is a "one-off" and normally you thoroughly enjoy the people that you work with, then maybe this is a case of poor cultural fit. If you dial up the Resilience Foundations in this book, and you still can't find a supportive person at work it might be time to find a new employer with a better suited culture for you.

Coaching tales: Collaboration Cards

One organisation in New Zealand has designed "Collaboration Cards" for on tables in their recreation room.

Like the idea of "Table Talkers", they include work related questions to help people who don't like small talk.

They found that despite designing their recreation room to encourage collaboration and connection, people were still sitting in cliques and not talking to others in the company.

The questions are rotated depending on the time of the year, to stay topical and encourage conversation about what's going on at work.

Questions include:

- What did you think of the news article about our Auckland project?
- Who do you know that could help us organise the Red Nose Day charity event?
- What are the coolest things about the goals for our company this year?

Reflection: sometimes collaboration or connections need a little nudge, you're likely to be one amongst many who are a little shy of starting conversations with somebody new.

Management corner

If you're a manager reading this chapter, then hopefully you will have built some ideas for yourself to increase your connections and grow your resilience at work.

Connecting is so often cited as being a powerful tool for building career success, never mind resilience, and it's very rarely trained in businesses. The potential power for its effect on both the engagement and resilience within your team is huge.

Consider discussing this with your HR team to explore the possibility for training or direct your team to the tools and resources presented here.

Consider the role you might play in encouraging your own team to learn from this chapter on networking, along with how it could contribute to the growing success of your team.

Here are some ideas for you to talk through with them:

1   What could we do to increase the number of interactions we have with other teams in the organisation?
2   Who could come and talk to us about <insert topic> from another part of our business or another company?
3   What would be the potential benefits for us creating better connections with other parts of our business/teams in our company/ organisations in our industry?

Tell me more!

Read

- The Success Code. John Lees, 2017
- Dig Your Well Before You're Thirsty. Harvey Mackay, 1999
- Click: Ten truths for building extraordinary relationships. George Fraser, 2008

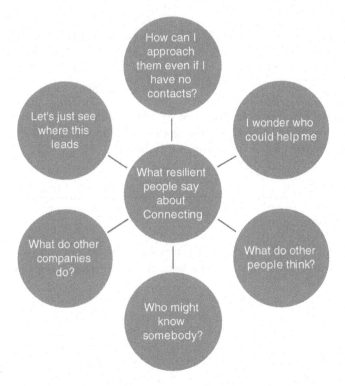

Figure 8.3 Connecting "flower": what people say

- The Science of Introverts (and Extraverts and Everyone in-Between). Peter Hollins, 2017
- Quiet: The power of introverts in a world that can't stop talking. Susan Cain, 2013
- How to Win Friends and Influence People. Dale Carnegie, 1936
- Social: Why our brains are wired to connect. Matthew Leiberman, 2013
- Conversational Intelligence. Judith Glaser, 2016
- Tough at the Top. Sarah Bond and Gillian Shapiro, 2015
- Braving the Wilderness. Brené Brown, 2017

Watch

- www.youtube.com/watch?v=Po-QOVodPhU (Rediscovering Personal Networking. Michael Goldberg.)
- www.youtube.com/watch?v=IjSPfGsaC3g (The Art of Active Networking. Mark E. Sackett.)
- www.youtube.com/watch?v=D4cV8yfgNyI (How to magically connect with anyone. Brian Miller.)

- www.ted.com/talks/brene_brown_on_vulnerability (The Power of Vulnerability. Brené Brown.)
- www.ted.com/talks/susan_cain_the_power_of_introverts (The Power of Introverts. Susan Cain.)
- www.youtube.com/watch?v=NNhk3owF7RQ (The Social Brain and its Superpowers. Matthew Leiberman.)
- www.youtube.com/watch?v=J6EjBwrdHgE (Why to Sell is Human. Dan Pink.)

Apps to Connect

- Sevn
- Lunchback
- Yepstr
- Shapr

Five vital facts: Connecting

1 **The N-word terrifies most people:** networking is likely to be high on most people's feared things to do list. You are not alone in being concerned about what to say and how to get the conversation started.
2 **Connections must be created AND maintained:** if they are not created, then connecting becomes impossible, if they are not maintained then connecting becomes futile.
3 **Not all connections are created equal:** by prioritising your connections you will be able better to maximise the time you have available for them.
4 **Connecting is fundamental:** if we do not feel connected, this will have a direct impact on the chemicals in our body which create trust and bonds at work.
5 **Consider inbound and outbound options:** connecting can be dialled up by reaching out to more people, or it can be dialled up by creating a need for people to reach out to you.

Do: it's time to write your story (Action Plan)

This chapter about Connecting has underlined the importance of . . .
It has given me a better understanding of . . .
What I've learned about myself is . . .
What I'm particularly thankful for is . . .
What I'm going to do immediately as a result is . . .
What I'm going to do over the next twelve months is . . .
The impact this will have is . . .

(continued)

(continued)

What could get in the way is . . .
(If this happens I'm going to . . .)
I will know I have succeeded because . . .
I am going to check what I've achieved on . . . (date)
The person who will help me to stay accountable to this plan is:

CONNECTING

GRID	Here are some questions for you to consider as you reflect on what you have learned in this chapter. They have been designed to help you decide how to use what you have read. You may wish to consider the questions alone, with a friend or with your manager at work.
GOAL	• If you were amazing at creating connections at work, how would that impact your resilience? • What are the main reasons that you would like to increase the amount of energy you are giving to connections right now? • If the connections you had at work could help you, what would they be doing for you? • What are the connections you already have (your tribe, your friends, your team) and how are they helping you? • How will your resilience be affected by increasing the amount of focus on your connections at work?
REALITY	• How would you describe your connections at work right now? • How well connected are you already to people who mentor, encourage and support your career success? • How do you normally meet people in your life and your work? • What has previously been the impact of neglecting your connections? • How would you describe the connections in your workplace now? • When did you feel like you made a really great connection? You felt like "you" and the conversation flowed. Explore. • What is getting in the way of creating connections to support your career ambitions? Explore. • Who are the amazing connections you already have and how do they already help your resilience at work? • What impact is social media having on your sense of connectedness? Is it helping you? Hindering you? Explore. • How skilled are you at the skills of great connectors; asking questions about other people and listening?
IDEAS	• Who do you know that's awesome at creating connections? How do they do it and what could you learn from them? • What have you learned in this chapter about connecting which could help you to achieve your goals? • What is your learning preference and how could it help you grow your confidence in connecting at work?

- How could you reach out to your connections to show them how much they mean to you at work?
- Who do you know that you could introduce to another person to support THEIR resilience at work?
- What are the topics at work that you'd like to talk to your connections about, in order to grow stronger?

DO

- What one small step could you take towards growing your connections at work?
- What changes could you make immediately?
- What will you have to plan to introduce over time?
- How could other people in your workplace support you with achieving your goals?
- What are you going to do as a result of your learning about connections in this chapter?
- What signs are you going to see that your strategies are working?

9 Learning

The golden difference that decides
if you're simply coping or growing
more resilient from your experiences

Resources in this chapter:
  Coaching moments:

- Choosing to learn
- Learning right now
- Impact of learning
- Signature Strengths and learning
- Your Goal for learning
- Feedback and development
- Career lifeline
- Learning mission
- Feedback and resilience
- Learning Review (1 and 2)
- Feedback Review
- Identifying obstacles
- Career lifeline
- Learning Zones
- GRID learning
- Learning decision matrix
- Coaching sandwich
- Thinking matrix

What is this chapter about?

In this chapter, the Coaching moments and Coaching tales have been designed to support you in growing the Resilience Attributes associated with dialling up your Learning Foundation. We will focus on cultivating your ability to be self-confident, determined, enterprising and anticipating.

By the end of this chapter you will have:

- Explored how intellectual wellbeing can impact your levels of Resilience
- Learned how to dial up Evidence-Based Learning
- Used two frameworks for seeking more feedback about your work
- Found out how developing Signature Strengths at work can influence resilience
- Cultivated your growth mindset

Alice: Would you tell me, please, which way I ought to go from here?
The Cheshire Cat: That depends a good deal on where you want to get
to. Alice: I don't much care where. The Cheshire Cat: Then it doesn't
much matter which way you go. Alice: So long as I get somewhere. The
Cheshire Cat: Oh, you're sure to do that, if only you walk long enough.

("Alice in Wonderland" by Lewis Carroll.
Originally published 1865)

One of the exciting things about learning at work today is how easy it is to
access, for our professional (or personal) growth, at any time we want.

In the space of a generation, we now have access to global insights about
pretty much every single topic you could imagine in the time it takes to click
the mouse, read or watch the information we find.

Much of the learning available to us in this way is free, or low cost – so if we
want to get better at something that's going to help achieve our career ambitions,
we are no longer constrained by needing "management approval" for spending
thousands of dollars, euros, pounds or yen on attending a development programme
at work. We can quite literally choose to learn and grow at any time, often for free.

Of course, if you work for an employer that does support professional development you might also be able to access very tailored programmes to help you
grow in a way specific to your company, which is rather lovely.

However, because we're now realising that there's a dark side to everything
if it goes to an extreme, you might notice that it's also a bit easy to be bamboo-
zled with the different learning options available to us.

How do you narrow it down? How do you decide what to believe? How
do you stay on top of reading everything? How do you make sure something
changes after you invest your time in learning?

Coaching moment: choosing to learn

For the next 24 hours make a note of all the training ideas you receive:
Facebook advertising, direct emails inviting you to attend, LinkedIn recommendations, friends and colleagues' suggestions, updates about the
latest findings or regulation changes which you now need to learn.

1   What impact does this have on you? Consider using our Emotional
    Word List.
2   How are you deciding what to lean into (to read, to attend) and
    what to ignore?
3   When you learn something new, what do you do with that learning?

Alice's question to the Cheshire Cat is beautiful.

It demonstrates the opportunity for us to consider where we would like to
go, what options are available to take us there, permission to decide to take any

of the options or choose specifically, and the surety that whatever we choose we're going to arrive somewhere in the end.

The Cheshire Cat applies our GRID coaching framework perfectly by inviting Alice first to consider where she would like to go (her Goal), before making a plan to get there.

If we applied this to our consideration of dialling up our Learning Foundation, we might find that we have an opportunity to get clearer on where we want to focus our learning, allowing ourselves to do any learning that we choose, or simply trusting that whatever we decide we will grow ourselves somehow, if we commit to putting one foot in front of the other.

What else does the story about Alice in Wonderland's dilemma represent to you?

My story: Teagan

Teagan sat down with her coach and sighed.

It was the end of a very long week, and she had her performance review the following Thursday. She worked as an apprentice in a road-ing related company and had been asked to talk about what training she wanted to do.

"I really want to make sure that I stay ahead of the game" she said.

"There's so much happening in work just now, all these changes. As well as this, I'm constantly getting emails from my industry training organisation because of my apprentice status and it seems like there's just so many things I need to attend – but I'm not sure how I'm going to find time"

"What training should I ask for at work when I meet with my manager?"

Instead of telling her what to do or making recommendations her coach asked what she hoped to achieve from her apprenticeship (her Goal).

During the ensuing conversation using the GRID coaching framework, Teagan considered the journey ahead for her as an apprentice. She realised there were many options which she could consider for her "wish list" to support her performance discussion:

- Learning linked to the work that she enjoyed
- Training focussed on feedback that she had received
- What was required for the apprentice programme
- Simply what she was interested in
- Learning that specifically focussed on developing skills which were in high demand for her industry.

She realised that she could ask for any of the training interventions that she wanted, but there were some choices which would help her to achieve the goals of her apprentice programme faster than others, and some that she might enjoy more than others. She understood that even if her employer wasn't able to support all of her "wish list" she was much clearer on what she wanted to develop and could do so alone if she chose.

Reflection: making sure you have a clearer reason for your learning can help you to prioritise and take some pressure off because you plan it out.

Teagan wanted her coach to tell her what she should do to grow in her role, and yet she hadn't given any thought to where she wanted to focus her learning. That's a bit like saying you want to grow your fitness and asking what exercise you should do. Without knowing whether you have injuries, whether you prefer to exercise outside, with equipment, alone or in a team it's impossible for suggestions to add anything other than noise to your thinking.

To dial up our Learning Foundation then, we must have an idea about what we are trying to develop and why. Otherwise, there's a risk that we just run around signing up for lots of learning and development opportunities that aren't taking us nearer to where we would like. This could have a negative impact on our desire to grow resilience because it could become pretty time consuming and put us under even more pressure.

According to a study by PricewaterhouseCoopers ("Workforce of the Future"), up to 42% of employees say they are likely to leave because they aren't learning fast enough. While on the one hand this sounds very dramatic and likely to strike fear into the heart of any leader, on the other hand it creates an amazing opportunity.

What if we took more responsibility for our own learning at work?

When we apply for a job that's outside our organisation, we tend to put our very best foot forward. We polish up our CV, we prepare or practice for our interviews by identifying what we've achieved at work and we dress up in our finest interview outfits.

Compare this to what we do when we want to be considered for another role in our existing organisation (whether it is a promotion or a move into different responsibilities). How many of these are you guilty of?

- Waiting until your quarterly performance discussion to request consideration for something new
- Sending the same CV that you applied for your current job (and it's been over a year since you started)
- Hoping that somebody will notice all the effort you put into your current role
- Accepting a "not now, dear" with a brave smile instead of asking specific questions to get clearer on what's required for success next time.

- Sharing your sense of disappointment with other colleagues if you are unsuccessful in achieving something
- Forgetting that to be considered for something new, you need to demonstrate your ability BEFORE you ask for the opportunity
- Expecting your manager or team leader to know you inside out. What motivates and excites you at work, what your values are and what you love to do with your skills – without ever really telling them.
- Keeping your career dreams secret from your manager (the things you REALLY want to do) in case they think you're not really committed to your current role
- Avoiding the "feedback" discussion – finding out how well you are doing in your job, along with ideas where you might consider change or improvement
- Dressing for the job you have, rather than the job you want to have
- Expecting to be promoted because you've been in the job X number of years
- Complaining to colleagues about the selection process
- Assuming that you are underpaid compared to your market worth and therefore being taken advantage of at work.

Coaching moment: learning right now

Consider your own views on the amount of learning that you get in your work right now.

1 What would you like to learn more or faster? How else could you go ahead and achieve this learning goal without waiting for your employer to give you the green light?
2 How are you staying informed about the main changes and trends in your industry, or your role? Where do your tribe go for information – the online forums, the MOOC's, the online learning opportunities? What's happening in your country, or overseas?
3 How are you actually using what you've learned? What are you doing differently? What impact is this having on you or on others?

Coaching tale: Beth

Beth worked at a non-profit organisation as a counsellor. She enjoyed her work overall, but with almost twenty-five years in the industry she was starting to feel a bit tired, and uninspired in her role.

When the company decided to bring in an external consultant to deliver a company-wide programme teaching solution focussed approach to their work, she was furious.

She couldn't help but notice that the consultant was costing the non-profit organisation a considerable amount of money and taking extra time to get familiar with the different elements of their practice, to bring a solution focus to all their activities. This really grated with her personal values and she resented the work, bringing a very negative attitude to the training events.

Beth realised that she had all the experience that her company needed to be able to do this work; she had the qualifications, the experience in solution focussed therapy and the credibility within her peers. However, she had never explored her desire to use these skills to grow capability in others at her employer.

Luckily, Beth realised this early in the programme and instead of remaining angry she used this as a catalyst to talk about her frustrations and boredom with her manager. She began to act as a mentor for colleagues who were new to the methodology and took on responsibility for designing some in-house materials to support the project.

Without realising this, and then using the situation as an opportunity to ask for more of what she wanted to do, Beth might have simply resigned from a role where she felt undervalued and overlooked.

Reflection: employers aren't mind readers. If there is something you'd like to achieve at work then ask for it or look for ways to make it happen yourself. Don't become one of the 42% who are frustrated that they aren't learning fast enough – you deserve to be in a job that you love.

What is learning?

When we are at work, we often find that the plans we put in place for our learning are those "areas for improvement" that have been identified or imposed on us by our team leaders, our managers or our supervisors.

Sometimes this can be a little bit demotivating, particularly if we're being encouraged to learn in areas that we don't actually want to use, or in skills that aren't going to take us closer to our career ambitions.

If we want to grow our resilience so that we can achieve our career ambitions, we need to think a little bit differently about how we define and achieve our learning:

1   **Learning about me:** this sort of learning is aimed at helping us to understand more about who we are. It is a curiosity about now rather than a desire to grow. For example, it can be as simple as realising that you do your more focussed work in the morning and therefore that's the best time to attempt anything difficult in your role. Or it can mean exploring psychometric assessments to understand things like whether

you prefer detail, if you do best by talking through ideas or if you thrive in roles where you are responsible for organising. This is a critical place for our Signature Strengths reflections.

2   **In the Moment Learning:** this happens when we stay focussed on events that give us an opportunity to decide if we're OK with what just happened. It is an evidence-based approach to learning, in that we see and experience the event personally. For example, a meeting that didn't go to plan, a report returned as unacceptable, a CV rejected. In that moment, we could choose to ask for information that will help us both understand the reason for the "failure" and identify things we could do differently for future success. It helps us to grow right now and helps us do our current job even better.

3   **Future Learning** – this happens when we consciously plan our learning for something that we would like to achieve in the future and is often more formal in nature. For example, we would like to be promoted into a specific role but haven't quite got the required knowledge, skills or experience. It's likely to be aimed at ensuring we can do a job for the future with more capability. It can either be focussed on helping us to do our current job better in the future, or achieve a different role.

Remember that learning doesn't just mean attending workshops.

Figure 9.1 Word cloud: types of learning

Coaching moment: impact of learning

Think about the learning that you have done during the last twelve months. Include as much as you can in your reflections; the articles you've chosen to read, the training you've attended, the investment you've made in growing your understanding.
   Consider:

1   Out of the learning you've just identified, what has been directly aimed at achieving your career ambitions; your future learning?
2   What has been more focussed on In the Moment Learning, as a result of things that haven't gone to plan?
3   What impact has this learning already had on you at work? (For example, the things that you're doing differently.)

What are Signature Strengths?

In our chapter on Self-Care we discuss the power of Signature Strengths at work so, if you've already read that, you may wish to skip through this paragraph.

Signature Strengths are the character strengths that are the most essential to who we are. They are foundational to the school of Positive Psychology and represent some of the science behind understanding what it takes to live a flourishing life. They are the traits that come naturally to us, and if we find that we must repress them, or cannot use them to some extent then we lose our sense of fulfilment and purpose.

Remember our consideration of how Psychology was disrupted by Positive Psychology because it focussed on identifying and finding ways to strengthen the traits which enable us to thrive and live a flourishing life? Well, Signature Strengths are foundational to this.

They play an enormous role in our Self-Care at work, but we can also take them into consideration when planning to dial up our Learning Foundation for resilience. Each of us possesses every single one to a different degree, and knowing our strengths can help us significantly in times of resilience.

The VIA Institute on Character has a free online survey which lets you work out your unique profile. It also has an enormous amount of research available if you're at all interested (or sceptical!) about how the Signature Strengths can influence us, along with tools and resources to support your learning.

In 2017, The University of Canterbury is embarking on an extended study into the impact of Signature Strengths at work; specifically focussing on how we can use them to decrease stress and/or increase wellbeing. The findings

Table 9.1 Signature Strengths

Wisdom	1	Creativity (thinking of new ways to do things)
	2	Curiosity (exploration and discovery)
	3	Judgement (examine from all sides)
	4	Love of learning (passion for mastering new skills, etc.)
	5	Perspective (people who know you consider you as wise)
Courage	6	Bravery (not shrinking from challenge, threat, difficulty or pain)
	7	Honesty (living an authentic honest life)
	8	Perseverance (working hard from start to finish)
	9	Zest (approaching everything you do with excitement and energy)
Humanity	10	Kindness (kind and generous to others)
	11	Love (valuing close relationships with others)
	12	Social Intelligence (know how to fit into social situations)
Justice	13	Fairness (treat all people fairly)
	14	Leadership (encouraging a group to get things done)
	15	Teamwork (excel as a member of a group)
Temperance	16	Forgiveness (forgive those who wrong you)
	17	Humility (recognised and valued for modesty)
	18	Prudence (a careful person)
	19	Self-Regulation (a disciplined person)
Transcendence	20	Appreciation of Beauty (notice and appreciate beauty and excellence)
	21	Gratitude (aware of good things, and don't take them for granted)
	22	Hope (expect the best and work to achieve it)
	23	Humour (bringing smiles to others is important)
	24	Spirituality (your beliefs shape actions and are a source of comfort)

will no doubt contribute greatly to the evidence-based approach that is already used by Engagement Consultancies (like Gallup and Kenexa). This is such an exciting new world that we can learn from.

It would of course be impossible to aim to be all these things, all the time . . . but the research highlights that when we consciously focus on bringing more of what makes us "us" into our work and our lives, we are more able to thrive.

Visit www.viacharacter.org and take the online survey or highlight what you think are the three Signature Strengths that are the most important to you, and the one Signature Strength that is the least important to you.

The shadow of strengths

Every Signature Strength can become a problem if it's over extended, so it's important to recognise when this might be happening to you. Strengths are to be used for supporting our best selves, and not for creating issues for ourselves or others.

For example:

- If Zest is a Signature Strength – be mindful of being exhausted by over zealousness, or exasperating others in your team who need a rest.
- If Fairness is a Signature Strength – consider how this may influence your tendency to assume how others want to be treated.
- If Humour is a Signature Strength – be mindful that not all situations or people will be equally receptive.

In addition to recognising that there is sometimes a "wrong time, wrong place", it can also be helpful to realise that what's important to us in our life might not be important to another person. Consider for example if you worked for a manager with Bravery as a top Signature Strength, and your main Signature Strength was Prudence. How might this influence your relationship? What are the areas which could cause the most friction? What would need to happen to resolve this?

The power in supporting ourselves to be who we truly are, and using our Signature Strengths to enrich our life, is no doubt enormous. Research to understand the impact of this within our workplaces is just taking off but there are already significant findings to suggest that understanding our Signature Strength at work will support our ability to be resilient at work.

For example, a study of over 10,000 workers in New Zealand, by Lucy Hone et al., reported those who were aware of their Strengths were 9.5 times more likely to be flourishing and those who were frequently using their Strengths at work were 18 times more likely to be thriving.

Also, a three-year study of employee engagement in the UK, by Shane Crabb, found that employees who are encouraged to identify, use and alert others (like managers) to their Signature Strengths were more likely to be engaged in their work.

I wonder how it would impact your resilience if you were one of those people who was thriving and engaged at work?

Coaching moment: Signature Strengths and learning

Reflect on the reasons that you are reading this book; the goals for developing your own resilience for achieving your career ambitions and the things that you believe are getting in the way.

1 How could your top three Signature Strengths help you to achieve your goal(s)? What could you do to experience more of them in your career journey?

(continued)

(continued)

2   How could your top three Signature Strengths be getting in the way? To what extent are their shadows impacting your goals?

3   How might the Signature Strengths of other people in the equation be influencing what's going on? (For example, if your Strength is Humility and your manager's Strength is Gratitude you might feel self-conscious by their continued thanks.)

Goal: what do you want to achieve?

Dialling up our Learning Foundation to become more resilient can be done at any time, although it is most powerful when we have a clear reason (or reasons) for doing so.

Perhaps your career ambitions are being thwarted by your perception that your gender is holding you back; in which case, you might create a Goal about learning how to achieve career success as a male/female/transgender/asexual in your industry.

If you need to develop resilience to stay strong because you have lost your job; you might focus on a Goal which helps you to confirm that your CV and interview techniques are strong, and you learn how to cultivate your networks.

If you discover something about yourself as a result of reading this book (for example, to be more resilient you want to develop your self-care strategies); you might set a Goal of learning from the resources recommended in the Tell me more! sections (and seeking out extra ones).

Coaching moment: your Goal for learning

1   Look back at the overall reason that you are reading this book; the Goal that you created for growing your own resilience.

2   Now look at all the obstacles that you've identified; the things that are stopping you from achieving your career ambitions.

3   Looking at what you have written down, what are the areas where you might benefit from more learning? (For example, if one obstacle you have identified is that you keep getting rejected for a promotion you could consider asking for feedback about why, and design your learning to grow skills that you are lacking for the next role ahead).

Reality: How much learning are you doing already?

Before we design ideas about how you could dial up your Learning Foundation, let's consider how much learning you're already doing.

Using an evidence-based approach, we can explore the impact that your current level of learning is having on your overall resilience, so you can decide whether you want to dial it up or dial it down to achieve your Goals.

Bearing in mind our plans for this chapter are to seek feedback, tailor your development plans and use a Strengths based and growth mindset we need to consider what you're already doing in these four areas.

Coaching moment: feedback and development

Reflect on the last twelve months in your career.

1   How much feedback have you received or asked for during this time? What have been the main themes of this feedback? The areas where you are performing well or could improve? What action have you taken because of this feedback?
2   Look at the development plan that you have in place at work. To what extent has it been tailored to meet the needs of your own career ambitions? How will the development plan that you already have in place influence your goal to become more resilient? How does your development plan make use of your Signature Strengths?
3   From your reflections above, what are the main areas of concern for your Learning Foundation – the things you'd most like to focus on?

Coaching tales: Jude

Jude is a highly ambitious employee at a retail organisation in New Zealand. She signs up for pretty much every learning opportunity that comes along in her company. Her top Signature Strengths are Curiosity, Love of learning and Zest.

Her super power is therefore the Learning Foundation, which sometimes gets over extended because of her Signature Strengths, because they are largely in the same Wisdom classification.

Jude began to recognise that every time she hit a speed bump in the process of achieving her career goals, she immediately dialled up her Learning. In some instances, this became obsessive and at the expense

(continued)

(continued)

of her Connections and her Self-Care. She found that she preferred to research instead of taking some time out for healthy activities, she became so enthralled in workshops that she didn't talk much to people she attended them with and she found it very hard to switch off in the evenings.

Jude also found that this was beginning to impact her self-confidence at work, because she felt there was always so much to learn (which was, to her, exciting) but she occasionally felt overwhelmed at the enormity of the learning journey ahead.

After considering the Resilience Foundations, she realised that she was perceiving knowledge as the only way to stay strong and be more resilient. She saw new knowledge as a way of regaining control every time something went wrong.

She realised that she wasn't taking time to reflect on existing knowledge; for example, what she already knew, how it might help her and how well she was already performing in skills that were critical to her role.

She also realised that to become more resilient she would need to dial down her Learning Foundation a little; cutting back on new learning and make more time for Self-Care, Emotional Honesty and Connecting. She quickly became excited by this idea (of course, because she had Zest as a Strength) and immediately planned to research more in these three areas.

Reflection: Signature Strengths are a source of great energy and power where they are used consciously and with good intent. If we are unconscious in how they are impacting us at work, sometimes we can find ourselves undermining our own career ambitions.

Career lifeline

Another way to explore the Reality of our Learning Foundation is to consider the journey we have already had at work. This will help us to identify when we have already been at our most resilient, and therefore what are the likely conditions that we need to recreate this.

Consciously noticing the highs and lows can contribute greatly to finding the sense of purpose behind our career ambitions.

- Start with a blank sheet of paper.
- Draw a horizontal line, left to right through the middle of the page.
- The left represents your first ever job, the right represents today.
- Above the line represents an overall sense of positivity at work, below the line represents an overall sense of negativity at work.
- Plot above and below the line to create a visual of your work so far. You may wish to break this down into projects if you prefer, or if this is early

in your career you may prefer to focus on identifying overall positivity or negativity in life, instead of work.

- Now you are going to write between three and five bullet points, which describe why you have placed each point above or below the line. Write as much detail as you can (for example, "Inspiring manager supported my development" instead of just "manager").
- Now you are going to add the trigger. What caused you to move from one job to the next?
- Finally, you're going to approximate the time between jobs, to look for patterns and trends.

Learning is so incredibly powerful to our resilience that many of us reach a point when we feel like we're no longer learning in our role and move on. Learning often correlates to enjoyment, energy and engagement, so when we stop learning the effect can be enormous.

Look at your patterns for moving on and consider when you would benefit from a conversation about finding new ways to grow in your current role; perhaps three to six months before your usual trigger point. Maybe you could discuss taking on a stretch assignment, try a secondment in another area of the business or find somebody to mentor you into readiness for a promotion?

Notice that even if you haven't had a specific role in mind for your career, you are likely to have created a pattern for yourself in another way. Perhaps you love working with a specific type of person, or you are attracted to organisations which stand for something you believe in. Perhaps you have been following a feeling, rather than a destination role.

Notice too, if there are any side effects to finding work that you absolutely love. For some people, when they find themselves doing what they are passionate about it becomes exhausting because they don't ever want to switch off, while for others it can be totally energising. The power is in noticing, and then considering, if this is the way you want to be.

Coaching moment: career lifeline

Reflect on the career lifeline you have just designed. Consider talking about what you have designed with another person, who can ask you questions and help you to clarify your thoughts.

1   What do you notice about the jobs, projects or experiences that are above the line? What are the patterns or trends? Do the same with those that appear below the line.
2   What do you notice about the trigger points which cause you to look for new opportunities?
3   What do you notice about the timeline between jobs?

Coaching moment: learning mission

Reflect on what you have learned about your Signature Strengths and what you noticed during the career lifeline exercise. Creating a consciousness of when we have been at our most resilient in the workplace can help us to look for more; we are learning about the conditions that we would like to create for ourselves in order to be more resilient.

- The **Strengths** I would love to use (or use more) at work:
- The **People** I would love to impact:
- The **Difference** I would love to make:
- The **Way** I would like to do this:

My story: Sarah

Sarah was a professor who specialised in entomology. She had worked for her employer for the last twenty years and had enjoyed a career as a professor for eleven years prior to this. She was starting to think about retirement and noticing that when she did, she felt apprehensive.

Approaching the end of full time employment represented a lot of different things to Sarah; she was concerned about losing touch with her colleagues, she felt that the access she had to inspiring research would decline and she was worried that she would no longer feel the excitement she experienced every day at work.

Reflecting on her career, Sarah realised that she was at her most motivated when she was researching and writing. She noticed that her Signature Strengths included Love of learning, and Curiosity.

Exploring this with a coach led her to notice that losing her connection to learning was the thing that stressed her the most and caused her sense of resilience to dip.

During her coaching sessions, Sarah explored how she might use this knowledge to create a more exciting picture for her retirement and she decided that there were several options she wanted to explore; retaining a part time role as an editor for supporting the organisation she worked for (contributing to shaping and refining articles that were presented for publication), supporting one-off projects in the industry (working with other organisations in the industry as an occasional consultant to research and present data) and exploring other more general opportunities for researching and writing, like for the New Zealand organisation, Grey Power.

She decided to dial up her Learning Foundation because of this realisation to find out more about how to achieve these things.

Reflection: creating consciousness of when we have been at our most resilient during our career lifeline can also give us clues about the Foundation we may want to focus on dialling up.

What you've already learned

Coaching moment: feedback and resilience

Consider your career so far. If you are new into the workforce, use this Coaching moment to think about your experience at school, or in further education.

1   On a scale of 1–5 (with 5 being the highest) how confident are you about your ability to do your job?
2   What causes you to believe this? (What are the evidence-based clues about your confidence levels? What feedback have you had? What information do you have to reinforce your confidence?)
3   What impact is this having on your resilience at work?

Now consider the last twelve months at work. What feedback have you had about the way you do your job?

1   Who did the feedback come from?
2   What have you done as a result?
3   How have these changes affected the way you do your job?

What's your learning zone?

Finding a framework to help you consider your learning needs can be helpful, particularly when you're exploring whether learning is something you want to dial up, and understand the implications of doing so.

One framework to support us is the psychology based Four Stages of Competence Model, originally designed in the 1970s by Gordon Training International. The model has been evolved through the years and can help us to understand where we are with our learning.

Figure 9.2 Learning zones

Reflect on your overall Goal for dialling up your Learning Foundation, or the things that you are "learning about your learning" and then compare where you think you are on this framework. This can give you clues about the best possible actions to help you achieve your Goal.

> For example, if you keep being rejected from promotional opportunities and genuinely don't know why then you are likely in the zone of Unconscious Incompetence. Asking for feedback about what's perceived by your employer as holding you back will likely help you step into the zone of Conscious Incompetence; you might find that your professional brand isn't seen as strong enough, or your skills aren't quite up to scratch – but at least now you know, so you can put a plan in a place to train, practice and reflect.

Coaching tales: Braden

Braden wanted a role in a bigger organisation. He had been in the management team at his current employer for six years and felt it was time for change. He had received regular feedback about his work and knew that he was perceived as a good performer so he decided to apply for roles which represented a step up on the management ladder.

After six interviews where he got down to the final two candidates, Braden admitted defeat. He had been gradually getting more and more disheartened with the process of progressing his career and decided to approach a career professional for advice.

Together, they reviewed the job descriptions that he was applying for and looked for evidence to demonstrate his capability. There were heaps of examples that he could use during interviews. It was a puzzle how he was missing out.

So, the career professional decided to run some practice interviews with Braden, so he could explore first-hand what the problem might be. Together they selected a potential advert, and Braden prepared as if it were a real interview.

What his career coach noticed almost immediately was that Braden was talking in the third person when discussing his achievements at work. Instead of talking about what he had been personally responsible for achieving, Braden was sharing examples about the roles that other people had played in his successes at work.

In exploring this, Braden shared that he did not like to talk about himself because he believed that as a manager he was only ever as good as how well his team were performing.

His career coach also noticed that Braden was very hesitant in his responses; faltering and rephrasing as he worked through what he was trying to say.

Both observations would no doubt have an adverse impact on how Braden might present during an interview, and he was not aware of either of them. He was in a state of unconscious incompetence.

A responsible interviewer could have shared this observation with Braden at any time during his six interviews, and there are many recruiters that share feedback or practice with candidates before important final-stage interviews so they can do just this.

However, Braden confessed that he had never been in touch with any of the hiring managers to seek feedback about his interview performance, and therefore accepted there was also some accountability on his part too.

(continued)

(continued)

Armed with this information, Braden could then dial up his learning about how to talk about achievements during interviews in an authentic way, and how to overcome his interview nerves.

Reflection: where you are experiencing obstacles, or blocks to achieving your career ambitions, look for ways to get advice, guidance or feedback as soon as possible.

Another framework to use for considering your current Learning state is that of New Zealand based Neuro Linguistic Programming coach, Jane Pike.

Her three-step framework gives us an interesting take on exploring the potential impact of a Growth Mindset on our need to develop strong coping strategies to avoid stress.

Quite simply, if we want to grow ourselves to become more resilient we will likely need to move beyond our Comfort Zone and therefore we will enter either the Sweet Spot or the Survival Zone. Understanding our own personal responses to both these zones is critical to support our resilience, in that by recognising the signs (both physical and emotional) that we are leaving the Sweet Spot and entering our Survival Zone can help us to remain resilient.

The inference of ownership in this framework is interesting. It gives us the opportunity to consider culpability in the often-quoted global stress epidemic. If "pushing our boundaries" for personal growth at work is self-driven, we must therefore consider how to strengthen our coping strategies so that we recognise we are entering the Survival Zone and can put steps in place to manage ourselves back to the Sweet Spot.

In other words, yes, our employer or our role may cause us distress which requires us to become resilient, but it might also be our desire to grow ourselves even more generally (in our role, in our lives) that also causes stressors, for which we must take ownership. We might find we can get rid of much of the stress in our world by simply being, rather than focussing on growing and changing.

Settling into our Comfort Zone could therefore be an answer for some of us, though it won't help us grow stronger so we won't be influencing our longer term resilience.

Staying in our Comfort Zone will also likely impact our ability to achieve progression – whether with our current employer or a different employer. Josh Bersin, Deloitte, shares an awesome quote: "the learning curve is the earning curve". If we want more money, we usually must grow our skills and capabilities and the only way we do this is to push out of our Comfort Zone.

Combining our Learning Foundation with our Emotional Honesty and Self-Care Foundations can help us to ensure that we do this by staying in our Sweet Spot, and not straying into the Survival Zone.

Zone Three – the Survival Zone. At this point, we have pushed our boundaries so hard that we are likely to experience the fight, flight or freeze response associated with increased adrenal and cortisol response. Realising we have reached this place is part of our Emotional Honesty Foundation, and then we can choose to dial up or down our Resilient Foundations as a result.

Zone Two – the Sweet Spot. This is the place where optimal learning happens; where we're firing on all cylinders, pushing our boundaries and taking ourselves to the next level of our capability. At times, this can feel a little messy as we play with new competencies but it's the best place for us to operate without blowing a fuse.

Zone One – the Comfort Zone. This is a lovely place to hang out, and we could stay here all day because it's such a cruisy place to be. Anxiety levels are low to non-existent, and we can pretty much nail all the skills required of . . . except not much happens here, and it can get a bit boring unless we are here for a specific reason. Sometimes during our career staying in our Comfort Zone can be a strategic decision – for example if we are dealing with stressors outside work or have chosen to take the pressure off ourselves at work.

Coaching moment

Consider what you have learned about the Learning Foundation so far.

1   What have you learned about the Reality of your Learning Foundation?
2   What impact is this having on your resilience right now?
3   How would you like to use this observation to support your Learning Foundation Goals?

Ideas: what could you do?

Having reviewed your current Goal for dialling up your Learning Foundation at work, we can now explore different Ideas for how you could do this – so you can tailor the things you decide to Do.

These Ideas are all designed positively to influence your ability to be self-confident, determined, enterprising and anticipating. You can choose what you focus on depending on what you want to achieve, and modify the exercises to suit you.

The GRID coaching framework

The whole book has been designed using a GRID coaching framework to help you tailor your own resilience programme.

The GRID coaching framework can also be used to help you to consider Ideas and then make a plan for any Learning that you consider.

For example:

> **Goal:** your Goal is to find a job after being made redundant. (If you have created a Specific, Measurable, Achievable, Realistic, Time-bound (SMART) Goal then it might even more specific, like finding a marketing role in the education industry that falls within a salary of NZ$60,000–80,000 within the next eight weeks.)
>
> **Reality:** consider your Reality using the evidence that accompanies your job search; how many CV's have you sent out? How are you deciding where to send them? What is their success rate? How many contacts do you have within the education sector that you have followed up? How do your knowledge, skills and experience compare with the roles you're applying for? What are the actual salaries attached to the roles you're applying for? Consider how your Reality is impacting your Goal.
>
> **Ideas:** once you've established your reality, consider the actions you might take to help you achieve your Goal; could you get CV feedback from an agency? Could you pay for a professional CV? Could you use your social media connections to help you find somebody in the education sector to meet with and seek advice? Could you follow up an unsuccessful application and get feedback? Could you consider moving to another city or country where salaries for this role are higher? Check that your Ideas will help you achieve your Goal.

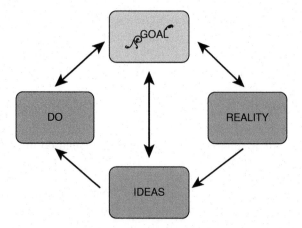

Figure 9.3 GRID coaching framework (from Chapter 2)

Do: after fully considering all the things you could do to achieve your Goal, you're going to plan what you will actually do, how and by when. Ensure that what you are planning to Do is going to have a direct impact on achieving your Goal.

Any time that we are using a GRID framework to support our thinking, we are dialling up our Growth Mindset, because we're looking for the opportunity to use the experience of a current situation to achieve something better, or different.

We are also creating a solution focussed approach, by exploring different actions that we could take to achieve something specific – we aren't just staying stuck in the current circumstances.

Learning Decision Matrix

Deciding what to focus on helps us to make sure that the learning we do is as closely aligned as possible to growing our resilience and achieving our career ambitions.

The Learning Decision Matrix is one way of doing this, it helps us to consider two specific variables:

- **Impact**: this refers to whether the effect of the learning we are considering is likely to have a high impact on our ability to achieve our career ambitions.
- **Interest**: this refers to whether we are interested or excited in the learning that's on offer.

It is an adaptation of the Ease and Effect Consulting tool which is often used to prioritise actions in project management.

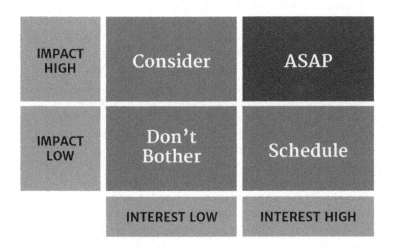

Figure 9.4 Learning Decisions Matrix

This helps us to see that if there's something that we could do to develop ourselves which is likely to have a high impact on achieving our career ambition AND we are excited by it; we should do it as soon as we possibly can.

If we are not so excited by something that's going to have a high impact on achieving our career goals, then we should consider it more fully – it can still contribute to helping us achieve our ambitions but we may need to do a bit more thinking about it. For example, reflect on why it doesn't excite you; perhaps you are accidentally working towards achieving somebody else's career goal for you? Or maybe you haven't fully researched what you will actually do in the job you're aspiring to achieve?

Anything that interests you a lot, but is unlikely to help you achieve your career goals, can still be planned into your journey – but with less of an urgency than the learning which will have a high impact on achieving your goals. This learning is more likely to be for fun, rather than for professional achievement.

Anything that neither interests you nor takes you closer to achieving your career goals should be avoided at all costs. This may be harder in an environment where some training is "compulsory" so it is important to consider whether you might benefit from an honest conversation with the person insisting that you attend (for example, you might discover that you're being asked to attend the training because the organisation is introducing new tools or resources for everybody . . . or you might discover that the perception you have of your capability in something is very different to the perception that your manager has).

Future proof your career

At work, many of our learning conversations are driven by leaders and managers in the organisation. We have quarterly reviews of our performance, we organise post implementation reviews when a project has completed, we wait to be told if we are doing a good job (which is interesting because too often we have a "no news is good news" approach, but we still get cross when nobody tells us anything about how we are doing).

Many of the companies we work for are really committed to encouraging their managers and leaders to do a great job; investing both time and money in growing their abilities to hold better conversations with their team.

Since the ground breaking Hawthorne experiments during the 1930s, which indicated both the importance and impact of being heard and seen at work, organisational research has continued to explore the potential for people in leadership and management roles to influence the extent that we all enjoy the work we're doing and want to stay to pursue our career ambitions.

For those of us not lucky enough to work in organisations that are committed to this, or who work for managers who have done the training but have chosen not to do anything differently in their conversations, how could we override this?

If we want to grow our resilience at work we need to explore our opportunities for learning and growth, but if nobody is telling us what those opportunities are, what are our options to grow our confidence and get on the front foot for a continued and successful career?

Cultivating learning confidence

There are several ways you might want to consider to find out how you're perceived to be doing and grow your confidence in the work that you do, by creating a structured learning plan. Three of them are:

- Asking for more feedback
- Using your Signature Strengths
- Remembering your successes

Coaching moment: Learning Review

Take a moment to reflect on the things you have achieved at work in the last three months. Consider reviewing your job description to support your thinking, considering the knowledge, skills and abilities you've officially been hired to use.

1 What are you most proud of having done? The things that have gone especially well for you? What impact have these things had on your team, or your company?
2 What are the additional levels of knowledge, skills and abilities you've used at work in the last three months which are not formally noted on your job description?
3 What are the things that haven't gone so well, and if you could do them again you would choose a different way of achieving them?

Asking for more feedback

Often you don't ever know how you're performing unless you know how you compare to others doing a similar role; for example, if we want to be a World Class Athlete, we need to know what World Class looks like in our area of sport – how fast do we need to be? What should our training look like? What extras should we consider (nutrition, diet etc). This helps us not only set our goals but check how competitive we are staying.

One of the main things we can do to increase our resilience at work using a learning approach is to be a bit brave and ask for feedback.

Let's face it, if you leave it to your manager or team leader to provide you with an update on how well you're doing (or not) you might be waiting for a LOOONG time, depending on how confident they are at having this sort of discussion, so seeking feedback is a great skill to have in your Learning Foundation box of tricks.

You see, the thing is, most leaders are absolutely terrified of feedback discussions. They tend to think they must deliver bad news, let you down or break your heart and they forget that these discussions can be an incredible opportunity to have a truly honest discussion about what you love and what you'd like to improve. Leaders forget that much of the time we are already aware of our strengths and our failings and we will usually be harder on ourselves than anybody else when we discuss them. And they forget that the best sort of feedback is discussed regularly (in the moment) as well as during annual reviews or career discussions and is an opportunity to share guidance which can inform and support you to an amazing place at work.

If there really is something unexpected that comes up which disappoints, frustrates or angers you then ask to park the conversation while you roll around with what they have shared with you. Use the tools in this book to build evidence to decide whether you agree or disagree with what you have heard and create a plan of what you will do as a result.

Try arranging a meeting with your manager or team leader to chat about how you're doing at work. Let them know what you'd like to talk to them ahead of the catch up, so they are able to feel prepared.

Use or adapt the following template and be as specific as possible with your examples; make sure you complete the first three questions before you send it through:

1   Here are three things that I am proud of achieving in the last <six> months:
2   This is what I believe the impact has been on the business of achieving these things:
3   Here are three things I want to do better (or differently) in the future:
4   What do you think I should be most proud of having achieved in the last <six> months?
5   What impact do you think I have on the business (or on you, my manager)?
6   What are three things I could do better (or differently) in the future?

Preparing for the conversation by using this template will help you to use a feedback framework called a **Coaching Sandwich**.

The Coaching Sandwich

Most of us have heard of a Feedback Sandwich conversation (sometime called a S**t Sandwich because it implies that there is likely to be bland positive feedback surrounding a rather nasty bit of something in the middle). It's typically a conversation where your manager or team leader shares: something you do well, something you need to do differently then something you do well.

The Coaching Sandwich is a conversation with your manager or team leader where they ASK YOU to share something you do well and then something you'd like to do better or differently . . . and then they share something THEY have observed you doing well.

It can be a very positive starting block for seeking feedback about what you do at work, by the end of the conversation you should have discussed your own ideas for what you do well and what could go better, and reinforced your own observations about what you do well (or surprised yourself by hearing new things that your manager or team leader appreciates).

From this point, you can build more general conversations about how you do your job into regular meetings . . . just three questions considered on a fortnightly or monthly basis can totally revolutionise your learning and confidence at work:

1   What were you trying to achieve?
2   How did it go? (What went well, what didn't go so well?)
3   What could you do to improve next time? (Take ideas and ask for ideas.)

Using Signature Strengths

We all have days when we know we are utterly nailing our work and our life. We feel energised and uplifted and like we will get through whatever comes our way.

Chances are, these are the days when we have been really leaning into our Signature Strengths, or what motivates us at work.

This book has already presented several suggestions for noticing your Signature Strengths, and the impact that using them has on your resilience levels.

Coaching tales: David

David wanted to grow his conscious use of Signature Strengths at work along with an understanding of how they influenced his resilience.

After learning about what they were, and how to recognise them he created a tool to help him work out the impact they were having.

For two weeks, he had an A4 sheet of paper next to the coat rack, and at the end of the day he drew a smiley face representing the sort of day he had experienced; he chose to notice whether he had felt resilient or stressed to the max. He also wrote a couple of bullet points to remind himself what had contributed to his choice of smiley face.

(continued)

(continued)

After two weeks, David noticed that in order to experience more resilience at work he needed to spend some time outside reflecting. For him this was critical to his sense of wellbeing, and therefore resilience. He noticed that his core Signature Strength was Appreciation of Beauty, and that for him this meant being outside to enjoy the natural environment.

Working with a coach, he created a strategy for building his resilience on days when he was unable to take time outside; ensuring his screen saver had images of natural beauty, printing and framing some photographs of his favourite natural places to go and finding a quiet office space where he had a view to the outside world that included "green".

David shared that in this simple action he boosted his self-confidence because he felt like he could truly be himself at work. He shared that he felt calmer and more in control, which influenced his sense of being able to cope with the challenges of his job.

Reflection: finding a way to lean into our Signature Strengths at work not only influences our wellbeing, but also the confidence that we bring to our work.

Remembering successes

Something that career professionals often hear from their clients is that they don't like "boasting" at work. By boasting, this is deemed to mean anything that includes sharing what they've achieved, any action to raise their profile or conversations about how well they've performed.

We know that one way to boost our confidence is to remind ourselves what we have achieved and the impact it's had, so instead of sharing this with other people, what if you were to start by simply reminding yourself?

By consciously writing and remembering not only what you have done, but the impact your actions have had you can begin building a self-esteem which focusses on what you have achieved and the impact your learning is already having.

Updating your CV every four to six months can be a great way to achieve this, particularly because it will ensure that you're in a very strong position to apply for any internal promotion (your story is ready) or if you need to apply for a role externally (either because you want to, or because you need to).

Of course, if you choose to use the information to support the feedback discussions you have with your manager, then even better.

Coaching moment: Learning Review

Think about your last twelve months at work.

1 What are the three things that you've learned which have made the biggest difference to how you do your job?
2 What difference is that making to the team, or the company you work with?
3 Who needs to know about this? (for example, do you need to update your CV?)

Coaching tales: Rebecca

Rebecca works in the Healthcare industry and is very motivated to make a difference in the lives of others. Her strongest two Signature Strengths are Kindness and Humility.

Her work doesn't currently mean that she receives a lot of feedback about her work; her manager is not very interested in feedback conversations, and the area where she works does not currently use client focussed surveys (though this is something that she is currently exploring). Yet Rebecca is still incredibly proud of what she does, and the difference it makes to other people.

Rebecca keeps something called an "Awesome Folder" in her emails, which she looks at regularly to remember the successes she has had. In this folder, she saves any emails (or scans and includes letters) which share a story about what she's done, and the effect it's had.

This has included comments from patients, kind words from other staff members and letters of thanks from the community.

She looks at this folder when she's having a bad day, when she needs a boost or any time she wants to remind herself of the impact she has in her job. This helps Rebecca to remember the difference that she makes to other people, and she has shared that this increases her confidence and makes her feel good every time she reads it.

She has told her manager about the Awesome Folder, but she hasn't yet specifically shared anything in it with him. She is building her own sense of confidence.

(continued)

(continued)

> **Reflection: using our Signature Strengths to build our self-confidence can be helpful because it enables us to tailor our approach and build confidence within ourselves (regardless of the input of others). Rebecca chose to focus on feedback about her acts of Kindness, she could easily have chosen to save feedback about when she has been brave, persevered or worked in a team if those had been her strengths.**

The impact of self talk

How often have you heard statements like these at work:

- "I hate work, nobody ever takes my ideas seriously."
- "I didn't get the job because my manager doesn't like me; now I'll never get a pay rise."
- "It just goes to show I'm far too old to learn how to use that IT system."

The way that we interpret both successes and setbacks is critical to either supporting or undermining the resilient approach that we bring to our learning.

The explanation we give to ourselves about the cause of what is happening (or has happened) to us at work, can result in some powerful inner dialogue. This can either be helpful, or unhelpful.

For example, when we believe that if something goes wrong it will always go wrong ("nobody took my ideas seriously yesterday, or last month, or in my last place of employment . . . therefore nobody will ever take my ideas seriously and I will only ever hate work"), at this point, we often give up or become the person who moans that their ideas are never taken seriously.

A more helpful way of thinking about this might be:

> Nobody took my ideas seriously in today's meeting, so I need to do things differently next time; what could I do? Perhaps I should include some case studies of how my idea has worked in other companies? Or some graphs showing the expected impact? Maybe I could talk to the person who objected the most to find out what their concerns are? Next time, I'll include a case study and some graphs that target the perceived problems.

Great questions to consider if you find yourself thinking like this could be:

1   Has there ever been a time when somebody did take your ideas seriously? (Explore in work and outside work. Try to work out what you did.)
2   Have you ever worked with somebody whose ideas were widely understood? (Explore what they did, and therefore what could be learned.)
3   How useful is my belief that nobody takes my ideas seriously? What could be a more helpful thing to believe?

Another example might be if we make one problem leak into other areas of our life: "I didn't get the job because my manager doesn't like me – now I'll never get a pay rise". We have made the circumstances personal to us, and in doing so have disempowered our ability to change any future outcome.

A more helpful alternative might be: "I didn't get the job, but at least now my manager knows I am keen to be promoted. I can always apply for the same job in another company if I want to".

Great questions to consider if you find yourself thinking like this could be:

1   What real evidence do I have that my manager doesn't like me? What else could this evidence (or my managers behaviour) be suggesting?
2   How could I use this rejection to make sure I've got a much stronger chance of success next time?
3   What other ways could I try to achieve my goal of a new job, or a pay rise?

The personalisation of failure is also one to watch out for during our inner dialogue. That sense that the reason you haven't succeeded is entirely down to your personal failings. For example: "It just goes to show I'm far too old to learn how to use that new IT system".

Compare this with:

The training for the new IT system was very fast-paced and the trainer didn't give me enough time to practice what I was learning. I need to ask for a bit of extra support, maybe somebody can come and work one-to-one with me for a few hours until I understand it.

Great questions to consider if you find yourself thinking like this could be:

1   What other things in your life and your work have you managed to learn, despite your age? (And how did you do this?)
2   How would your job be different/easier/more enjoyable if you did manage to learn the new IT system?
3   What other ideas do you have to change the outcome here? (E.g. are there other jobs that you could do which don't require you to use the IT system? Could somebody else do the IT part of your job instead?)

Ralph Brown combines his experience in psychology, business and journalism to train organisations in New Zealand and has designed a matrix to explore the impact of our inner dialogue when things happen to us at work.

The matrix builds on Martin Seligman's work about "Explanatory Styles" which suggests that whether we talk to ourselves with an optimistic or a pessimistic style can influence how successful we are with creating a resilient outcome.

Seligman's Explanatory Style model is made up of three elements:

1   **Permanence:** people who are optimistic (and therefore have more resilience) see the effects of unforeseen/unfortunate/bad events as temporary rather than permanent. For instance, they might say "My boss didn't like the work I did on that particular project" rather than "My boss never likes my work".

2   **Pervasiveness:** resilient people don't let setbacks or bad events affect other unrelated areas of their lives. For instance, they might say "I'm not very good at having feedback discussions" rather than "I'm no good at being a manager".

3   **Personalisation:** people who have resilience don't blame themselves when bad events occur. Instead, they see external circumstances as the cause. For instance, they might say, "I didn't get the support I needed to finish that project successfully" rather than, "I messed that project up because I can't do my job". This is an interesting twist; there's a fine line between blaming failure on external factors and taking responsibility for creating a better outcome in the future. We need to find a way to leave our belief in our capability intact, while also learning from the experience. If we just blame others, then our belief in our capability remains – but we might lose the opportunity to learn from the experience. Or sometimes others are indeed to blame, and yet there's nothing we can learn from the experience.

Breaking our thoughts down in this way can help us to consider whether the inner dialogue we have is creating a healthy optimistic or unhealthy pessimistic way of thinking about our setbacks and our achievements. What are our thoughts saying to us: Are we brushing things off? Exploring what happened? Owning the outcome?

Ralph's matrix looks like this:

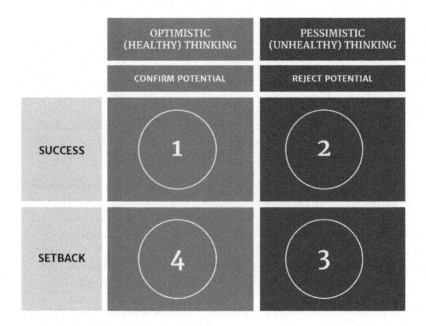

Figure 9.5 Inner dialogue matrix

Regardless of whether we succeed or fail, an optimistic and healthy mindset will have a cheeky little inner voice that will let us know we've got this. We might not have got this right now, but if it hasn't worked out yet, we will find a way to make it work.

A pessimistic and less healthy (or helpful) mindset will brush off any of our successes as a fluke or coincidence and use failure as an excuse to remind us that we aren't cut out for doing what we were attempting to do.

Things we might tell ourselves:

1 **Box One** (I am responsible for my success): "This shows I have potential", "I knew I could do it", "my hard work has paid off"
2 **Box Two** (my success relies on other things): "I was just lucky that time", "that worked because my boss helped me", "I got the job because I was in the right place at the right time"
3 **Box Three** (failure is all my fault): "I just don't have the skills to achieve my goal", "I'll never be able to achieve it", "the odds are totally stacked against me"
4 **Box Four** (failure is an opportunity to learn): "I'll do better next time", "what can I learn from what just happened", "how could I do it differently next time?"

Coaching moment: thinking matrix

For one week, keep a note of where your natural thoughts gravitate when things happen for you at work (this includes both successes and setbacks).

1 What are the situations that cause your thoughts to land in the right-hand column? What impact is this having on your resilience?
2 What are the situations that cause your thoughts to land in the left-hand column? What impact is this having on your resilience?
3 What could you do instead to support your thoughts into a more helpful, optimistic and resilient mindset?

Schedule a Learning Review

One of the biggest gifts you could give yourself to develop your Learning Foundation would be to schedule a regular Learning Review. This idea is so simple, and yet made one of the biggest differences to the teams at SCIRT, in Christchurch.

They found that too often, personal discussions about learning were overlooked and their diary filled with conversations about projects, updates on deliverables and meetings to resolve issues. Their definition was that their diary was so filled with sand, there was no room for any rocks. They believed the rocks to be the foundations for their career success and resilience; and so they needed to prioritise them.

- Instead of wishing your employer did monthly reviews instead of quarterly reviews; book your own monthly review (either alone or with your manager). Book this into your diary now for the next couple of years (or book them at the interval you'd prefer if you want more/less than monthly).
- Instead of wishing your manager would talk to you about how you're doing at work; review your own strengths and areas for development by using the approaches outlined in this book, then schedule a meeting to talk about what you've observed. Alternatively, find another person at work who you could bounce around your ideas with. There's no need to hold back your progress – and it's highly likely your boss will be delighted you've taken this on.

Here are some questions to get you started which were designed by SCIRT employees for their Learning Reviews:

- What do I love most about my work, and what do I wish I could do differently?
- What are my skills or strengths and what skills do I need to improve? (consider using your Job Description to help you)
- What ideas have I had for training or development which would help me to achieve this?
- What training or development have I done since my last Learning Review and how am I using what I learned?
- What is the career vision, mission, goal or aspiration that I have for the next three months?
- What will I need to do more of, or less of, to achieve this vision/mission/ goal or aspiration?
- What topics are the online learning forums trending in my role? What are the discussions about around the world?

The Learning elephants

It's all very well focussing on dialling up your Learning Foundation so that you can be more resilient at work, but what if you're faced with any of the following:

Learning is not supported

Suppose you use the tools and resources in this book to plan your learning, and then take your ideas to work but are told that they are not going to be supported? After all, what you're looking for might not be seen as priority for investing in.

One thing you could consider is to create a business case. Think about why it would be of benefit to the business to support your request. Consider what the current issues are at your workplace (look for topics in newsletters about coming work etc.) and find ways to present your request so it contributes to solving or improving some of the things that are important to your work.

Find out if there is a precedent, for example has anybody else ever achieved approval for this sort of learning in your work before, if so, ask what they did to help their success.

Of course, for many of our learning needs we can consider accessing the free online learning resources available to us that we discussed at the start of this chapter.

Social media and the ease of internet searches have massively increased our ability to access research and resources to support our ability to learn and discover at will. However, some of the data available is based purely on opinion, speculation and personal experience.

While this can be helpful for growing a richer understanding of how other people are learning and then growing from what they have learned, there is a risk that we miss the opportunity of hearing from experts.

Using data and evidence from industry specific sites, professional organisations, specialist LinkedIn groups and qualified bloggers are more likely (though not guaranteed) to be based on information that has been rigorously researched, tested and verified.

Mixing up your knowledge is likely to result in a more robust learning experience, in fact even better would be to deliberately look for ideas that contradict what you believe, or radical polar opinions because they will help you to make a much stronger decision about what you believe, and why.

Find somebody to mentor you; a person who has strength and skill in the area you'd like to learn. Taking an enterprising approach like this will help you to feel that you're still progressing your learning goals, and you might even impress your employer with your determination along the way.

A dreadful manager

Some of the people who are in positions of authority (and who therefore we would approach for feedback) aren't the best at sharing their thoughts.

This can range from providing absolutely no feedback because they have no time or interest in doing so, through to vanilla feedback that is seriously unhelpful ("you need to get better at time management") through to vicious feedback that feels like a personal attack.

If you're worried about this, consider seeking feedback in different ways:

- Are there other people on your team who you could approach?
- Who are the external people; clients or customers who could share their thoughts?
- What is the additional evidence that could help you (e.g. the extent to which you're achieving performance targets?).
- Could you speak to somebody you have worked with in the past?

Using the feedback frameworks in this book will help you to position the conversation as positively as possible.

If you really do have nobody to talk to about your work performance, it might be worth reflecting a little more on the extent that you're suited to the company which employs you.

Not liking what you hear

One of the risks of asking for feedback is that you get feedback.

Even if you set up the conversation to focus on what you do well, you could well end up hearing something about what you could get even better at.

If you find that you're having a very emotional reaction to what you hear, consider calling a time out on the discussion; let your manager know that you'd like some time to think about and process what they have told you and then visit the chapter about dialling up Emotional Honesty to find some coping strategies for reflecting on what you learn.

Ask to meet with them again when you have used some of our strategies for creating a more helpful emotional state, and consider asking the following questions:

- What would I need to be saying or doing differently to be perceived as successful?
- How could you, or the organisation, support me in achieving that?
- When can we meet again to discuss how I'm progressing?

Coaching moment: feedback review

If you're receiving or reflecting on feedback, you could use the template in Table 9.2 which is based on a Johari Window communication model.

When we receive feedback, our natural temptation can be to look straight for things that we feel we want to "get better at". We often disregard other areas that are highlighted to us in our hurry to work out what's broken, so we can fix it.

Using the template can help you to consider feedback in a much more balanced way and look for patterns and trends: make a note of the results that you expected and the results that you didn't expect, and then divide them into what you perceive to be positive or negative feedback.

The template in Table 9.2 represents YOUR interpretation of results (for example, you might receive feedback that you are very assertive and you might interpret this as either positive or negative, depending on your personal views).

Table 9.2 Feedback review

	Encouraging – desirable	*Disheartening – undesirable*
Expected feedback	**Your strengths** This area largely represents the things that you are already conscious of being good at. You can celebrate these results because they are your known strengths. If you've previously identified these as an area for development, then it's likely that your training initiatives have to some extent succeeded and your new skills are being enjoyed by others. Consider how you might use these strengths more often – to bring you joy – or support others in developing them.	**Your development choices** This area represents those things that you already know you need to get better at – or sometimes they are the controversial skills you need to use in your work, but not everybody enjoys experiencing them. Perhaps you've already undertaken some training, but don't feel results have changed. Ask yourself what additional action you might take and what benefits would be gained from making a change in this area. Who do you know who is good at these things and how can they help you to develop?
Unexpected feedback	**Your surprise gifts** This area represents things that other people think you are good at, but which you weren't aware of. You might be surprised by these results and feel a bit embarrassed about them. It's likely that you perform these things subconsciously and these are your natural strengths. Consider how you might adjust your sense of self with this insight.	**Your blind spots** This area represents the things that you didn't realise could be perceived as negative by those providing feedback to you. They may be surprising and offer a totally new opportunity for you to consider growth. Try not to become defensive or look for excuses to write off this feedback. It's likely that by acting on this feedback you will make a big difference to how others experience you.

Designed by Kathryn Jackson

Avoiding evidence

Sometimes we tell ourselves to avoid looking for evidence which could actually help us to work out where to dial up our learning. We avoid contacting the recruiter to seek information about why we weren't offered the job, we pretend that our manager is picking on us at work but we're not really performing to the level we should or we find reasons not to have "a chat" with our team leader because we know they are going to share things that aren't exactly good news about our work.

This avoidance is actually a pretty good coping strategy under some circumstances (for example, we've heard about counsellors who have to suppress their emotional responses to the personal circumstances of the person they are working with), but it can result in increased stress over time where we do not lean into that which we know is true.

The result can be we increase pressure on ourselves by avoiding the emotion that goes with looking at evidence. Worrying about this can also result in a sense that we cannot control the outcome; we effectively self-sabotage.

Ironically, looking at the evidence can help us to dial up our learning in a less subjective and therefore less emotional way. It helps us to regain control and create a black and white picture of our options.

Evidence-based learning includes looking for examples of real things that confirm what you think you probably need to get better at; for example, if you think that you need to practice your interview technique to be successful in your job search, then look at how many times you have been invited for an interview and rejected versus how many times you've been successful.

If you believe you need to get better at delivering presentations at work, consider how many presentations you've done – asking yourself what people said or did after you presented. What did they tell you about the presentation? What impact did the presentation have on achieving what you hoped it would? Did attendees do what you wanted them to?

This can help to make sure that you are investing your learning in areas which are truly going to make a difference to achieving your Goals. It will also help you to use information that is based on fact, rather than simply the opinion of another person about what you should focus on developing.

Coaching moment: identifying obstacles

Consider the things that you believe are holding you back from achieving your career ambitions.

1   What is the evidence that you have to support these beliefs?
2   How could you find out more about this evidence to get a sense of perspective?
3   Who could help you to create a plan to address them?

My story: Conrad

Conrad had been for several interviews and was getting increasingly frustrated by his lack of success. Because he kept being rejected from jobs he applied for, he was also starting to feel even more trapped in his current role, which added considerable pressure to his already low resilience starting point.

Conrad approached a coach to help him and together they realised that he was not comfortable with asking for interview feedback, and as a result he had simply been accepting the rejection and walking away.

Together they designed a script to support Conrad in exploring outcomes from interviews, and he called several of the recruiters he had been interviewed by.

This is the script he used:

"Hello, this is Conrad calling, you interviewed me for the position of <insert position> on <insert date> and I'm really keen to get some feedback from you, so that I can continue to develop my skills during interviews.

Do you have a couple of minutes to answer some questions for feedback to me about the job?

- On a scale of 1 to 10 how suitable did you see me for the job on my CV or during the interview?
- In your opinion what attribute or skill, that if I'd had it, would have made me a __ (*add 1 to the score given in answer to previous question*)?
- What impressed you the most about me regarding the job application?
- What impressed you the least about me regarding the job application?
- What impressed you the most about the candidate that you offered the job to?
- What were you looking for in a successful candidate that you didn't see in me?
- What advice would you have for me, if in future, I was applying for a similar job in a different company?

Thank you very much for giving me the opportunity to interview for the job and for the feedback you've just shared. I have really appreciated the time that you've given me.

I wish you the best of luck in the future and with the successful candidate."

Not all the recruiters answered his questions fully but he got a much more detailed and evidence-based insight into his interview performance and was able to take specific, targeted action with his coach to grow his interview skills for the future.

(continued)

(continued)

Reflection: using What, When, How, Who and Where questions to explore evidence can help us to really tailor our learning and avoid wasting time growing our skills in areas we don't need to grow. Developing this exploratory style can help us become more confident in the current Conceptual Age, where exploring evidence, linking together ideas, building our case and then deciding action are perceived as critical.

My story: Hanna

Hanna was a new graduate who had accepted a dream job, but for a lower salary than she really wanted. She recognised that this was a strategic move to help her achieve her longer term career ambitions, and that the low pay was a short term decision.

After seven months in her role, Hanna realised that she wasn't getting much feedback, and would therefore find it tricky to make a strong case for a pay rise when the time came, so she met with a career coach to design a conversation.

As a result, she designed a conversation guide to discuss with her boss which included these questions:

- What do I need to do more of to be considered for a raise in six months?
- What do I need to do less of to be considered for a raise in six months?
- How can I make use of the organisation training and development resources to support my growth in the areas where I need to grow? (aligned to her formally recorded development plan).
- Who would you recommend I meet with to talk about growing my capability further?
- How could I make changes so that I still feel like I'm going in the right direction for my longer term career goals?
- Thank you for your guidance, wisdom and advice.

As a result, Hanna was able to create clarity about the specific areas where she could focus to grow her chances of a pay rise. She didn't choose to develop all of them, but by targeting what was important to her employer she did get a rise at her first review period.

Reflection: use every situation that doesn't go to plan as an opportunity to ask questions and then decide where to act.

Too much learning

Remembering that our Resilience Foundations need to be dialled up or down depending on how what we are experiencing compares with what we want. If things aren't going to plan we need to consider whether we have over extended one of our Foundations, and therefore need to adjust our focus.

My story: Andrew

Andrew works in the construction industry. Originally from Canada, he moved to New Zealand to support the Christchurch City Rebuild. He describes himself as a "continuous work in progress" regarding resilience.

When he first arrived, he threw himself into his work while waiting for his family to join him (they had stayed behind to sell the family home). This was an easy task, because there was so much to do and the pace of work was like nothing he had ever experienced before.

Determined to do not just well but REALLY well in his new job, he focussed all of his energy on learning about the challenges which lay ahead, researching both inside and outside his employer and staying in touch with the latest trends of his professional associations. He was determined that the solutions he created were best in class. He constantly asked for feedback about the work he delivered, which resulted in even greater opportunities for him to deliver better solutions and created such a good impression on his employer that they put him in charge of more teams.

For nearly four months, Andrew believed that he was resilient, and relished the ride. His work gave him energy, focus and inspiration.

The arrival of his family to join him in Christchurch changed everything immediately.

The immediate concern for Andrew was helping to settle his children into their local school, a task that he shared with his wife. Despite working with a sympathetic manager who allowed him to take time out during his day to support this, Andrew found that his feelings about work had changed.

Within a few weeks, he was feeling very stressed and agitated. He found it hard to manage his diary and was frequently late for meetings or missing deadlines. He felt like he had lost his sense of resilience and was no longer enjoying coming to work. Because of the visa he had entered New Zealand on to work, he now felt trapped by his job. And this sense of having no power began to impact him physically, as he began suffering from frequent coughs and colds.

(continued)

(continued)

Andrew realised that a very emotional response had taken place; he no longer felt powerful at work and decided to explore what had happened so that he could act and get into a more resilient place at work.

The first thing he realised was that all his energy had been concentrated on the Learning element of resilience. To some extent he had also focussed some of his energy on building Connections, but they were purely with the intention of building his Learning further.

He realised that the arrival of his family had exposed his lack of focus on Self-Care, and that because his time was already chock full of Learning and Connecting there was no more time available for this equally important part of his resilience. He decided that he needed to dial this up and needed to dial down the Learning element to make some space.

Andrew decided that he wanted to have an honest conversation with his immediate manager at work. Because he knew that his manager was supportive of his desire to support his children into schools, he was hopeful about a similar supportive conversation about this new emotional place that Andrew found himself in.

In preparation for this discussion, Andrew decided to create a couple of scenarios to allow him to do his work in a different way, which went more towards meeting the needs of both his employer and his family. His manager was impressed that he had considered some options for them to discuss, though he challenged a couple of ideas, and together they worked out a solution.

Reflection: having a resilient state is not static. It constantly needs to be reflected upon and dialled up or down as the need arises.

HR and Business reflect

- "It's so difficult (but so important) to manage the dual challenge of supporting employees whilst remembering to nurture and keep an eye on your own career."
- "Always ask yourself, 'what can I do to grow in my current role?' Seek out new opportunities, get better at things you do already, maximise your involvement at work and don't wait to be managed by your employer."
- "Consider asking what are the skills or experiences that the company values the most (pays most for) and exploring how your pay compares to other companies' pay (by looking at pay scale websites). Knowing your worth can help you to realise that you're in a well paid job, or it can give you a case for consideration. Ask yourself: do I 'stay and thrive' by realising

I'm well paid, or growing my skills into an area that is better valued, or do I 'leave and thrive' by applying for roles that meet my $ value needs. Don't just 'stay and survive'."

- "Cultivate a mindset of experimentation – learning creates innovation – finding that something doesn't work and then exploring what happened; so you can try again differently and see if there is a better outcome. This leads to resilience because we know we can't fail, we just might have to try a few times before we succeed."

- "I want employees who are rocking out of bed each day (to come to work) and if for some reason you're not rocking it, I want you to have full licence to discuss this with me. I would rather have a difficult conversation that allows me to support your next steps, than a disgruntled employee – even if that means you are going to leave the company."

- "If the role isn't right for you and you can't see yourself ever enjoying it, I will support you in finding another one which is either in or out of the business. Tell me what you'd like from your role, and what you don't enjoy and together we can plan out a map."

- "Test the market; either you'll realise you have a great job and the pay isn't that bad after all, or you will find evidence to build a case for improving your existing role, or you'll decipher the skills you need to develop to move on up, or you'll find something new and exciting."

- "Focus on small things; one thing I learned today, one person I touched positively today, one thing I contributed to the business today."

My story: Adam

Adam was a self-employed consultant who relied on building networks and connections to achieve business success. One method that he used was delivering training programmes. These half day or full day workshops introduced attendees to the tools and methods of his business and he invariably picked up several new clients as a result.

The attendees at his workshops gave great feedback and he was confident that delivering the training was one of his strengths.

Adam wanted to extend his ability to find new clients outside Australia and as a result, he organised a series of webinars. Having never run a webinar before, he researched on the internet and attended a few webinars run by other people to see what sort of thing would work well.

On the day, he was surprised by how nervous he felt while waiting for the clock to tick to start time and, as his guests logged onto their computers, he found his heart racing. He bombed – completely and utterly

(continued)

(continued)

bombed – leaving awkward silences, asking for opinions (which never came) and grasping to stay with his script.

Adam realised this was not his normal way of being during workshops, so he reviewed his performance immediately afterwards. He realised just how much he relied on audience participation and visual interaction to run successful workshops, something that was very hard to achieve online.

Instead of abandoning the idea of webinars, Adam dialled up his Learning and his Connections Foundations. He met with everybody he knew in the industry to get their advice on webinars and he attended some high cost webinars run by incredibly experienced hosts, so he could learn from the very best. The bombed webinar wasn't a disaster at all, it was a launchpad for Adam to ensure more quickly that his webinars were top class.

Reflection: everything that does not go to plan is an opportunity to learn.

Tell me more!

Read

- Flourishing in New Zealand Workers: Associations with lifestyle behaviours, physical health, psychosocial, and work-related indicators. L. C. Hone, A. Jarden, S. Duncan and G. M. Schofield. 2015. www.ncbi.nlm.nih.gov/pubmed/26340286
- The Use of Coaching Principles to Foster Employee Engagement. Shane Crabb, 2011.
- Positive Psychological Capital: Beyond human and social capital. F., K. and B. Luthans. https://digitalcommons.unl.edu/managementfacpub/145/
- Radical Candour. Kim Scott, 2017
- www.glassdoor.com (For insight that will empower and inform your employment choices straight from the horse's mouth.)

Watch

- Brighttalk.com
- www.ted.com/speakers/emilie_wapnick (Multipotentialite at Work.)
- www.coursera.org/learn/learning-how-to-learn (Learning How to Learn; a highly respected online option to develop learning capability.)
- www.ted.com/talks/ramsey_musallam_3_rules_to_spark_learning (3 rules to spark learning.)
- www.ted.com/talks/diana_laufenberg_3_ways_to_teach (How to learn from mistakes.)

Play

Here are some of the coolest online assessments to support your learning: I do not receive any recommendation fees from them, they are recommended by HR, Business and Career professionals from around the world.

- Fuel50
- Strengthfinder
- Morrisby
- VIA Strengths
- EAP Mindset Tools
- Appraisal360

Five vital facts: Learning

1   **Learning is yours:** any learning that you choose to do should be your own learning. There is great power in understanding from feedback what knowledge, skills or experience your employer will most value from you, but you will learn most effectively when it's something that you personally want to grow from, and you have tailored your approach to your learning preferences.

2   **Learning builds confidence:** despite what you might think, feedback contributes directly to helping us grow stronger – if we see it as a sign that something could be better. The tools and resources in this book are strengths based and designed to support a conversation about where you excel and where you could consider growing. Be curious.

3   **Learning needs a reason:** learning will be most impactful where it is evidence-based. Don't just attend interview training because you think you should do so – attend interview training because you've been turned down and you want to explore ways to get better at interviewing. Ask your manager to share examples of why they believe you need training in something, it may simply be that you haven't quite understood a process. Use the Learning Decision Matrix to help you plan.

4   **Sometimes Learning creates our pressure:** deciding to move out of our Comfort Zone and dial up Learning can result in creating pressure, as we begin using knowledge or skills that we haven't necessarily used before. This can create a pressure source, which we know might cause us distress at work depending on how we interpret the pressure.

5   **Learning can be for now or the future:** learning can happen any moment of every day, whenever we get a sense that something is not quite right (for example, by dialling up our Emotional Honesty) we have an opportunity to ask ourselves if this is a potential learning moment. Conscious learning for the future requires us to have a destination in mind, so we can cross check our learning plans are going to take us where we want to go.

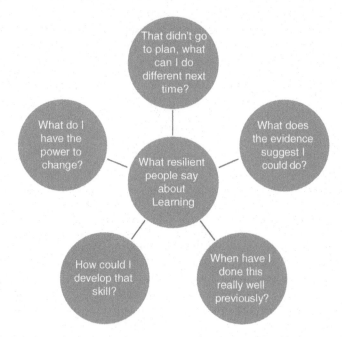

Figure 9.6 Learning "flower": what people say

Do: it's time to write your story (Action Plan)

This chapter about Learning has underlined the importance of . . .
It has given me a better understanding of . . .
What I've learned about myself is . . .
What I'm particularly thankful for is . . .
What I'm going to do immediately as a result is . . .
What I'm going to do over the next twelve months is . . .
The impact this will have is . . .
What could get in the way or prevent me from achieving this is . . .
(If this happens I'm going to . . .)
I will know I have succeeded because . . .
I am going to check what I've achieved on . . . (date)
The person who will help me to stay accountable to this plan is:

LEARNING

| GRID | Here are some questions for you to consider as you reflect on what you have learned in this chapter. They have been designed to help you decide how to use what you have read. You may wish to consider the questions alone, with a friend or with your manager at work. |

GOAL
- What are the obstacles to your resilience that you would like to overcome because of increased focus on learning?
- What is the reason that you would like to focus more energy on your learning?
- How will you know that your focus on learning is positively influencing your resilience at work?
- What outcomes are you hoping to achieve by giving more attention to learning at work?
- How is your attitude to learning at work holding you back or preventing you from being your most resilient?

REALITY
- What are the things that are preventing you from achieving your career ambitions and how could you look for learning from them?
- How much feedback do you currently get about your achievements at work?
- What frustrations do you currently experience which might be a learning opportunity in disguise?
- What are the areas of learning where you are expecting your workplace to mind read? (e.g. trying new skills, growing capability).
- What role have you already played in your learning so far? How has this helped your resilience?
- What learning have you already done which could help you?
- How can you use your knowledge of the Comfort Zone, Sweet Spot and Survival Zone to help you plan your learning?
- What evidence can you use to create a more targeted approach to your learning (e.g. if you've been rejected from a promotion how can you look for learning?)

IDEAS
- What do you know about your learning preferences and how could this help you?
- What have you learned in this chapter which might help you to increase the learning opportunities for building your resilience at work?
- How could your Signature Strengths help you?
- Who do you know that has developed their learning in the same area as your learning goals? What could you learn from them?
- How could you grow your confidence in asking questions to seek information or advice to help your learning?

DO
- Who will you talk to about this?
- What are you going to do immediately?
- What are you going to do as a result of these reflections?
- What are the tools and resources at work that can support you?
- How could your employer or manager potentially help you?
- What might prevent you from achieving your goals and if this happens, what will you do to overcome it?
- How will you know you're doing the right thing? What will be different?

Part IV

Concluding thoughts

10 Planning for resilience and measuring your progress

The heart of this book suggests that resilience is something that we need to become more conscious of, and then regularly dial up or down our four Foundations to put ourselves in the best possible place to be our strongest ever version of us.

This means that we can't just take resilience for granted; the approach that works for us in January might not be quite right when life throws us a curve ball in March . . . so taking a moment on the first day of each month to reflect on the energy and focus you're giving to your four Resilience Foundations (and the impact that is having) can be helpful.

This won't guarantee that you are able to adjust your focus immediately, or ensure you have perfect resilience at all times, but it might prevent you from sleepwalking your way into a place of low or no resilience . . . which is likely to be harder to come out of.

You might decide to take a resilience Selfie using the tools in this book, or you might simply ask yourself this question: "Do I feel confident and ready to handle the things that I know are ahead of me this month?"

If the answer is "no", consider each of the Resilience Foundations in turn to explore how dialling them up my have a positive impact on your readiness . . . where would you like to focus on increasing or decreasing your efforts.

Resilience, rejected

One of the realities of resilience at work is that if you have dialled up and down to your heart's content and are still being met with obstacles, blocks and resistance then you may need to consider whether you are suited for the employer.

Decide on your deal breakers; the things that you have learned through this book without which you cannot be resilient. Make sure you've considered enterprising ways to achieve your ambitions – that you're not just giving up before thinking around the problem.

Consider a table top analysis of the risks to each of your Resilience Foundations if you stay, versus if you leave (or flip a coin). You can still choose to stay even if the odds are stacked against you, but you will do it consciously, and knowing that the road ahead will likely be hard . . . so you can shore up your resources.

Use the results to make a plan so that you don't make an emotional decision which you regret later.

My story: Katelyn

Katelyn worked in a legal company as a project analyst. This was her third job since graduating and she had always performed very well, enjoying accolades and positive reviews from all her previous employers.

During her first year, Katelyn enjoyed getting to grips with the challenge of new systems, new colleagues and researching the projects that she was assigned to. During this time, the feedback that she got from her manager was limited, and while surprised, she didn't have any reason to doubt her capabilities given her previous experience at work.

During her end of year review however, Katelyn was shocked to hear that her performance was perceived as significantly below standard and she was going to be put on a formal performance management process.

Dialling up her Learning Foundation, Katelyn asked for specific information about where she was perceived to be failing but received vague responses. There was an indication that attention to detail was an issue, yet she had never been corrected in any project report that she had submitted. Looking for evidence, she asked for feedback on the project she was currently writing and was met with resistance; one meeting after another was cancelled as she searched for objective information from which she could learn.

The impact across all her Resilience Foundations was astounding. Her usually buoyant and optimistic personality changed beyond recognition, she withdrew from friends both inside and outside work and her health deteriorated into a series of flu like symptoms.

Katelyn spent four months spiralling in this way, until she realised what was happening. The moment that she was emotionally honest with herself about the impact this situation was having on her mental and physical health, Katelyn became energised because she realised something had to change, and the one thing she had control over was her.

Dialling up her Self-Care strategies she took more time to focus on eating well and exercising, and it was during one of her runs that she decided: her experience in this role was so alien to anything she had ever experienced before, at work and at school. Combining this with the lack of evidence presented by her employer suggested to her that this must simply be a total mismatch of employment.

The decision made, Katelyn focussed very consciously on dialling up her Connections and as a direct result of this identified a role in another organisation that she was perfectly suited for. Realising that she might not be at her most confident during interviews, Katelyn talked with a career coach to practice her techniques and nailed the application process.

In the fifteen years since working at that employer, Katelyn only ever received very positive feedback about her work, including her attention to detail. She has never looked back and will always be conscious of when she is (or is not) feeling resilient as a result of her experience.

Reflection: realising there is a problem means there is an opportunity to get even closer to what you are looking for; to create a solution. Embrace your need for resilience as an opportunity to become an even stronger version of who you are at work.

Coaching moment

Consider everything that you have learned and reflected on during this book.

1   What do you know to be truths? What do you now believe are untruths, and what evidence do you have to support these beliefs?
2   What are the contingency plans that you need to make to ensure your learning continues?
3   How could you now support yourself to a more helpful way to achieve your career ambitions at work?

Proof of progress

How do we know it's working? How can we measure our own resilience and whether it's changed (or is changing)?

What an incredible journey you've taken. You've explored the history of resilience; where it originated, how it's evolved and heard from some of the latest research about how to develop it.

Together, we've explored the idea that Change isn't always the same – and that some elements of Change might even be a little bit exciting, although we've also acknowledged that some areas of Change are perhaps contributing to our need for resilience. We've considered how the world of work is currently changing, along with different ways we might stay connected to the changes within our own role or industry, so we can try to anticipate and respond to any changes down the line.

We've heard about the four Foundations for growing resilience at work and are better equipped to tailor a journey of resilience that dials up (or down) our Emotional Honesty, Self-Care, Connecting and Learning as we focus our energy on developing resilience for any personal circumstance.

At the start of our book, we considered some of the things that we might notice as our learning evolved and our resilience at work grows.

Reflect on how you might answer the following questions:

1   What do you think is changing?
2   What does your employer think is changing?
3   What do your friends and family think is changing?
4   What are you the proudest of having achieved on this journey?
5   What do your quiz results tell you? If you complete the quiz again now, you should notice that there are changes. You may be dialling up your resilience in one or more Foundations, or dialling down your resilience in one or more Foundations. Consider what impact this is having on your resilience at work.
6   What does the research suggest? You should notice some of these things happening to you; increased energy and positivity, decreased distress, illness and sadness and a better quality of sleep.

We asked employers to describe what they would see when employees were becoming more resilient; this is what they shared:

- Proactive
- Realistic
- More Positive
- Contributing
- Build connections internally
- Build connections externally
- Ideas focussed
- Supportive
- Increased confidence

Coaching moment: what are you noticing?

Consider these questions about becoming more resilient:

1   What are the main things that have changed for you during your resilience journey?
2   What impact has this had on achieving your resilience goals?
3   What do you need to do to continue to grow and maintain your Resilience Foundations?

The Prochaska Stages of Change framework is an excellent framework to help us to understand the next steps you could consider for your journey of resilience. It was designed in the 1980s to help professionals who were working with addiction problems understand how people modify their behaviours.

At the **Pre-contemplative** stage of change, you were likely not even aware that growing your resilience at work would be helpful for you. Perhaps you were experiencing the same challenges over and over again or being turned down during promotion processes or rejected from interviews – but you just kept trying over and over again, with the same outcomes. It's a pretty demoralising place to be, and now that you know how to dial up your Emotional Honesty you can avoid being here too long in the future, because you can short circuit the stage by noticing there's an opportunity for change.

This noticing helps you to enter the **Contemplative** stage of change. This is when we start wondering whether we might do something different or explore new ways to approach the issue that we are facing, or the change we want to make. Our thinking shifts and we start wondering what the journey could look like; we will likely imagine the benefits of acting on feedback so we do get that promotion, or practising interviews so we have a better chance of success. We may begin to gather facts about what we will need to do. We'll also be very aware of the downsides of the change too, telling ourselves how hard it is to change, or how expensive it will be to do the training. This stage can go on for quite a while as we psyche ourselves up to do something about changing, because we will likely keep listening to that voice that reminds us that change can be tricky.

Once we've overcome that voice, we enter the **Preparation** (or **Determination**) stage of change, where we start preparing to do something towards the change we wish to see. Perhaps we will have identified the development or training we want to do, or the mentor we want to work with. We will have found a career professional to support us and we're ready for action.

Action is the next stage of the framework, we are not only doing the training we are also changing as a result – this is key for this stage, we don't just attend the training, or meet the mentor for a chat, we actually make a change towards the outcomes we want.

Maintenance occurs when we have made changes to how we operate and are working hard to avoid relapse. Perhaps we seek more feedback about the changes we have made to make sure they are hitting the mark, perhaps we ask interviewers how we are doing.

Termination (or **Exit**) can occur for a variety of reasons, including that the new specific behaviour or skill is now embedded and there is no need for maintenance to check it's still working. Another reason might be if we decide the new behaviour or skill is no longer required, and we have a different focus for change we might choose to terminate, or exit, our change strategy.

Coaching moment: Stages of Change

In considering the Stages of Change identified above, where do you think your journey currently sits?

1   Perhaps it is multiple, and you have taken significant Action in one or more Resilience Foundations, but you are still Contemplating change in another foundation.
2   Perhaps you have decided that all you require from now is Maintenance, a regular check in using the resilience quizzes or the questions in this chapter.
3   If you are stuck in any of the Stages of Change, what support could help you make a decision to move on (or out) of the framework?

GRID *your resilience journey*

We know that we can never be perfectly resilient at all times, and so our resilience journey will be one of continuous Maintenance, if we use the Proschaka Stages of Change. However, we now have a more conscious approach to noticing our resilience and taking action towards dialling up (or down) our Resilience Foundations.

If you want another way to consider the progress you are making, use our GRID framework to consider what you've achieved:

Goal

•   What were the main goals that you had for your resilience journey?
•   Which chapters of the book have been your main focus?
•   What changes were you hoping to achieve as a result of reading this book?

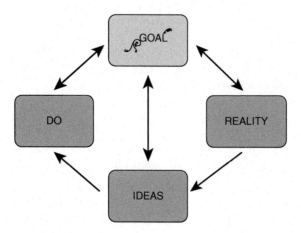

Figure 10.1 GRID coaching framework (from Chapter 2)

Reality

- How has your experience of those goals changed as you have put into action the learning from this book?
- Which Resilience Foundations have you focussed on dialling up? What has been the impact of this on your goals?
- What have you achieved in the way of change since you began your resilience journey?
- What has got in the way or prevented you from acting on what you learned from the book?

Ideas

- What other things could you try, to achieve your resilience goals?
- Who else could support you in your journey towards resilience at work?
- What extra learning could you do to achieve this?

Do

- Of the ideas that you just designed, what are you going to commit to?
- When are you going to achieve it by? What difference is it going to make?
- How can you use the "It's time to write your story (Action Plans)" at the end of chapters to support you in achieving this decision?

Overcoming obstacles

For one week, keep a diary of all the negative thoughts that you have – the little voices that whisper to you that you're not going to make it, you haven't got the strength, you're wasting your time. Make a note of what they are telling you, and start facing the obstacles that you perceive. Then for each obstacle, identify at least three things that you could do to overcome it – get your friends or colleagues to help you if you're feeling stuck.

Obstacles	Possible actions
	1
	2
	3
	1
	2
	3
	1
	2
	3
	1
	2
	3

Resilient reminders

Take two minutes right now to book a recurring appointment into your diary so you can check into your resilience levels.

It might be a monthly appointment, or an annual appointment (or anything in between). It might be a half hour self-coaching coffee appointment, or it might be an appointment with a career professional or your manager . . . remember this is your journey, you get to choose.

During this meeting, reflect on what you have learned and what you're doing differently. Identify anything that's getting in the way, or new challenges and obstacles that you didn't originally foresee.

Celebrate the successes, achievements and changes that you've made as a result of your commitment to learn about the resilience journey of Christchurch, New Zealand. Commend yourself for taking time to learn from the academics, practitioners and companies around the world who are dedicated to understanding not only how to survive when things don't go to plan – but use it as an opportunity to thrive.

You are already stronger.

11 Extending the reach of resilience

Reach

For over twenty years I worked in Human Resources or People Consulting roles. I loved my job, which was largely working in global corporations to understand the drivers of employees, supporting their development and finding ways to lead them into even stronger performance at work.

However, I never failed to be amazed by how many of the people I met who were in jobs they didn't enjoy.

Friends confided they were waiting to be invited to apply for more senior roles (instead of just asking for the promotion), colleagues complained that they were never encouraged to use skills they secretly wanted to develop, peers shared their plans for what they "really" wanted to do.

Too many people resigned from their work and went somewhere new in the hope that things would be different.

For the many who stayed in touch, it very rarely was. Patterns of disappointment and frustration were repeated, until for some people work has become somewhere to be tolerated until home time, and ultimately retirement.

So, I decided to do something. I decided to extend my reach and train so that I could work with a larger group of people, not just those employed by the organisations I worked for.

After training as a coach, specialising in career and performance related coaching, I established my coaching practice.

There are so many incredible resources available to help us evaluate, reflect upon and define our hopes and dreams for the place we spend so many years of our life; our workplace. Many of them are highlighted through the Tell me more! sections of this book.

The reality, however is that this is only part of the story.

Defining what you'd like to achieve, do more of or develop is just the start. Finding the words to share your aspirations and then finding the persistence and strength to keep putting one foot in front of the other towards your destination (regardless of what happens around you and how long it takes) is another thing altogether.

Working in an environment dedicated to consciously increasing resilience at work for the past five years has exposed me to some of the best minds and latest ideas about how we might do this, so in writing this book I have tried to translate some of the core messages about what we have learned, to help you stay the course.

During my writing journey, I also researched the latest global thinking about resilience to check these learnings can be helpful for you wherever in the world you may be.

Thank you so much for choosing my book.

Reach

- If you're an HR professional, please consider this book as a resource to reach out to your employees and encourage them to find their own way to enjoy a thriving career at your business for longer. Consider designing workshops around the chapters, consider sharing this book with your teams, consider finding a way to create a common language for resilience in your workplace. Imagine what a difference your workplace would be if teams were dialling up or down their Resilience Foundations more consciously, and the potential impact of self-managed resilience at work.

- If you're a Business leader, please use this book to reach out to your team and help them find the words they would dearly like to share with you and explore ways to stay strong in achieving their career ambitions. Just picture the enormous impact on how they perceive you as a leader, and the difference you will make to their world. Invite them to choose a chapter at a time, encourage them to read it and ask them questions about what they are learning.

- If you're a Career professional, please reach out to Routledge, and talk to them about using the materials to design your own workshops and programmes to build resilience with the people whom you work with. I'm determined that what we have learned in Christchurch should be shared in as many ways as possible, and Routledge have the means to support this.

Please reach out to your friends and talk to them about what you've learned.

Share this book with them, talk about your story; what's worked for you because of what you've learned from this book and what you would do differently.

Reach out to me with your thoughts. Tell me where I need to write more, or write less. Share your story for future editions, so that others can grow their resilience from your own experience.

Wouldn't it be amazing if we were all just a little bit more resilient, as we leaned into our career aspirations together?

And feel free to experiment with the Resilience Foundations too; I noticed that when I was a new mum I had to constantly dial up and down the way I was leaning into Emotional Honesty, Self-Care, Connections and Learning . . . just imagine all the other potential ways we could positively impact our resilience in other areas of our lives, by trying out what we have learned as a result of reading this book.

Index